Briefcase on

MEDICAL LAW

Second Edition

Alasdair Maclean, BSc, MBBS, PG Dip Law, M Jur
The School of Law, University of Glasgow

Cavendish
Publishing
Limited

London • Sydney • Portland, Oregon

Second edition first published in Great Britain 2004 by
Cavendish Publishing Limited, The Glass House,
Wharton Street, London WC1X 9PX, United Kingdom
Telephone: + 44 (0)20 7278 8000   Facsimile: + 44 (0)20 7278 8080
Email: info@cavendishpublishing.com
Website: www.cavendishpublishing.com

Published in the United States by Cavendish Publishing
c/o International Specialized Book Services,
5824 NE Hassalo Street, Portland,
Oregon 97213-3644, USA

Published in Australia by Cavendish Publishing (Australia) Pty Ltd
45 Beach Street, Coogee, NSW 2034, Australia

© Maclean, Alasdair	2004
First edition	2001
Second edition	2004

British Library Cataloguing in Publication Data
Maclean, Alasdair, MJur –
Briefcase on medical law – 2nd ed – (Cavendish briefcase)
1 Medical laws and legislation – Great Britain
I Title
344.4'1'041

Library of Congress Cataloguing in Publication Data
Data available

ISBN 1-85941-954-2
ISBN 978-1-859-41954-0

1 3 5 7 9 10 8 6 4 2

Printed and bound in Great Britain

PREFACE

Medical law is a relatively new area of law. It draws on, and overlaps with, many other areas of law such as tort, family law, human rights and criminal law. Apart from this hybrid legal basis it is also informed by bioethical theory. This book draws those elements together to form a comprehensible and succinct overview. The cases – and other relevant material – will be linked by short comments that help to explain and clarify their legal relevance. A brief introduction to the ethical principles that govern the provision of healthcare will provide a framework for considering the issues that arise in the cases. This ethical framework will include discussion of the principles of autonomy, beneficence, non-maleficence, justice and veracity. Following this, relevant cases and important judicial *dicta* will illustrate the legal rules and principles of each key area of healthcare law. Some relevant statutory material will be included, as will appropriate extracts from professional bodies' codes of practice.

The primary aim of this book is to provide students with a rapid and easy access to the important cases within the area of healthcare law. By highlighting the principles and rules that may be abstracted from the cases, it is hoped that the reader will be able to better understand the law in this area. It will provide a valuable adjunct to more substantial texts as well as being an essential revision tool. It will also provide a useful springboard from which a student could dive into the deep waters of research. A secondary aim of the book is to provide a summary of healthcare law to students and practitioners of other disciplines. Doctors, nurses, other healthcare workers and bioethicists will all find the book a ready source of relevant case law.

The author has made every effort to ensure that the law is correctly stated as of 30 August 2004.

PREFACE

ACKNOWLEDGMENTS

I would like to acknowledge Professor Sheila McLean, Sarah Elliston, Colin Gavaghan and Shanti Williamson, my medical law colleagues, for their forbearance in putting up with my hermit-like behaviour while updating the book and for their help in discussing points of law. I would also like to thank Professor Jonathan Montgomery for his support during my time at Southampton.

CONTENTS

TABLE OF CASES

TABLE OF LEGISLATION

SECONDARY LEGISLATION

CHAPTER 1

MEDICAL ETHICS

1.1　Ethical theories

1.1.1　Teleological theories

These theories are goal orientated or consequentialist. They aim to provide a theory for action based on the consequences of the act. The preferred alternative is the one that produces the most good and least harm. Teleological theories stress that it is the consequences of the act and not the motive behind the act that should be judged. Thus, they separate the moral judgment of the act from the moral judgment of the actor. Utilitarianism is perhaps the foremost example of a teleological theory. It combines two theses: (1) all actions and rules are judged solely by the contribution they make to increase human happiness or decrease human misery; and (2) pleasure is the only thing that is inherently good and pain is the only thing that is inherently evil. Notable exponents of utilitarianism include Jeremy Bentham and John Stuart Mill. An important aspect of utilitarianism that Bentham argued for is that every person counts for one and no person for more than one.

Other consequentialists adopt a 'pluralist' approach and believe that things other than pleasure can be inherently good. Ross (1930) argues that at least four things are intrinsically good:

(1)　pleasure;
(2)　knowledge;
(3)　virtue;
(4)　justice.

Specific medical goods might include: absence of disease; absence of pain or suffering; and a 'trust-filled' professional-patient relationship (Graber, 1998).

Because utilitarianism risks riding roughshod over the individual for the good of society, some philosophers have incorporated deontological principles (see below) within a utilitarian framework. 'Rule utilitarianism' argues that such principles should be followed if institutionalisation of the principle maximises welfare. In that case the rule should be followed even though there may be occasions when breaking the rule would maximise welfare. Mill (1991), for example, argues that a respect for autonomy will maximise happiness; see also Hare (1981).

1.1.2　Deontological theories

These theories are based on the premise that we owe certain duties to others. These duties may arise from the other person's right, such as a 'right to be informed', or from the idea of 'respect for persons'. Immanuel Kant is the most notable deontologist. Two important principles that Kant described are:

(1) treat both yourself and other people as ends and never simply as means to an end;
(2) only base your acts on maxims that you would want to be applicable universally.

The moral duties that derive from these principles act as constraints upon an individual's actions that may be performed in pursuit of his goals. Examples of moral duties include: do not lie; do not kill another person; do not harm another person. Some deontologists believe that the most important moral duties are 'absolute' and cannot be overridden. This can lead to problems where moral rules conflict. The rules could be qualified but this weakens their value. Instead, other deontologists argue for *prima facie* duties, which means that where two moral duties conflict their relative moral weights must be determined in order to give primacy to the more compelling rule. This is necessarily situation-dependent. Ross lists seven fundamental *prima facie* duties:

(1) fidelity;
(2) reparation;
(3) gratitude;
(4) justice;
(5) beneficence;
(6) self-improvement;
(7) non-maleficence.

In the medical ethics setting, Beauchamp and Childress (2001) lay down four essential principles:

(1) autonomy;
(2) beneficence;
(3) non-maleficence;
(4) justice.

Some medical ethicists would add a further principle to this list:

(5) veracity.

1.1.3 Religious theories
Each religion has its own views on morality. Although secular ethics has evolved from the religious approach, it is not appropriate to consider them here as this book takes a secular approach. For a consideration of medical ethics from a Christian perspective see Ramsey (1970).

1.1.4 Contractarian theories
Strictly speaking, these theories are political but they are relevant to medical ethics – especially when considering resource allocation and other issues of justice. Perhaps the most notable contractarian theory is Rawls' *A Theory of Justice* (1972). This social theory requires a hypothetical 'veil of ignorance' that prevents the individual from knowing his role in society – whether a leper or politician. From this impartial viewpoint Rawls argues that an individual would choose a system of justice with two main principles:

(1) each person should have a maximum liberty that is compatible with the same degree of liberty for everyone within the community; and

(2) an unequal distribution of goods and resources would be unjust unless such a distribution improved the lot of the least advantaged.

1.1.5   Feminist theories

In the space available it would be impossible to do justice to the various feminist approaches to bioethics. It should be noted that there is no single feminist approach; however, important considerations that inform feminist theories include the importance of: a care-based approach to ethics; the body; dealing with the ethics of difference (sex, race and disability); and developing a relational approach that accounts for the individual situated within a complex network of relationships rather than the more individualistic approach to autonomy found in some liberal writing (see Donchin and Purdy, 1999; Tong, 1997).

1.2   Ethical principles

1.2.1   Autonomy and respect for autonomy

Autonomy literally means self-governance. There is no universal agreement as to its exact meaning and the term is often used interchangeably with self-determination. It is valued because it is through autonomy that our character is shaped. It is the exercise of our autonomy that makes us the person we are and provides us with our dignity. Definitions include:

- 'The idea of autonomy is a blindingly obvious one. It simply means that if I am to act in an ethical or moral way I must choose for myself what I am going to do' – Charlesworth (1993).

- '... the capacity to think, decide, and act on the basis of such thought and decision freely and independently ... In the sphere of action it is important to distinguish between ... simply doing what one wants to do and, on the other hand, acting autonomously, which may also be doing what one wants to do but on the basis of thought or reasoning' – Gillon (1985).

- 'Autonomy is a second order capacity to reflect critically upon one's first order preferences and desires, and the ability either to identify with these or to change them in light of higher order preferences and values' – Dworkin (1988).

- '... freely and actively making one's own evaluative (requires true beliefs and rationality) choices about how one's life should go' – Savulescu and Momeyer (1997).

- 'Personal autonomy is, at a minimum, self-rule that is free from both controlling interference by others and from limitations, such as inadequate understanding, that prevent meaningful choice. The autonomous individual freely acts in accordance with a self chosen plan' – Beauchamp and Childress (2001).

Autonomy may be used in three senses (Mappes and Zembaty, 1991):

(1) Liberty (freedom) of action – lack of coercion, intentional action, voluntary action.

(2) Freedom of choice – implies a positive obligation on others to ensure that an adequate range of choices is made available.

(3) Effective deliberation – implies rational thought, the ability to form appropriate goals and determine how best to achieve those goals.

A distinction should be made between an autonomous person and an autonomous action. This is very relevant to the assessment of decision-making capacity, which is a pre-requisite for the legal validity of consent. The English law of consent recognises this distinction since it protects *any* decision of an autonomous person. An autonomous person is one who is capable of acting autonomously but this does not mean that all of his actions will be autonomous. Beauchamp and Childress argue that an autonomous action has three components: (a) an intentional act; which is (b) based on an understanding of the circumstances; and (c) is without controlling influences. To this, it might be added that for an act to be autonomous it must be rational.

It is also important to note that autonomy is not an all-or-none characteristic. Individuals will possess a greater or lesser degree of autonomy. Even where the individual's autonomy is extremely limited it is still important to respect that autonomy and to maximise it as far as possible. It should be borne in mind that one goal of medicine is to return the individual to their pre-illness level of autonomy. However, where the individual is incapable of making an autonomous decision, paternalistic intervention can be justified, as it will promote or protect that individual's autonomy. In fact, respect for autonomy demands paternalistic intervention in situations where the individual lacks the requisite capacity. Paternalism is not justified where the individual has the capacity to make an autonomous decision even if the decision they make is not an autonomous one.

A respect for autonomy demands that both the state and other members of the community respect the decisions and actions of an autonomous person. This is not simply a negative duty of non-interference but also requires the positive obligation that choices are made available to the individual. However, autonomy and respect for autonomy are not absolute.

The negative duty of non-interference with another's autonomy may be justifiably constrained by liberty-limiting principles. The most widely accepted of these principles is Mill's 'Harm principle', which states that the only justification for interfering with an individual's autonomy is where it prevents harm to a third party. Some authors, more controversially, would extend this to include the prevention of self-harm (Raz, 1989).

The positive obligation entailed by a respect for autonomy may be justifiably constrained by the following:

• This duty does not exist universally but requires a 'special relationship' between the parties. Such relationships exist between the state and the members of its community, between the professional and his client, and between parent and child.

• This duty is owed equally to all individuals within the community and thus one person's choices cannot be legitimately promoted at the expense of another's.

- The duty only exists where there are sufficient resources available to make the choices meaningful.
- There is no duty to provide choices that are 'futile' and will not promote an individual's autonomous life plan. There is no obligation to promote the non-autonomous choices of an individual simply because he is autonomous.
- There is no obligation to promote an individual's autonomy if it compromises the promoter's moral integrity.

An individual's autonomy may be unjustifiably infringed or constrained by the following:

- coercion;
- misinformation – including lying;
- withholding information;
- restricting or not offering choices.

Additionally, internal factors such as illness, pain, strong emotion, inadequate mental capacity and mental disorders such as phobias or compulsive disorders may limit autonomy.

As a principle, the concept of autonomy provides a broad guide as to how to treat others. By considering the ways in which autonomy may be infringed it is possible to develop more specific rules based on autonomy. Beauchamp and Childress (2001) provide some examples of these more specific rules, which include:

- tell the truth;
- respect the individual's privacy;
- protect confidences;
- ensure that consent is obtained for medical interventions;
- when asked, help others to make decisions.

To this list may be added:

- make an adequate range of choices available.

It is worth remembering that Kant's notion of autonomy was rational self-governance constrained by universal moral rules. Thus, Kant's autonomous act is one that flows from a sense of universal moral duty and not from selfishness, or even self-interest. This is somewhat different to the more egocentric, modern 'Kantian' notion of autonomy (see Secker, 1999).

1.2.2 Beneficence and non-maleficence
In its book, *Medical Ethics Today*, the BMA quotes Ranaan Gillon (1993) who wrote: 'The central moral objective of medicine ... is to produce net medical benefit for the patient with as little harm as possible. Today we may add to that Hippocratic objective the moral qualifications that we should pursue it in a way that respects people's deliberated choices for themselves and that is just and fair to others' (BMA, 2003). This statement, which begins the BMA's discussion of medical ethics, emphasises the dominant, if constrained, position that beneficence holds in healthcare practice.

The principle of beneficence owes its origin to three influences: the Hippocratic Oath, the Good Samaritan Christian ethic, and the Noblesse Oblige ethic of the Order of the Knights Hospitallers of the Crusades (see Jonsen, 1990).

Put simply, the principle of beneficence is the moral duty to act for the benefit of others. It is a positive obligation that requires both the provision of benefits, and the prevention and removal of harm (such as pain or ill health). The obligation extends to all healthcare professionals by virtue of their professional role. Thus, a surgeon would be expected to perform the most appropriate operation for the patient rather than performing an alternative that they would prefer because it would be good experience for them and enhance their career. However, it would not require the professional to offer his own kidney for transplantation if none other was available.

Beneficence also exists as an imperfect obligation, which means that, outside of special relationships, it is morally good to act for the benefit of others but a failure to act in this way is not morally bad.

Beauchamp and Childress (2001) suggest a number of moral rules supported by the principle of beneficence:

- protect and defend the rights of others;
- prevent harm from occurring to others;
- remove conditions that will cause harm to others;
- help persons with disabilities;
- rescue persons in danger.

Beneficence may be constrained by the choice of the autonomous person. If the patient refuses an intervention that the professional believes would be of benefit, then the professional must respect that choice. A caveat is that the professional must ensure that the patient has all the necessary information, and has given proper consideration to the issue. A contentious issue is whether the professional should override a non-autonomous choice made by an autonomous individual. Legally, the professional must respect the patient's choice, but morally there is a strong argument for overriding a choice that will adversely affect that patient's future autonomy. A problem arises in this area in deciding what counts as a benefit. Should benefits be objectively or subjectively determined? If subjectively determined, should the patient or the healthcare professional determine what is a benefit? Traditionally it has been the physician who decides but this is a paternalistic approach that is no longer acceptable. It is disrespectful of the patient's autonomy not to take into account the patient's view of what constitutes a benefit.

Another constraint on beneficence is that of justice. The professional owes an obligation of beneficence to all of his patients. It might be unjust for the physician to provide the best treatment to one patient if it is so expensive that it uses up resources that would have benefited other patients.

Non-maleficence is simply the obligation not to cause harm. Because it is a negative obligation, it has a wider application and is universally applicable. Unlike beneficence, it is a perfect obligation. However, it may be trumped by other principles, such as beneficence, if the overall result is beneficial and maximises utility. This is the justification for surgical operations. The harm caused by the incision and removal or damage to tissue must be less than the benefit that the patient will receive from the operation. The decision as to what constitutes a net benefit is one that should be made by the patient with the expert advice of the professional. It is important to note that overriding an autonomous person's wishes is itself a harm irrespective of any physical harm that the treatment causes.

It is also worth noting that medical decisions involve a greater or lesser degree of uncertainty that may affect the balancing of harms and benefits. Consider a man with a gangrenous leg. Surgical amputation offers a good chance (though not 100%) of survival but with the certainty that the man will lose the affected limb. Medical treatment with antibiotics offers a much lower chance of survival (say 15–20%) but the man retains his leg and so will not be disabled. The patient is the only person who can ultimately provide a value rating for such a disabled life that will allow a proper balancing judgment to be made against the risk of death. The role of the healthcare professional is to assist the patient in making the decision and not to make that judgment for him. For this reason, beneficence and non-maleficence must be constrained by the wishes of the autonomous patient. The professional's duty of beneficence and non-maleficence in these circumstances is to ensure that the patient has made a truly considered decision.

1.2.3 Justice

In this context, 'justice' refers to fairness or equity and not to lawfulness. Aristotle argued that an unjust act was one that caused the actor to gain more than their fair share. He distinguished two forms of 'particular justice' (1953):

(1) rectificatory justice – remedies an inequitable transaction between two parties; and
(2) distributive justice – remedies an inequitable distribution of community resources.

It is the second of these two types of justice that is most relevant to healthcare ethics. Aristotle believed that equals should receive equal shares and unequals should get unequal shares in proportion to their inequality. The judgment of equality should be based on some form of merit. Aristotle noted three different types that may be used:

(1) the democratic criterion of free birth (ie, not being born a slave);
(2) the oligarchic criterion of wealth or good family;
(3) the aristocratic criterion of excellence – this type of merit judgment would, for example, allow that an Olympic athlete should get preferential treatment to a 'fun runner'.

Another type of merit judgment that might be made is based on the criterion of 'need'. This raises the conceptual problem of what is meant by 'need'. Relevant factors in assessing need include:

- seriousness of illness or disability;
- capacity to benefit from the resources available – it would be unjust to give the last dose of an antibiotic to someone with a viral illness rather than to someone with a sensitive bacterial infection, because the individual with the viral infection has no capacity to benefit from the antibiotic;

- likelihood of further harm, or deterioration of the individual's condition;
- rapidity of any deterioration.

In making judgments of equality or inequality, the Rawlsian system discussed earlier might be a suitable mechanism. By operating behind the 'veil of ignorance' there would be less tendency to make decisions based on criteria that act to our advantage.

Utilitarian justice aims to maximise overall welfare. Although Mill argues that each person counts for one, and no-one for more than one, this does not mean that resources should be equally distributed. Instead, the aim is to maximise happiness regardless of its distribution amongst the members of the community. Thus, Mill states that 'equal amounts of happiness are equally desirable, whether felt by the same or different people'. Take three persons, A, B, and C, and 6 units of a resource, X. Let A gain 1 unit of happiness from each unit of X; let B gain 3 units of happiness from the 1st unit of X, 1 unit of happiness from the 2nd unit of X and none from any more units of X; and let C gain 1.5 units of happiness for the 1st three units of X followed by 0.5 units of happiness for the next 2 units of X and nothing for any more units of X. Consider distribution (1):

A: 2X = 2 units of happiness.
B: 2X = 4 units of happiness.
C: 2X = 3 units of happiness.

The overall happiness produced is 9 units and is unevenly distributed even though the resource was shared equally. Consider distribution (2):

A: 3X = 3 units of happiness.
B: 1X = 3 units of happiness.
C: 2X = 3 units of happiness.

Here the overall happiness is still 9 units but now it is evenly distributed although the resources were not. Finally, consider distribution (3):

A: 2X = 2 units of happiness.
B: 1X = 3 units of happiness.
C: 3X = 4.5 units of happiness.

Now the amount of happiness is maximised at 9.5 units but neither the distribution of resources nor the distribution of happiness is equal.

From the utilitarian's perspective, distribution (3) would be the most just. However, from the perspective of equality based on the capacity to benefit, distribution (2) would be the most appropriate. Distribution (1) would be favoured by a system that regards all men as equal and distributes resources accordingly.

1.2.4   *Veracity*

Traditionally, truth-telling has not received prominence in healthcare relationships. The argument is that a healthcare professional is justified in lying to a patient when the deception is used for the patient's benefit. Lipkin (1991) argues that: (1) telling the 'whole truth' is a practical impossibility; (2) patients are unable to interpret medical information accurately; and (3) patients do not always want to know the truth. This argument is still recognised by English common law in its concept of 'therapeutic privilege' (see Chapter 2). The argument for deception is based on the principles of beneficence and non-maleficence.

Telling a patient about serious risks may prevent the patient from consenting to a procedure the doctor believes is in the patient's best interests. The concern is that the severity of the potential outcome is blown out of all proportion relative to the probability of the risk materialising. Why worry the patient with unlikely possibilities? The counter-argument derives from the principle of autonomy; that is, the patient will be prevented from making a truly autonomous decision if they are not in possession of the relevant information. If they have been lied to about a particular risk, then their autonomy has been constrained. It might be argued that lying will prevent the patient from making a decision they later come to regret but this argument falls down for two reasons: first, there may be factors that the doctor is unaware of that are relevant to the decision and thus affect whether withholding the information is actually beneficial; and secondly, failing to respect the patient's autonomy – as discussed earlier – is a harm in its own right that would need to be entered in the benefit-harm judgment.

Another instance in which deception may occur is when the healthcare professional tries to 'protect' the patient from a poor prognosis. This is also unjustified for the same reasons as given in the first scenario. If a dying patient is not informed of this fact, they may lose the opportunity to ensure their affairs are in good order and to say goodbye to loved ones. Furthermore, deception can lead to uncertainty, anxiety, stress and depression. In addition, in an on-going relationship a lie will necessitate further lies in order to maintain the deception.

Deception is also unacceptable because it breaches the trust that is essential in the therapeutic relationship. Without trust the relationship breaks down. The patient will be reluctant to divulge information or rely on the advice of a person that they do not trust. Trust and respect are the cornerstones of the therapeutic relationship and a lack of veracity erodes both of these.

One argument against telling the truth arises from the philosophical difficulty in ever being able to know what the absolute truth is. Most medical advice and decisions are based on probabilities and uncertainties. However, this objection to veracity falters if we add the caveat that the healthcare professional's duty is to honestly tell the truth as he believes it to be based on the available evidence.

Another argument against truth-telling is that patients do not want to be given bad news or told of serious risks. Although there are individuals who do prefer to leave the decision up to the doctor, this does not justify a global policy of lying or deception. Most studies suggest that patients generally want more information and not less. In one study the doctor underestimated the patient's desire for information in 65% of the encounters (Waitzkin, 1984). Withholding information or lying is the type of behaviour characteristic of a relationship in which the physician retains a high degree of control over the encounter and is paternalistic in nature.

Ellin (1991) distinguishes between lying and deception. Lying is the provision of false information while deception is the provision of true information that in some way fails to convey the whole picture. This may be achieved through a combination of withholding some information and providing other information that appears to be sufficient. Ellin argues that there should be an absolute prohibition on lying but deception should not even be considered a *prima facie* wrong. He suggests that deception should just be another medical tool, which is justified providing it is used in the patient's best interests. This model places beneficence above autonomy. The difficulty with it is that the doctor will have to make a judgment about the patient's best interests when that role is really the prerogative of the autonomous patient. It is arguably over-paternalistic.

One final problem with the practice of lying and deceiving is that, although purported to be in the patient's best interests, it may simply be a result of or a defence to an inability to communicate effectively in a sensitive and compassionate way. Randall and Downie (1996) argue: 'The high value which we place on truth in the community, in conjunction with our concept of individuality and of ownership of our bodies, leads to the conclusion that we are entitled to the truth about our health which intimately relates to our welfare.' As Sissela Bok (1978) notes: 'we are coming to learn much more about the benefits ... [information] ... can bring patients. People follow instructions more carefully if they know what their disease is and why they're asked to take medication ... Similarly, people recover faster from surgery and tolerate pain with less medication if they understand what ails them and what can be done for them.'

1.3   Paternalism

Buchanan (1978) defines paternalism as 'interference with a person's freedom of action or freedom of information, or the deliberate dissemination of misinformation, where the alleged justification of interfering or misinforming is that it is for the good of the person who is interfered with or misinformed'.

Gerald Dworkin (1972) provides a simpler, but less broad definition: '[Paternalism is] the interference with a person's liberty of action justified by reasons referring exclusively to the welfare, good, happiness, needs, interests or values of the person being coerced.'

Mappes and Zembatty (1991) state: 'Paternalism is the interference with, limitation of, or usurpation of individual autonomy justified by reasons referring exclusively to the welfare or need of the person whose autonomy is being interfered with, limited, or usurped.'

A simple conception of paternalism is to view it as treating another person as a child.

Mill argued that the only justification for interfering with another person's liberty is to prevent harm to others. He tempered this strong stance against paternalism by arguing that it did not apply to children or the mentally incompetent.

There are three reasons why paternalism is generally unjustified:

(1) The idea that doctor knows best is unfounded. It falters because the doctor is unlikely to know enough about the individual patient to enable him to make such a judgment.
(2) Very often, in making such a 'best interests judgment', the healthcare professional is simply substituting their own moral values for those of the

patient. There is no reason to think that the healthcare professional has any expertise, qualification or right to believe that their moral values are preferable to the patient's.

(3) Paternalism infringes the right of the individual to control what happens to them. It fails to respect the person, his personality, individuality and autonomy.

Paternalism is, however, occasionally justified. 'Weak paternalism' is consistent with Mill's position. It holds that paternalism is justified:

- to prevent those with a significantly reduced autonomy from harming themselves; and
- to temporarily restrain a person from an apparently irrational self-harming act while it is determined whether that person has sufficient autonomy. This justifies the non-consensual treatment of persons who have attempted to commit suicide until their competency can be formally assessed.

1.4   Virtues

A moral approach that can be used as an alternative, or supplement, to the principles approach is to focus on self-development and the characteristics that a moral person should strive to enhance. These characteristics are called 'virtues'. Both Kant and Mill support the idea of personal development. As Mill (1991) puts it: 'In proportion to the development of his individuality, each person becomes more valuable to himself, and is therefore capable of being more valuable to others.' Randall and Downie (1996) suggest that healthcare professionals have a duty to maintain their own self-development because this ensures the professional is a 'morally developed person who happens to follow a given professional path … [which] … is good both for its own sake and for what it gives to patients, friends, and families'.

Virtues that are particularly valuable in a healthcare setting include:

- compassion (caring);
- kindness;
- forgiveness;
- generosity;
- integrity;
- humility;
- courage;
- fidelity;
- trust;
- justice or fairness;
- understanding.

1.5   Power

A number of writers focus on issues of power. There is a disparity in power between the healthcare professional and the patient. In most settings, the healthcare professional enjoys the balance of power because:

- he has a greater knowledge of health matters;
- the interview is usually on his 'home ground' (where the patient is seen on a home visit, the power balance shifts);
- his autonomy is unaffected by illness, disease or the need for someone else's help;
- the language, discourse and institution of medicine all favour the healthcare professional;
- he has 'control' over what treatments to offer, the timing of the treatments and the place of the treatments.

Howard Brody (1992) argues that the physician's power can be divided into three components:

(1) Aesculapian: derives from the medical skills and knowledge he possesses.
(2) Charismatic: derives from the physician's personal qualities.
(3) Social: derives from the social standing of physicians.

Brody argues that 'The central ethical problem in medicine is the responsible use of power'. For this, the physician must 'own' (acknowledge), 'share' (with the patient) and 'aim' (direct its use for the benefit of the patient) that power.

A post-modern approach decries the rational principles approach that retrospectively focuses on ethical dilemmas at the professional-patient level. Instead, the principles should be applied within an approach that 'includes issues of discourse, power, control and subjectivity' (McGrath, 1998). This involves applying the principles, such as autonomy, within an institution whose discourse provides a way of approaching autonomy that empowers the patient, offers them real choices, enables them to make a choice and supports that choice in a non-judgmental manner. A failure to take a global view of the situation risks the possibility that the application of the principles will simply promote the current biomedical discourse and further the physician-patient power imbalance.

1.6   Models of professional-patient relationships

Various models (see Veatch, 1972) have been described to try and explain the ideal relationship that should exist between healthcare professional and patient. None of the models are perfect as the relationship probably varies depending on the context. The reality is more complex than can be defined by a single model and a combination of these models is necessary. However, the models may be useful in defined circumstances.

1.6.1   The fiduciary or trustee model

In this model the patient places his body and his health 'in trust' with the physician. The physician is morally obligated to act in that patient's best interests. The physician must consider the wishes of the patient but ultimately it is he who must take responsibility for the decision. While there are elements of this model in all professional-patient relationships, it is perhaps best suited to the medical care of an incompetent patient. It also applies where the patient requests that the physician (assuming he accepts the responsibility) make the decision for him.

1.6.2   The priestly model

This represents the traditional paternalistic doctor-patient relationship. Its main ethical principle is 'Benefit and do no harm to the patient', which takes precedence over the patient's autonomy. It is a paternalistic model that ascribes a religious or spiritual authority to the doctor and creates an unbalanced ethical situation that devalues individual freedom and dignity, truth-telling, promise-keeping and justice. It enhances the doctor's power at the expense of the patient, and tends to focus on the patient's medical needs to the exclusion of other considerations such as respect and autonomy.

1.6.3   The engineering model

This results from the impact of science. The doctor behaves like an applied scientist and vainly attempts to divorce himself from all value judgments. The physician presents all the facts to the patient and leaves the entire responsibility of making the decision to the patient. Veatch (1972) suggests that this 'would make him an engineer, a plumber making repairs, connecting tubes and flushing out clogged systems, with no questions asked'.

1.6.4   The customer-salesperson model

In this model the patient takes the role of the customer. The essential feature of the model is that 'the customer is always right'. The duty of care of the physician is simply to respond honestly to any requests for information but he is under no obligation to volunteer the information. The physician is under a duty to only provide 'goods' that are suitable for their purpose and must also warn of any dangers or risks. Ultimately, however, sole responsibility lies with the patient and the physician accepts no moral responsibility for the treatment decision. This model gains credibility from the political drive to run healthcare along the lines of a market economy. However, it reduces the role, duty and moral responsibility of the physician too far. It also means that a healthcare professional may sometimes have to provide a service to which they are morally opposed (see Randall and Downie, 1996).

1.6.5   The collegial or partnership model

The physician and patient are colleagues working in partnership towards the common goal of restoring and maintaining the patient's health. It enhances the roles of trust, confidence and commitment creating an 'equality of dignity and respect' (Veatch, 1972). Both parties share the responsibility for decision-making. This model is wholly inappropriate when the patient lacks sufficient autonomy. It also fails to recognise the reality that the doctor usually has a far greater knowledge than the patient. Furthermore, the doctor's autonomy is not diminished by ill health and the interaction is usually on the doctor's 'home ground'. All these factors result in a power imbalance that makes a truly equal partnership difficult to achieve. It is perhaps also unrealistic, because of ethnic, class, religious, economic and value differences, to expect doctors and their patients to share common goals.

1.6.6   The contractual model

This is to be seen as a symbolic contract or covenant, which provides expected obligations and benefits for both parties arrived at through negotiation. It recognises that there may not be common goals and it respects the 'basic norms of freedom, dignity, truth-telling, promise-keeping and justice' (Veatch, 1972). It requires the trust and confidence of both parties and respects the autonomy and moral values of both doctor and patient. It means that a doctor is not obliged to provide a treatment they disagree with and it means that a patient cannot be treated against their will. The patient accepts moral responsibility for his decision while the doctor retains responsibility for the choices offered to the patient, assistance given to help the patient understand and make their decision, and in the performance of the treatment agreed upon. Again, it is an inappropriate model for incompetent patients. Also, since the provision of the goods is in the hands of the doctor, there may be an undue imbalance of power. This is especially true in a healthcare setting where the patient does not directly pay for the doctor's services. Theoretically, the patient can shop around for a doctor willing to provide the required service but this is not often practical in a system that operates through regional funding. It may also be impossible if the patient is seriously ill. As Randall and Downie (1996) note: 'It tells you how you must not act but not how you should act.' Thus, a contractual model may not always enable a consensual decision that is in the best interests of the patient as an holistic person.

Feminist philosophers have criticised this individualistic approach to medical relationships as failing to take into account the effect of prevailing social and cultural conditions. It views the doctor-patient relationship from the perspective of an educated white middle class male. The autonomy of less privileged individuals may preclude such a relationship. Instead we should view these interactions in context, taking notice of the power imbalance created by the patient's race, sex, social class, etc. Apart from the fact that these individuals may require a more proactive approach on the part of the doctor to ensure they are enabled to make an autonomous choice, the entire social institution of medicine – including the patriarchal training of doctors – needs to be reconsidered within a social and cultural context (see Parks, 1998).

1.6.7   The educational model

The educational model was proposed to account for healthcare provision by teams of professionals and to allow consideration of patients whose previous lives have been so radically altered by disease or injury that they need time to adjust. The model allows a greater leeway for paternalism in the early stages of an encounter while the patient is 're-educated' to understand the potentials and limitations that their new condition has placed on their prior autonomy. The process should always aim to enhance the patient's autonomy. Caplan (1988) states: 'In the earliest stages of care which follow the onset of unexpected, irreversible, and severe impairment, the healthcare team has an obligation to act in ways that encourage patients to participate in their own care, not simply to present options.' The aim is to gradually increase the patient's involvement in making decisions for themselves about the rehabilitation programme. It thus requires regular assessment and review. The model also encourages the involvement of the patient's relatives and agreement with the patient should be sought as to the extent of his family's involvement. The patient should also be made aware of the team approach and where the power and responsibility lie within the team. Caplan stresses that the model does not justify non-consensual invasive interventions.

1.7   The goals of medicine

1.7.1   Traditional goals

- The saving and extending of life.
- The promotion and maintenance of health.
- The relief of pain and suffering.

1.7.2   Definition of health

... the experience of well-being and integrity of mind and body ... characterized by an acceptable absence of significant malady, and consequently by a person's ability to pursue his or her vital goals and to function in ordinary social and work contexts (Callahan, 1996).

1.7.3   Four goals of medicine

- The prevention of disease and injury and the promotion and maintenance of health.
- The relief of pain and suffering caused by maladies.
- The care and cure of those with a malady, and the care of those who cannot be cured.
- The avoidance of premature death and the pursuit of a peaceful death.

A premature death is one that occurs before the person 'had an opportunity to experience the main possibilities of a characteristically human life cycle ... Within an individual life cycle a death may be premature if, even at an advanced age, life could be preserved or extended with no great burden on the individual or society' (Callahan, 1996).

1.7.4   The BMA and the aim of medicine

For many patients with serious conditions there comes a stage where no more can be done to save or prolong life and the aim of medicine shifts from curative treatment to keeping the patient comfortable and free from pain ... The aim of medicine is not, and should not be, to avoid death for as long as possible, but to recognise and accept what is inevitable and to make the dying process as positive as possible for all concerned (BMA, 2003).

CHAPTER 2

CONSENT AND INFORMATION DISCLOSURE

The moral basis of consent is founded on the principle of autonomy. In the US case, *Schloendorff v Society of New York Hospital* (1914), Cardozo J famously stated that 'every human being of adult years and sound mind has a right to determine what shall be done with his own body; and a surgeon who performs an operation without his patient's consent commits an assault'.

Consent transforms a morally forbidden act into a morally permitted act and this transformation is recognised and given legal force in both criminal law (eg, rape and battery) and in the civil law of trespass against the person. Thus, in the Court of Appeal hearing of *F v W Berkshire HA* (1990), Neill LJ stated that 'Treatment or surgery which would otherwise be unlawful as a trespass is made lawful by the consent of the patient'.

Generally, there are three conditions that must be satisfied for consent to be legally effective: (1) the patient must be competent to make the decision; (2) the patient must understand the nature and purpose of the act; and (3) the decision must be voluntary (free from coercion and undue influence). A further constraint is that the act is one that is not contrary to public policy or made unlawful by statute (see 2.7 below).

Because of a judicial reluctance to find doctors liable for battery, which has criminal connotations, only gross failures of consent will succeed in battery. Most cases in the UK involve a failure to disclose risks (in the US the physician's experience has also become an issue, as in *Johnson v Kokemoor* (1996)) and are brought as claims of negligence. Traditionally, the standard of disclosure has been determined by the *Bolam* test (see 12.4 below). Recently, the courts have become more willing to question common medical practice and the test has arguably inched towards the prudent patient standard (see *Pearce* (1999), 2.4 below) applied by some US states, Canada and Australia.

2.1 Competence

Re T (Adult: Refusal of Medical Treatment) (1992): The patient must be competent to give consent, but there is a presumption of competence in favour of the patient

Facts

T, a pregnant woman, was admitted to hospital following a car accident. T herself was not a Jehovah's Witness, but following a private conversation with her mother – who had raised T and was a practising Jehovah's Witness – refused any blood transfusions. When an emergency Caesarean section became necessary she repeated her refusal. After the operation her condition worsened and she was kept sedated and ventilated in the intensive care unit. Her father and boyfriend appealed to the court to authorise a blood transfusion despite her earlier refusal of consent. At first instance the judge held that T had neither consented nor refused consent and it would be lawful under the doctrine of necessity for the doctors to administer blood. T appealed.

Decision
The Court of Appeal dismissed the appeal. It was lawful for the doctors to administer the transfusion. Lord Donaldson MR stated: 'The right to decide one's own fate presupposes a capacity to do so. Every adult is presumed to have that capacity but it is a presumption that can be rebutted. This is not a question of the degree of intelligence or education of the adult concerned.'

Comment
The draft Mental Capacity Bill 2004, if it becomes law, will give the presumption statutory force.

Re C (Adult: Refusal of Treatment) (1994): Even where the patient is suffering from a mental disorder or disability there is a presumption of competence

Facts
C was an elderly chronic schizophrenic who had been resident in Broadmoor for 30 years. He had developed a gangrenous foot and the risk of his death without amputation was estimated to be about 85%. C refused consent because he was born with four limbs and he intended to die with them intact. He also believed that God did not want him to have an amputation. One of his delusional beliefs was that he was a great doctor with the ability to cure damaged limbs and had never failed to cure his patients. He did accept that without the amputation he might die.

Decision
Thorpe J, sitting in the High Court, granted an injunction to prevent amputation, and held that there was a rebuttable presumption in favour of C's competence.

Comment
The Law Commission (1995) proposed that 'a person should not be regarded as unable to make a decision by reason of mental disability merely because he or she makes a decision which would not be made by a person of ordinary prudence'.

Re MB (Medical Treatment) (1997): An irrational decision may be evidence of incompetence but it is not the same as incompetence

Facts
MB was a 23-year-old pregnant woman who first sought antenatal care at 33 weeks. A Caesarean section was advised because the baby was in a breech position. She consented to the Caesarean operation but, because of a needle phobia, refused consent to the anaesthesia. Initially she agreed to inhalational anaesthesia but then withdrew that consent when she saw the mask. The risk to her baby was assessed as a 50% likelihood of serious injury if delivered vaginally. There was, however, little physical risk to the mother. The hospital sought a declaration that it would be lawful to operate. At first instance, Hollis J granted the declaration on the basis that the needle phobia rendered MB temporarily incompetent to decide. MB appealed.

Decision

The Court of Appeal dismissed the appeal. Because her needle phobia rendered her incompetent, the declaration that a non-consensual Caesarean section was lawful was upheld. Butler-Sloss LJ said: 'A competent woman who has the capacity to decide may, for … rational or irrational reasons or for no reason at all, choose not to have medical intervention even though the consequence may be the death or serious handicap of the child she bears or her own death.'

Comment

Butler-Sloss LJ defined an irrational decision as one that is 'so outrageous in its defiance of logic or accepted moral standards that no sensible person who had applied his mind to the question to be decided could have arrived at it'.

To truly respect the patient's autonomy, the test should be applied to the patient's *capacity* to make decisions rather than the actual decision. This has to be the case if Butler-Sloss LJ's *dictum* is followed. However, in many cases, including *Re C*, the test seems to be applied to the patient's actual decision (see also *Rochdale Healthcare (NHS) Trust v C* (1997), 3.1 below).

Re T (Adult: Refusal of Medical Treatment) (1992): The threshold for competence varies with the seriousness or risk of the decision

Facts

See above.

Decision

See above. In the Court of Appeal Lord Donaldson MR stated: 'What matters is that doctors should consider whether at that time [the patient] had a capacity which was commensurate with the gravity of the decision which he purported to make. The more serious the decision, the greater the capacity required.'

Comment

This risk-related standard is open to the criticism that the level of competence required varies with the complexity of the decision rather than its gravity. Certainly it does not always seem to be applied. It was not referred to in *Re C (Adult: Refusal of Treatment)* and appears not to have been applied in that instance. It was, however, referred to with approval in *Re MB (Medical Treatment)*.

2.2 The patient must understand the nature and purpose of the act

Mohr v Williams (1905) USA: The consent must be for the procedure performed

Facts

The plaintiff consented to an operation on her right ear. During the operation, while the plaintiff was anaesthetised, the surgeon found that it was the left ear rather than the right ear that required surgery. He successfully performed the operation on the plaintiff's left ear.

Decision

The Supreme Court of Minnesota held that the surgeon was liable for battery.

Comment

See also the English case, *Cull v Butler* (1932), in which a surgeon was liable for battery when he removed the plaintiff's uterus (womb) even though she had only consented to an abortion.

Devi v West Midlands RHA (1981): If the operation performed is not the one for which consent has been given, then it is irrelevant that it was in the patient's best interests

Facts

The patient consented to an operation to repair her ruptured uterus, which had been punctured during an evacuation of retained products following the birth of her fourth child. Because he believed it was in her best interests, the surgeon, while her abdomen was open anyway, sterilised her by occluding her fallopian tubes.

Decision

The Court of Appeal held that the surgeon was liable for battery.

Chatterton v Gerson (1981): Providing the patient has given a 'real' consent, there will be no liability for battery

Facts

The plaintiff suffered chronic pain in a scar from a previous hernia operation. The defendant administered spinal phenol to destroy the appropriate pain-conducting nerves. Following the second injection the plaintiff's right leg was left numb and her mobility was affected. She alleged that her consent was invalid because she had not been warned of these risks.

Decision

The High Court held that the plaintiff's action for trespass failed. Bristow J stated: 'It is clear that in any context in which the consent of the injured party is a defence to what would otherwise be a crime or a civil wrong, the consent must be real ... In my judgment once the patient is informed in broad terms of the nature of the procedure which is intended, and gives her consent, that consent is real.'

Comment

This case established the current conditions for determining whether a lack of information invalidates consent and gives rise to battery or whether the more appropriate cause of action is in the tort of negligence. Thus 'the cause of action on which to base a claim for failure to go into risks and implications is negligence, not trespass', *per* Bristow J. In the event, the plaintiff's claim for negligence also failed.

Hills v Potter (1984): It is not necessary for 'real' consent that the risks associated with a procedure be disclosed

Facts

The plaintiff was operated on to relieve the spasmodic torticollis affecting her neck. Following the operation, the patient was left paralysed. The plaintiff alleged that, because of the defendant's failure to inform of the risks, her consent to the operation was not 'real or effective' and the operation was a battery.

Decision

The High Court held that the plaintiff's consent was 'real' and the operation was not a battery. The plaintiff's claim in negligence also failed.

Comment

Hirst J stated: 'I should add that I respectfully agree with Bristow J [*Chatterton v Gerson*] in deploring reliance on these torts in medical cases of these kind; the proper cause of action, if any, is negligence.' His comment shows how reluctant the courts are to find a doctor liable for battery; hence the sometimes strained reasoning that can be found (see *Davis v Barking, Havering and Brentwood HA* (1993) (below)). The House of Lords in *Sidaway* (1985) (see 2.4 below) confirmed that risk disclosure is relevant to negligence liability rather than battery: 'I conclude, therefore, that there is room in our law for a legal duty to warn a patient of the risks inherent in the treatment proposed, and that, if such a duty be held to exist, its proper place is as an aspect of the duty of care owed by the doctor to his patient', *per* Lord Scarman.

Davis v Barking, Havering and Brentwood HA (1993): It is not necessary to get a separate consent for each part of a procedure

Facts

The plaintiff underwent a minor gynaecological procedure. The anaesthetist discussed a general anaesthetic but did not mention the possibility of a local anaesthetic. The plaintiff signed a general consent form. She was given a general anaesthetic and while asleep the anaesthetist performed a caudal local anaesthetic block. She was left with loss of sensation in her left leg and altered bladder control. The plaintiff claimed damages for battery because she had not specifically consented to the caudal.

Decision

The High Court held that it was enough that the patient understood, in broad terms, that she would have an anaesthetic. The explanation of the general anaesthetic satisfied that requirement. It was not necessary to 'sectionalise' consent to include a separate consent for every possible form of anaesthesia.

Comment

McCullough J's approach strains the concept of 'real' consent to breaking point and clearly originates from a judicial desire not to find doctors liable for battery. The GMC has adopted a different, and arguably more appropriate, approach. They held that an anaesthetist was guilty of serious professional misconduct when – although the patient had consented to the general anaesthetic – he failed to get specific consent for a rectally administered painkiller that he inserted while she was still asleep. For a greater discussion of this issue, see Maclean (2002a).

Brusnett v Cowan (1991): In determining what is included in a patient's consent, it is necessary to look at all the circumstances leading up to the signing of the consent form

Facts

The plaintiff consented to a diagnostic muscle biopsy. She signed a consent form that stated she agreed to any 'further or alternative measures as may be found to be necessary during the course of the operation'. The defendant performed the muscle biopsy but also biopsied the underlying bone. The plaintiff alleged that she had not consented to the bone biopsy and sued for damages in battery.

Decision

The Newfoundland Court of Appeal held that, looking at the whole set of circumstances, she had not simply consented to a muscle biopsy. Her consent was to an investigative procedure for the problem she was having in her right leg. This included, in such broad terms, both the muscle and bone biopsy.

Chatterton v Gerson (1981): It is the content, not the form, of a consent that is important

Facts

See above.

Decision

See above. The High Court held, *obiter*, that a pre-printed consent form signed by the patient is evidential only. It is not a substitute for 'real' consent but may provide evidence to support a claim that consent was in fact obtained.

Comment

It is common for consent forms to contain clauses that indicate the patient agrees to whatever further procedures may be necessary (or understands that such procedures will only be carried out if necessary in the patient's best interests). On the face of it this should only allow procedures that are essential to preserve life (or prevent a serious deterioration of health) and cannot wait. But, in *Pridham v Nash* (1986), Holland J argued that such clauses allowed the surgeon to therapeutically divide adhesions (unfortunately resulting in peritonitis) during a diagnostic laparoscopy. Holland J limited the clause to minor surgery: 'If the laparoscopic examination, an investigative procedure, had revealed a major problem requiring surgery then, in my view, the surgeon would not be entitled to rely on the original consent and the general words of the consent ... to carry out the major surgery.'

Freeman v Home Office (No 2) (1984): It is for the patient to prove an absence of consent

Facts

The plaintiff was serving a term of life imprisonment. He alleged that drugs had been forcibly administered to him without his consent. The plaintiff claimed that, because he was a prisoner, he was not capable of consenting.

Decision

The Court of Appeal rejected the claim: he was capable of consenting and had failed to establish that he had not in fact done so.

Comment

In the High Court, McCowan J considered Bristow J's judgment in *Chatterton v Gerson*. He stated: 'I would read this as indicating that Bristow J took the view that it was for the plaintiff to show the absence of real consent.' The Court of Appeal did not refer to the point but it is consistent with the law relating to rape from which the courts have carried over the principles relating to mistake, fraud and misrepresentation. The opposite is true in Australia, where the burden of proof lies with the doctor: see *Department of Health & Community Services (NT) v JWB and SMB* (1992).

2.3 The requirement for voluntariness

Re T (Adult: Refusal of Medical Treatment) (1992): Consent may be vitiated by duress or undue influence

Facts

See 2.1 above.

Decision

The Court of Appeal held, *inter alia*, that the plaintiff's mother had subjected her to an 'undue influence' which vitiated her decision to refuse the blood. Staughton LJ stated: 'In order for an apparent consent or refusal of consent to be less than a true consent or refusal, there must be such a degree of external influence as to persuade the patient to depart from her own wishes, to the extent that the law regards it as undue.'

Comment

Re T was relied on in *Mrs U v Centre for Reproductive Medicine* (2002) to deny the claim that the claimant's husband had been unduly influenced to withdraw his consent to embryo storage. Dame Butler-Sloss P stated: 'As Lord Donaldson said in *Re T*, it does not matter how strong the persuasion was so long as it did not overbear the independence of the patient's decision.'

Appleton v Garrett (1997): Consent may be vitiated by mistake as to the nature of the act

Facts

The plaintiffs had expensive restorative dental work carried out on healthy teeth. The work was unnecessary and the defendant dentist had carried it out purely for financial gain.

Decision

The High Court held that none of the plaintiffs had given a 'real' consent and the treatment was a battery.

Comment

This was a civil case but could equally have been brought under the criminal law. Although the dentist had deliberately misled his patients, neither fraud nor misrepresentation is theoretically necessary. In *Papadimitropoulos v R* (1957) the High Court of Australia stated: 'In considering whether an apparent consent is unreal it is the mistake or misapprehension that makes it so. It is not the fraud producing the mistake which is material so much as the mistake itself.'

R v Richardson (1998): Consent may be vitiated by mistake as to the identity of the actor

Facts
The appellant was a dentist who had been suspended from practising. Despite the suspension she continued to treat her patients. She was charged with assault occasioning actual bodily harm. The trial judge ruled that her patients' apparent consents were vitiated by her fraud in allowing them to think she was still registered. Because of this ruling she changed her plea to guilty. She appealed on the grounds that the judge's ruling was incorrect.

Decision
The Court of Appeal allowed the appeal. Only a mistake about the nature of the act alleged or the identity of the assailant vitiated consent in criminal law. A person's professional status or qualifications did not constitute part of their identity.

Comment
Otton LJ suggested that her actions were 'clearly reprehensible and may well found the basis of a civil claim for damages. But we are quite satisfied that it is not the basis for finding criminal liability in the field of offences against the person'. It is perhaps unlikely that any claim for damages in trespass would be successful. In the Court of Appeal hearing of *Sidaway v Board of Governors of Bethlem Royal Hospital and the Maudsley Hospital* (1984), Lord Donaldson MR stated:

It is only if the consent is obtained by fraud or misrepresentation of the nature of what is to be done that it can be said that an apparent consent is not a true consent. This is the position in the criminal law and the cause of action based on trespass to the person is closely analogous.

Although Lord Donaldson MR misstates the position of the criminal law, because the courts are reluctant to find doctors liable for battery unless their actions are wholly indefensible, his statement may well reflect the approach of a civil court.

R v Tabassum (2000): Although a person's qualifications do not alter his identity, they might affect the nature of the act

Facts
Three women consented to be shown how to perform a breast examination by the accused, who was preparing a computer software package on breast cancer. They knew that the act was a breast examination and that it was for the purpose of preparing the software package. The women all stated that they only consented to the examination because they believed the accused was medically qualified or properly trained. It was accepted that neither of these was the case. He was convicted of indecent assault and appealed.

Decision

The Court of Appeal upheld the conviction. The women had not given a true consent. Because he was neither medically qualified nor properly trained the quality of the act could not have been one of a medical examination. Thus, although the women understood the nature of the act, they had not consented to the quality of the act.

Comment

Richardson was distinguished because it related to the identity of the actor rather than the quality of the act. *Tabassum* would be incompatible with *Richardson* but for this distinction. Although the decision gives a greater protection to autonomy, it may be criticised as being achieved through judicial sleight of hand and legal sophistry. It is arguable that the judges were not sympathetic to the appellant solely because he was not medically qualified and that the manner in which they have extricated themselves from the *Richardson* decision merely confirms the judicial reluctance to find medically qualified professionals criminally liable. It also has the undesirable implication that success or failure could depend on whether the case is based on the 'identity of the actor' rather than the 'quality of the act'. An interesting variation occurred in the Canadian case, *R v Bolduc and Bird* (1976), where the Supreme Court held that misrepresentation of an observer's identity was collateral and therefore not relevant to consent.

2.4　The duty to inform and liability for negligence

Sidaway v Board of Governors of the Bethlem Royal Hospital and the Maudsley Hospital (1985): The standard of care required for information disclosure is measured by the *Bolam* test

Facts

The plaintiff had an operation to relieve her recurrent neck and shoulder pain. The operation carried a risk of damage to a nerve root of 1–2%. There was also a substantially smaller risk to her spinal cord. She was informed of the risk to the nerve root but the surgeon did not refer to the risk of paralysis that might result from damage to her spinal cord. The operation was performed competently, but the risk to her spinal cord materialised and she was left severely disabled. The plaintiff sued the surgeon for failing to inform of this risk.

Decision

The House of Lords held that the surgeon was not liable since he had followed a practice which – at that time – was accepted as proper by a responsible body of skilled and experienced neurosurgeons.

Comment

The Lords failed to agree on the appropriate standard. Lord Scarman dissented from the majority that the *Bolam* test was applicable (see Chapter 12). He preferred the 'prudent patient' test established by the US case, *Canterbury v Spence* (1972). He stated:

I think that English law must recognise a duty of the doctor to warn his patient of risk inherent in the treatment ... The critical limitation is that the duty is confined to material risk. The test of materiality is whether in the circumstances of the particular case the court is satisfied that a reasonable person in the patient's position would be likely to attach significance to the risk.

Lord Diplock preferred the *Bolam* test without qualification. The other three Lords agreed that *Bolam* was the appropriate standard but that this standard was subject to judicial scrutiny and approval. Lord Bridge stated:

I am of the opinion that the judge might in certain circumstances come to the conclusion that disclosure of a particular risk was so obviously necessary to an informed choice on the part of the patient that no reasonably prudent medical man would fail to make it.

Gold v Haringey HA (1988): *Bolam* applies to information disclosure in both therapeutic and non-therapeutic contexts

Facts
Following the birth of her third child the plaintiff underwent an operation to be sterilised. Following the operation she became pregnant. She sued the Health Authority in negligence for, *inter alia*, failing to warn her of the failure rate of female sterilisations. If she had known of the failure rate, her husband would have had a vasectomy instead. At first instance the judge held that the *Bolam* test only applied to therapeutic procedures and, on the evidence, the defendants had been negligent.

Decision
The Court of Appeal allowed the defendants' appeal. As far as the doctor's duty of care went, there should be no distinction made between advice given in a therapeutic context and advice given in a non-therapeutic context: the *Bolam* test was applicable in both instances. *Per* Lloyd LJ: 'The [*Bolam*] principle does not depend on the context in which any act is performed, or any advice given. It depends on a man professing skill or competence in a field beyond that possessed by the man on the Clapham omnibus.'

Comment
The Court of Appeal considered the judgment in *Sidaway*, but only referred to Lord Diplock's speech. They apparently interpreted the mixed judgment in *Sidaway* as affirming the application of an unmodified *Bolam* test.

Pearce v United Bristol Healthcare NHS Trust (1999): Significant risks that are material to the patient's decision must be disclosed

Facts
The claimant was two weeks beyond the due date of her sixth child. She asked the consultant obstetrician if she could have a Caesarean section or be induced. He explained the risks of those two procedures and advised that she allow her pregnancy to continue. The foetus subsequently perished and she was delivered of a stillborn child. She sued the defendants and alleged that had she been warned of the risk of stillbirth (0.1–0.2%) she would have insisted on a Caesarean section.

Decision
The Court of Appeal held that a failure to disclose the risk, which was not significant, was not negligent.

Note: in *Rogers v Whitaker* (1993), the High Court of Australia rejected *Bolam* as an inappropriate standard for risk disclosure. The majority opted for a 'prudent patient' standard and stated that 'the risk was material, in the sense that a reasonable person in the patient's position would be likely to attach significance to the risk and thus require a warning'. This standard is also applicable in Canada and some US jurisdictions. It is arguable that the courts in this country are moving towards that standard of disclosure, but see below.

White v Turner (1981): Material risks do not include 'ordinary', 'general' or 'obvious' risks

Facts

The defendant performed breast reduction surgery on the plaintiff, which left her breasts misshapen and badly scarred. She alleged that the performance of the operation was negligent and that he was negligent in not properly disclosing the risks of the surgery.

Decision

The Ontario High Court held that in this case the risk of asymmetrical nipples, misshapen breasts and scars that might stretch to a width of two to three inches were material risks. The defendant was negligent in not warning the plaintiff of these risks. *Per* Linden J: 'There are some common everyday risks that exist in all surgery, which everyone is expected to know about. Doctors need not warn about them, since they are obvious to everyone. Consequently, just as one need not warn that a match will burn or that a knife will cut, because that would be redundant, one need not warn that, if an incision is made, there will normally be some bleeding, some pain and a scar.'

Comment

In *Venner v North East Essex HA* (1987), a woman who became pregnant after stopping the oral contraceptive pill on her doctor's advice claimed that the doctor had been negligent in failing to disclose the risk. The court held that, since she had become pregnant before after stopping the pill, it was an obvious risk, which did not create a duty to disclose. In *Sidaway*, Lord Diplock stated: 'I find it significant that no common law jurisdiction either American or Canadian which has espoused the doctrine of "informed consent" appears to have suggested that the surgeon was under a duty to warn his patient of such general risks which, rare though they may be, do happen and are real risks.'

The concept of 'ordinary risk' may depend on the particular patient. In *Sidaway*, Lord Diplock stated: 'it may be that most patients, though not necessarily all, have vague knowledge that there may be some risk in every form of medical treatment: but it is flying in the face of reality to assume that all patients from the highest to the lowest standard of education or intelligence are aware of the extent and nature of the risks which ... are inevitably involved in medical treatment of whatever kind it be but particularly surgical.'

Pearce v United Bristol Healthcare NHS Trust (1999): A significant risk is material if a failure to inform a reasonable patient of that risk would affect her judgment in making the relevant decision

Facts

See above.

Decision

See above. Lord Woolf MR stated: 'it seems to me to be the law ... that if there is a significant risk which would affect the judgment of a reasonable patient, then in the normal course it is the responsibility of a doctor to inform the patient of that significant risk.'

Comment

The Court of Appeal noted with interest that Lord Bridge in *Sidaway* had referred to a significant risk as being greater than 10%. The expert witness commented that, had the risk in this case been over 10%, then it should have been mentioned. Since the risk was *only* 0.1–0.2% it was not significant. The Court of Appeal has apparently taken the remark out of context. Lord Bridge used the 10% risk as an example of an instance when a doctor could not rely on *Bolam* if he failed to disclose it to the patient. Under such circumstances the judge could hold that no reasonably prudent doctor would fail to disclose it. Thus, 10% is not the lower limit demarcating significance but is the upper limit demarcating when a judge should no longer accept the medical evidence that non-disclosure was reasonable.

Although the test of a material risk resembles the prudent patient standard, by requiring the risk to be significant and determining significance on the basis of expert evidence, Lord Woolf MR has pulled back from introducing the prudent patient standard into English law. In *Wyatt v Curtis* (2003) Sedley LJ gave Lord Woolf's judgment a generous interpretation when he explained that: 'Lord Woolf's formulation [in *Pearce*] refines Lord Bridge's test [in *Sidaway*] by recognising that what is substantial and what is grave are questions on which the doctor's and the patient's perception may differ, and in relation to which the doctor must therefore have regard to what may be the patient's perception.' Furthermore, the high standard of information disclosure required by, for example, the GMC may affect the standard of disclosure by affecting doctors' common practice. For example, GMC guidance requires that: 'You should provide patients with appropriate information, which should include an explanation of any risks to which they may attach particular significance. Ask patients whether they have understood the information and whether they would like more before making a decision' (GMC, 1999).

Sidaway v Board of Governors of the Bethlem Royal Hospital and the Maudsley Hospital (1985): The doctor may have a duty to answer truthfully to direct questions

Facts

See above.

Comment

Lord Diplock argued that if the doctor were asked he would 'no doubt ... tell him what he wished to know'. Lord Bridge more forcefully argued that 'when questioned specifically by a patient of apparently sound mind about risks involved in a particular treatment proposed, the doctor's duty must, in my opinion, be to answer both truthfully and as fully as the questioner requires'. However, since they were *obiter* to the judgment, although persuasive, they do not decide the point.

Blyth v Bloomsbury HA (1993): Where direct questions are of a general nature the standard of duty that the doctor owes is governed by the *Bolam* test

Facts

The plaintiff, a trained nurse, was given an injection of the long-acting contraceptive Depo-provera to prevent pregnancy while waiting for her rubella vaccination to become fully effective. She sued for damages and alleged that she was not warned about some of the side effects she suffered following the injection. She also alleged that the doctor had not answered truthfully to her questions. The trial judge awarded her damages and the defendant appealed.

Decision

The Court of Appeal allowed the appeal. On the facts it noted that the trial judge did not find that the plaintiff had asked the specific questions alleged. The Court of Appeal accepted that she had asked general questions but held that the *Bolam* test applied.

Pearce v United Bristol Healthcare NHS Trust (1999): The doctor must answer questions honestly

Facts

See above.

Decision

The Court of Appeal held (*obiter*) that if a patient asked about risks the doctor had a duty to give an honest answer.

Comment

The law regarding specific questions is not clear. While Lord Bridge in *Sidaway* stated that the doctor must answer 'truthfully and as fully as the questioner requires' (see above), Kerr LJ, in *Blyth*, argued: '... the *Bolam* test is all-pervasive in this context. Indeed I am not convinced that the *Bolam* test is irrelevant even in relation to the question of what answers are properly to be given to specific enquiries, or that Lord Diplock or Lord Bridge intended to hold otherwise.' This is in keeping with an earlier decision in *Hatcher v Black* (1954) in which a doctor replied to a direct question from the patient that a thyroidectomy did not involve any risks. Denning LJ stated: '[the doctor] told a lie because he thought ... it was justifiable ... [T]he law does not condemn the doctor when he only does that which many a wise and good doctor would do.'

Sidaway v Board of Governors of the Bethlem Royal Hospital and the Maudsley Hospital (1985): The doctor may claim 'therapeutic privilege' and withhold information that would cause the patient harm or be contrary to his best interests

Facts
See above.

Decision
Lord Scarman argued (*obiter*) that in raising therapeutic privilege the doctor must prove 'that he reasonably believed that the disclosure of the risk would be damaging to his patient or contrary to his best interests'.

Comment
In the earlier case *Hatcher v Black* (1954), it was argued that anxiety increases the risks of thyroidectomy and as such it was justifiable to withhold information from the patient to prevent her becoming more anxious. As far as English law is concerned, the privilege is not explicit but may be implicitly justifiable under the professional standard of care. The term therapeutic privilege comes from the US and was discussed in the US case of *Canterbury v Spence* (1972), in which the court held that the doctor may withhold information if disclosing it would risk making the patient so distraught that he is incapable of making a decision.

Newell and Newell v Goldenberg (1995): The courts have still reserved the right to decide that, notwithstanding *Bolam*, the body of medical men supporting the defendant's position is not a 'reasonable' body

Facts
The first plaintiff had a vasectomy and following the second of two negative sperm counts was advised that it was safe to have sexual intercourse without contraceptive protection. His wife, the second plaintiff, became pregnant because a natural process (risk of 1:2,300) had restored the first plaintiff's vas deferens. The defendant acknowledged that it was his normal practice to warn of this risk but that in failing to do so he had still conformed to the practice of a responsible body of medical opinion.

Decision
The High Court held that the defendant was negligent in failing to warn of the risk of failure of a vasectomy. The body of medical opinion was neither responsible nor reasonable.

Comment
See also *Smith v Tunbridge Wells HA* (1994) below; *Pearce v United Bristol Healthcare NHS Trust* (1999) above; and *Bolitho v City and Hackney HA*, Chapter 12 below.

Smith v Tunbridge Wells HA (1994): The doctor has a duty to take reasonable steps to ensure the patient understands the information

Facts

The plaintiff, a 28-year-old man, underwent an operation to repair a rectal prolapse. Unfortunately, although the surgery was performed competently, a nerve was damaged and the plaintiff was left impotent and with a significant bladder dysfunction. He sued the defendant and alleged that had he been warned of the risk of impotence, he would not have consented to the operation.

Decision

The High Court held that the defendant was negligent. Although some surgeons might not have warned patients in a similar situation to the plaintiff, that omission was neither reasonable nor responsible. Moorland J stated, *obiter*: 'the doctor, when warning of the risks, must take reasonable care to ensure that his explanation of the risks is intelligible to his particular patient. The doctor should use language, simple but not misleading, which the doctor perceives … will be understood by the patient so that the patient can make an informed decision as to whether or not to consent to the recommended surgery or treatment.'

Smith v Salford HA (1994): The surrounding circumstances may affect the reasonableness of steps to ensure understanding

Facts

The plaintiff was a window cleaner who suffered pain and restricted movement due to a problem with his neck. The surgeon advised that he should have a cervical fusion operation. The plaintiff suffered temporary tetraplegia and permanent disability preventing him from working. One of the grounds on which he sued was that he had been negligently informed of the risks associated with the surgery.

Decision

The High Court held that the doctor had breached his duty by failing to inform the plaintiff of the risks of paralysis. However, the plaintiff failed in this aspect of his claim because even if he had been warned he would still have gone through with the operation. (The plaintiff succeeded in establishing the defendant's liability for negligent practice on other grounds.) Potter J stated:

I am satisfied no specific mention of death or paralysis was made. Even if I am mistaken, I am satisfied that they were not mentioned in terms adequate to register upon the plaintiff who Mr Cowie [the surgeon] himself acknowledged was, at the time of the interview … suffering a headache and the adverse effects generally of the myelogram which he had recently experienced.

Comment

These last two cases suggest that it is not enough simply to make the information available to the patient. The doctor must take reasonable steps to ensure the patient understands the information and this includes providing the information at a time when the patient is likely to be in a suitably receptive state. See also *Lybert v Warrington HA* (1996).

2.5   Information disclosure, negligence liability and causation

Chatterton v Gerson (1981): Even if the failure to disclose has breached the standard of care, the claimant must still show that disclosure would have affected his decision

Facts
See 2.2 above.

Decision
Bristow J stated: 'When the claim is based on negligence the plaintiff must prove ... that had the duty not been broken she would not have chosen to have the operation.'

Comment
The test for causation in English law is subjective constrained by an objective test of credibility. In *Hills v Potter* (1984) (see 2.2 above), for example, Hirst J stated, *obiter*:

> For the sake of completeness, I should say that I am not satisfied on the balance of probabilities that even if the plaintiff had received a still fuller explanation ... she would have declined to undergo the operation. I wholeheartedly accept that in retrospect she sincerely believes that she would have so declined. But having regard to the evidence as to the gravity of her condition, I think it is more likely than not that she would have agreed to go head with the operation.

Chester v Afshar (2002): The claimant can satisfy the causation requirement without proving that ultimately he would have refused the treatment

Facts
The claimant was a 51-year-old journalist who suffered severe back pain. She was advised that surgery was her best option and she was referred to Mr Afshar, an eminent neurosurgeon. Although she was reluctant to undergo surgery, Mr Afshar reassured her sufficiently for the claimant to give consent. Unfortunately, following the surgery she was left with severe neurological deficit. At trial, she alleged that Mr Afshar had failed to disclose the risk of nerve damage or paralysis and that, had he done so, she would at the least have sought second and third opinions before deciding whether to undergo the operation. Mr Afshar claimed that he had warned her of the risks but the trial judge preferred the claimant's version and awarded damages for the failure to disclose. Mr Afshar appealed against the decision.

Decision
The Court of Appeal dismissed the appeal. The surgeon was liable for failing to disclose the risk despite the fact that even had it been disclosed the claimant might still have undergone the procedure on some future occasion and suffered the same consequences.

Comment
The Court of Appeal followed the judgment in the Australian case of *Chappel v Hart* (1998), and made it clear that causation was satisfied if the patient would not have undergone the intervention then and there.

2.6   Consent to medical research

The question of consent to medical research has not been tested in an English court. However, any research that involves physical contact would certainly require consent to avoid being a battery (such a failure may also be a breach of Article 3 (prohibition of torture and inhuman or degrading treatment), Schedule 1 to the Human Rights Act (HRA) 1998: see *X v Denmark* (1983) (Application No 9974/82)). Other types of research may – because of the ethical standards required by the professions – be negligent if no consent is obtained. In *Mink v University of Chicago* (1978), the defendants were liable for battery when they administered drugs to over 1,000 women without telling them that they were part of an experiment, nor that the pills – administered to them during their pre-natal care – were Diethyl Stilbestrol.

Montgomery (2003), while recognising the dangers of relying on overseas decisions, suggests that English courts may follow the Canadian case, *Halushka v University of Saskatchewan* (1965), which held that for consent to medical research to be valid there must be a 'full and frank' disclosure of the facts. It is also possible that the consent requirements for therapeutic research (ie, research that may also provide some clinical benefit to the patient) may only require the *Bolam* standard of information disclosure while non-therapeutic research would require the higher standard of disclosure (but see *Gold v Haringey HA* (1988), 2.4 above). However, since the *Bolam* test is based on the opinion of a reasonable body of medical opinion, the requirements for information disclosure in medical research will most likely be greater than for medical treatment. This follows because current professional and ethical guidelines (such as the Declaration of Helsinki 1964 (as amended 2000) and GMC guidance) demand it.

The European Directive on Good Clinical Practice in the Conduct of Clinical Trials 2001/20/EC was implemented in May 2004 by the Medicines for Human Use (Clinical Trials) Regulations 2004. Schedule 1 of the Regulations requires that a competent subject 'has given his informed consent', has been 'informed of his right to withdraw from the trial' and 'has been given an opportunity to understand the objectives, risks and inconveniences of the trial' (Part 3).

2.7   There are some instances where an otherwise real consent may be invalidated

Public policy may invalidate an otherwise valid consent where the act consented to is deemed immoral or not in the public interest (see *R v Brown* (1993)). Medical treatment generally does not fall within this category. However, female circumcision has been outlawed by the Female Genital Mutilation Act 2003.

2.8   There are occasions when treatment is justified in the absence of consent

As will be detailed in Chapter 3, treatment may be justified by the doctrine of necessity in the absence of consent where an adult is incompetent. Where the decision-maker is competent, however, non-consensual treatment may be justified to protect others under mental health law (also to protect the patient: see Chapter 9) and under public health law (see the Public Health Act 1984, eg, s 13).

Acmanne v Belgium (1984): Compulsory screening or treatment for communicable diseases may be a justifiable breach of the person's human rights

Facts

The applicants were fined for refusing to allow children in their care to undergo compulsory screening for tuberculosis. Four of the applicants were parents and the other six were secondary school teachers. The applicants argued that the law in Belgium – requiring compulsory tuberculin test and chest x-ray – was a breach of Article 8 of the European Convention on Human Rights. Article 8 provides:

(1)   Everyone has the right to respect for his private and family life, his home and his correspondence.

(2)   There shall be no interference by a public authority with the exercise of this right except such as in accordance with the law and is necessary in a democratic society in the interests of national security, public safety or the economic well-being of the country, for the prevention of disorder or crime, for the protection of health or morals, or for the protection of the rights and freedoms of others.

Decision

The European Commission on Human Rights found that, since even minor medical treatment against the patient's will may breach Article 8, the compulsory screening may amount to an interference with the right to respect for private life. However, the compulsory screening was in accordance with the law, and was justified to protect public health; and was 'proportionate to the legitimate aim pursued'. The compulsory screening for TB was therefore allowed as a legitimate derogation under Article 8(2) and so was not a breach of human rights.

Comment

Although this applies to screening, the same arguments would probably succeed for both compulsory examinations and treatment of persons with notifiable diseases. In addition, while European human rights judgments will not be binding precedents on English courts under the HRA 1998, the cases will be considered and may be persuasive.

CHAPTER 3

THE INCOMPETENT ADULT

One of the requirements for a 'real' consent is that the individual is competent to make the decision in question. If the individual is unable to consent, then they are unable to legitimise medical treatment even if they voluntarily agree to it. Obviously, from an ethical viewpoint it would be iniquitous if the inability to consent (which is, after all, a device meant to protect the individual) prevented the patient from getting medical care. Thus, unless someone else can give consent in place of the individual's consent, some other justification must be found so that incompetent patients can receive any necessary treatment while also protecting the doctor from liability for battery.

In 1960 the English courts lost their *parens patriae* jurisdiction over the affairs of incompetent adults. This occurred as a result of the Mental Health Act 1959 and revocation of the Warrant under the Sign Manual (see Lord Brandon's judgment in *F v West Berkshire HA* (1989) (below)). Following a Law Commission Report (1995), the Government indicated its intention to legislate (Lord Chancellor, 1999). Currently, the draft Mental Capacity Bill has undergone a consultation exercise and has been reported on by the Joint Scrutiny Committee (Session 2002–03). At the time of writing, the report has been considered by the Department for Constitutional Affairs (www.dca.gov.uk/menincap/legis.htm) and a revised Bill published. If it becomes law, the Act will allow the appointment of a welfare attorney who will have the power to make decisions for the incompetent adult, which will have to be predicated on the individual's best interests. In Scotland, the Adults with Incapacity (Sc) Act 2000 already governs the way in which incapacitated persons over 16 should be treated.

Prior to the Medicines for Human Use (Clinical Trials) Regulations 2004, the legality of research using incompetent adults rested on the question of whether it could be justified by their best interests under the doctrine of necessity. Thus, it was – at best – uncertain whether non-therapeutic research would be lawful. Part 5, Schedule 1 to the Regulations sets out the conditions when it will be lawful to include incapacitated adults as research subjects, but only in medicinal trials. One of the current problems with the regulations is that it requires involvement of the incapacitated adult's 'legal representative'. Until the draft Mental Capacity Bill 2004 is passed there is currently facility for anyone to perform this role. The draft Bill also includes provision to allow the inclusion of incapacitated adults in research more generally (clauses 30–33). In Scotland, the Adults with Incapacity (Sc) Act 2000 is already in force and provides authority for research under s 51 (although this has been amended by the Clinical Trials Regulations).

3.1   The definition of incompetence

Re T (Adult: Refusal of Medical Treatment) **(1992): There is a presumption of competence in favour of the patient**

Facts

See 2.1 above.

Comment

The Law Commission (1995) stated: 'We recommend that there should be a presumption against lack of capacity and that any question whether a person lacks capacity should be decided on the balance of probabilities' (clause 2(6) of the draft Bill). This has been accepted by the Government and in the future will be given a statutory footing (Lord Chancellor, 1999). See also clauses 1(1) and 2(3) of the draft Mental Capacity Bill 2004 (which is supported by the Joint Scrutiny Committee's Report Session 2002–03).

Re C (Adult: Refusal of Treatment) **(1994): There are three stages to determining competency**

Facts

See 2.1 above.

Decision

See 2.1 above. Thorpe J accepted the three stages suggested by the expert witness Dr Eastman:

(1)   comprehending and retaining treatment information;
(2)   believing it; and
(3)   weighing it in the balance to arrive at a choice.

Comment

In *St George's Healthcare NHS Trust v S* (1998) (see 5.1 below), the Court of Appeal laid down some guidelines, which included the determination of competence. It held that:

(iv) The authority should identify as soon as possible whether there is concern about a patient's competence to consent or refuse treatment.

(v)   If the capacity of the patient is seriously in doubt it should be assessed as a matter of priority. In many such cases the patient's general practitioner or other responsible doctor may be sufficiently qualified to make the necessary assessment, but in serious or complex cases involving difficult issues about the future health and well being or even the life of the patient, the issue of capacity should be examined by an independent psychiatrist ...

Re MB (Medical Treatment) **(1997): The requirement of 'belief' is not essential**

Facts

See 2.1 above.

Decision

See 2.1 above. The Court of Appeal stated: 'A person lacked capacity when some impairment or disturbance of mental functioning rendered that person unable to make a decision. Inability to make a decision occurred when a patient was *unable to comprehend, retain and use information and weigh it in the balance'* (emphasis added).

Comment

Butler-Sloss LJ based her test on the Law Commission's Report, *Mental Incapacity* (1995). The Law Commission recommended that: 'legislation should provide that a person is without capacity if at the material time he or she is: (1) unable by reason of mental disability to make a decision on the matter in question, or (2) unable to communicate a decision on that matter ...' (draft Bill, clause 2(1)). A person is unable to make a decision if 'he or she is unable to understand or retain the information relevant to the decision, including information about the reasonably foreseeable consequences of deciding one way or another or failing to make the decision' (draft Bill, clause 2(2)(a)). The Law Commission also required that the individual 'be able to use the information ... in the decision-making process'. The Law Commission's proposals will be given a statutory basis by future Government legislation (Lord Chancellor, 1999). Clause 2(1) of the draft Mental Capacity Bill 2004 states that: 'a person lacks capacity in relation to a matter if at the material time he is unable to make a decision for himself ... because of an impairment or disturbance in the functioning of the mind or brain.' Under clause 3(1), he is incapable if he is unable to understand, retain, or use the relevant information or communicate the decision.

Re C (Adult: Refusal of Treatment) (1994): A mental disability may be necessary for incompetence but it is not sufficient

Facts
See 2.1 above.

Decision
See 2.1 above. Thorpe J stated: 'Although his [C's] general capacity is impaired by schizophrenia, it has not been established that he does not sufficiently understand the nature, purpose and effect of the treatment he refuses.'

Re MB (Medical Treatment) (1997) CA: The mental disability may be caused by a temporary factor

Facts
See 2.1 above.

Decision
The Court of Appeal held that MB's needle phobia rendered her temporarily incompetent and a non-consensual Caesarean section would be lawful.

Comment
The Court of Appeal stated: 'Temporary factors such as shock, pain or drugs might completely erode capacity but those concerned had to be satisfied that such factors were operating to such a degree that the ability to decide was absent.' The draft Mental Capacity Bill 2004 also allows for temporary incompetence (clause 2(2)).

Rochdale Healthcare (NHS) Trust v C (1997): Being in labour may be a sufficient cause of temporary incapacity

Facts

The consultant obstetrician believed that without a Caesarean section both C and her baby would die. C refused consent because a previous Caesarean delivery had left her with backache and a painful scar. She declared that she would rather die than have another Caesarean. No psychiatric opinion was available but the consultant obstetrician believed that C was competent.

Decision

The High Court held that a non-consensual Caesarean section was in C's best interests and would be lawful as C temporarily lacked competence. Johnson J stated: '[She] was in the throes of labour with all that is involved in terms of pain and emotional stress. I concluded that a patient who could, in those circumstances, speak in terms which seemed to accept the inevitability of her own death, was not a patient who was able properly to weigh-up the considerations that arose so as to make any valid decision.'

Comment

This decision is only first instance and is open to criticism because the judge made a decision about C's competence based on her actual decision rather than her decision-making capacity. He also overruled the consultant obstetrician's opinion without even meeting – let alone assessing – C. In *Re MB*, although Butler-Sloss LJ considered this decision, she merely noted that there was little evidence to justify his decision but her only comment was: 'Nonetheless he made the declarations sought.' Thus, the decision appears to have been accepted without disapproval by the Court of Appeal.

Cambridgeshire County Council v R (An Adult) (1995): Competence only requires the ability to understand information in 'broad terms'

Facts

The family of a 21-year-old woman with a learning disability, who had been in local authority care since the age of 10, were seeking to re-establish contact with her. She had been taken into care after her father had been convicted of serious sexual offences against her. The local authority sought declarations that it would be lawful to prevent the family having contact without the local authority's consent and to prevent them from trying to persuade her to return to the family home.

Decision

The High Court refused the application. The court had no right to make a declaration that would interfere with her legal right of freedom of association where there was no demonstrable threat of violence or other injury to her person. Also, there was insufficient evidence to prove that she was incapable of making the decision for herself. Hale J stated:

… the question to be decided is whether the person's mental condition is such that he does not sufficiently understand the nature, purpose and effects of the proposed treatment … the Law Commission … proposed that the relevant information should be contained in an explanation 'in broad terms and simple language' so that people should not be expected to be able to understand everything about a complicated decision as long as they could understand the essentials.

Comment

The Law Commission (1995) recommended that: 'a person should not be regarded as unable to understand the information relevant to a decision if he or she is able to understand an explanation of that information in broad terms and simple language' (draft Bill, clause 2(3)). (The draft Mental Capacity Bill 2004 simply refers to the ability to understand relevant information (clause 3(1).) Although the Law Commission's recommendations are not legally binding, Hale J seems to have accepted them in principle (see above). Also, it is logical to suggest that the requirement for competence should mirror the requirement of information disclosure for a 'real' consent. There would be little point in requiring someone to demonstrate a greater level of competence than that needed to understand the actual information they will be given.

3.2   Incompetent patients and consent

Re S (Hospital Patient: Court's Jurisdiction) (1995): Spouses and relatives have no power to consent on behalf of incompetent adults

Facts

S had a wife and adult son living in Norway. He had set up home in England with Mrs A. S had a stroke. Mrs A had his power of attorney to operate his bank accounts, which she used to pay for the hospital bills. S's wife and son arranged to fly him to Norway. Mrs A obtained an injunction to prevent this transfer. She then applied for a declaration that it would be unlawful to take him out of England because it would not be in S's best interests.

Decision

The declaration was granted at first instance and upheld by the Court of Appeal.

Comment

Hale J stated (High Court approved by the Court of Appeal): 'Yet although his [the son] relationship to the patient is a close one, and his wishes are of course worthy of respect, he has no more legal right to decide the patient's future than has the plaintiff [Mrs A].' In Re T (Adult: Refusal of Medical Treatment) (1992), Lord Donaldson MR stated: 'There seems to be a view in the medical profession that in such emergency circumstances the next of kin should be asked to consent on behalf of the patient ... This is a misconception because the next of kin has no legal right either to consent or to refuse consent.' The law in this area is set to change with the statutory creation of the power to appoint a welfare attorney (draft Mental Capacity Bill 2004, clauses 9–14). The welfare attorney will be able to make decisions on behalf of the incompetent adult but need not be a relative. The Bill also requires, where practicable, that the doctor consult the views of 'any person named by him as someone to be consulted', even where that individual is not the welfare attorney. The doctor should also consult any person 'interested in his welfare'. These enquiries are not determinative of any decision but are part of the process of deciding that person's best interests (clause 4(6)).

F v West Berkshire HA (1989): The court has no jurisdiction to consent on behalf of incompetent adult patients

Facts

The plaintiff was a 36-year-old woman with a severe mental incapacity. She was a voluntary in-patient at a mental hospital and had formed a sexual relationship with a male patient. Psychiatric evidence suggested that it would be disastrous if she became pregnant. The medical staff wanted to sterilise her since other forms of contraceptive were unsuitable as either dangerous to her health or difficult for her to be able to use effectively. A declaration was sought that it would be lawful to perform the sterilisation.

Decision

The House of Lords held that the court had no jurisdiction either by statute or derived from the Crown as *parens patriae* to give or withhold consent on behalf of an incompetent adult.

Comment

(1) This case may also be found referred to as *Re F (Mental Patient: Sterilisation)* (1990).

(2) The position will change in the future when the Government legislates on the basis of the Lord Chancellor's report, *Making Decisions*. Under the draft Mental Capacity Bill 2004, the court may make Declarations, make decisions on behalf of the incapacitated adult or appoint deputies to do so (clauses 15–21).

3.3 Advance directives

In addition to what is discussed below, an advance directive must conform with all the other requirements of consent. Thus, the patient must have been competent (*The NHS Trust v Ms T* (2004)) when it was made, it must have been made voluntarily and with a broad understanding of the implications. As with ordinary consent, an advance directive does not have to be in writing (*Re T (Adult: Refusal of Medical Treatment)* (1992)) but a written directive may be more certain (see below) than an oral one. Although the Government initially indicated that it would not legislate on advance directives, clauses 24–26 of the draft Mental Capacity Bill will put them on a statutory basis and may require them to be in writing unless communicated to a doctor in the course of treatment (see the Joint Scrutiny Committee Report Session 2002–03).

Re AK (Medical Treatment: Consent) (2001): Advance directives are legally binding

Facts

AK was a 19-year-old man suffering from motor neurone disease (a progressive and incurable neurological disease). He was ventilator dependent and only able to communicate by blinking his eyelids to indicate 'yes' or 'no'. By this method of communication, AK requested that the doctors should withdraw treatment two weeks after he lost the ability to communicate. He was aware that this would result in his death. The doctors sought a declaration that it would be lawful to discontinue treatment as directed by the patient.

Decision

The High Court granted the declaration. Hughes J stated: 'It is … clearly the law that the doctors are entitled … [to treat the patient] if it is known that the patient, provided he was of sound mind and full capacity, has let it be known that he does not consent and that such treatment is against his wishes. To this extent an advance indication of the wishes of the patient of full capacity and sound mind are effective.'

Comment

Hughes J argued that particular care had to be taken to ensure that the anticipatory wishes still held true, bearing in mind: how long ago the directive was made; the way in which the directive was expressed (orally, written, etc); and all the circumstances that pertained at the time. Prior to this case, the courts had indicated, in *obiter dicta*, that advance directives would be lawful. For example, in *Airedale NHS Trust v Bland* (1993) (see 6.2 below), Lord Keith argued (*obiter*) that the patient's right to give or withhold consent 'extends to the situation where the person, in anticipation of his … entering into a condition such as PVS [Persistent Vegetative State], gives clear instructions that in such event he is not to be given medical care, including artificial feeding, designed to keep him alive'.

Re T (Adult: Refusal of Medical Treatment) (1992): To be binding, advance directives must be certain

Facts

See 2.1 above.

Decision

The Court of Appeal held that the circumstances under which T had refused the blood transfusion were different from the present circumstances and so her refusal was not binding. Other factors were also relevant (see 2.1 above).

Lord Donaldson MR stated that 'contact with the next of kin may reveal that the patient has made an anticipatory choice which, if *clearly established and applicable in the circumstances* – two major 'ifs' – would bind the practitioner' (emphasis added).

Comment

In *HE v A Hospital NHS Trust* (2003), a patient's advance directive (refusing blood) was invalidated by evidence that she had ceased to be a Jehovah's Witness and had expressed an intention to return to the Muslim faith. Her mother – who remained a Jehovah's Witness – opposed treatment and the High Court held that the burden fell on her to show that the directive was in force. Although the directive was signed by the patient, and in writing, it was not necessary for the revocation also to be in writing. The court additionally held that any doubt should be resolved by adopting the course of action most likely to preserve the patient's life.

Mallette v Shulman (1990): Broad catch-all phrases such as 'under any circumstances' are sufficiently certain even when the patient's life is threatened

Facts

The plaintiff was a Jehovah's Witness admitted to hospital following a road traffic accident. She was unconscious and so unable to give or refuse consent. She was carrying a card that stated: 'As one of Jehovah's Witnesses with firm religious convictions, I request that no blood or blood products be administered to me under any circumstances. I fully realise the implications of this position.' The doctor ignored these instructions and administered a life-saving transfusion.

Decision

The Ontario Court of Appeal held that the doctor was liable for a battery. Robbins JA stated: 'A doctor is not free to disregard a patient's advance instructions any more than he would be free to disregard instructions given at the time of the emergency.'

Comment

The draft Mental Capacity Bill states that 'An advance directive is not applicable to life-sustaining treatment unless P specified in the decision that it was to apply to such treatment' (clause 25(5)).

Re C (Adult: Refusal of Treatment) (1994): The court may grant an injunction to ensure that an advance directive is complied with

Facts

See 2.1 above.

Decision

The High Court granted an injunction to prevent the amputation of C's leg. The injunction included future circumstances such that an amputation could not be performed without his written consent.

Re C (Adult: Refusal of Treatment) (1994): An advance directive is binding until it is specifically revoked

Facts

See 2.1 above.

Decision

The High Court held that the injunction granted would protect C's refusal of the amputation until it was revoked in writing.

Comment

Just as the competent patient has no right to a specific treatment, so an advance directive cannot compel treatment. In *Making Decisions*, the Lord Chancellor (1999) states: 'An advance statement can request specific treatments. It is an important principle that health professionals are not legally bound to provide that treatment if it conflicts with their professional judgement.'

Doctors may not be obliged to comply with advance directives that are contrary to public policy such as the refusal of basic care. In para 5.34 of their Report No 231, the Law Commission stated: 'We *recommend* that an advance refusal of treatment should not preclude the provision of "basic care", namely care to maintain bodily cleanliness and to alleviate severe pain, as well as the provision of direct oral nutrition and hydration (draft Bill, clauses 9(7)(a) and (8))' (original emphasis). There is no case law on this and it is not referred to in the draft Mental Capacity Bill. The Law Commission recommendations are not legally binding but may influence the judiciary if a case ever came before them. Also note that this recommendation relates to direct oral nutrition such as spoon feeding or via a straw but both the BMA (1995) and the Law Commission (1993, para 3.26) state that an advance directive should be able to preclude artificial feeding such as through a naso-gastric tube. The BMA suggested to the Joint Scrutiny Committee that an advance directive should not be allowed to refuse basic care. The Committee has accepted a distinction between basic care and treatment, which includes tube feeding, and has recommended that, while treatment decisions are clinical based on best interests, 'basic care ... should always be available to people'. It is unclear from this whether the Committee is agreeing with the BMA's position or not (see Joint Committee on the Draft Mental Incapacity Bill Report, 2003).

3.4 The incompetent patient and the doctrine of necessity

F v West Berkshire HA **(1989): Justification of treating incompetent adults is found in the doctrine of necessity**

Facts
See 3.2 above.

Decision
The House of Lords held that the court had jurisdiction to make a declaration that the operation was lawful because it was in the patient's best interests. Lord Goff stated: 'On what principle can medical treatment be justified when given without consent? We are searching for a principle on which, in limited circumstances, recognition may be given to a need, in the interests of the patient, that treatment should be given to him in circumstances where he is (temporarily or permanently) disabled from consenting to it. It is this criterion of a need which points to the principle of necessity as providing justification.'

Comment

(1) Lord Griffiths argued that the justification was that medical treatment of incompetent adults was in the public interest.

(2) The draft Mental Capacity Bill 2004 allows the court, appointed attorneys, or deputies to make decisions on behalf of the incompetent adult and will also establish a 'General Authority' to provide care if it is 'reasonable ... to do the act'. Under the Bill, any act or decision must be in the incompetent adult's best interests. The Bill sets out a number of conditions that must be considered when determining the person's best interests (clause 4).

Norfolk and Norwich Healthcare (NHS) Trust v W (1996): If a court declares a treatment as lawful then the doctors may use reasonable force to carry out that treatment

Facts

A 32-year-old woman was admitted in a state of arrested labour. She had a past history of psychiatric treatment 'marked by non-co-operation by her with those seeking to help her'. The psychiatrist opined that she was not suffering from a mental disorder under the Mental Health Act 1983 and she was capable of instructing a solicitor. However, she had persisted throughout the day in denying her pregnancy. On the basis of the *Re C* test, the psychiatrist determined that she was unable to weigh treatment information in the balance and hence lacked the capacity to consent. There were two potential risks if the delivery of her baby was not assisted: the foetus might be deprived of oxygen and possibly die *in utero*; and secondly, the scar from her previous Caesareans might rupture. A declaratory order for a Caesarean was sought.

Decision

The High Court held that the court had a common law power to authorise the use of reasonable force. This was provided there was a 'necessity to act ... [and] the action taken must be such as a reasonable person would in all the circumstances take, acting in the best interests of the assisted person', *per* Johnson J.

F v West Berkshire HA (1989): The doctrine of necessity requires that it is not possible to wait until the patient is competent and that the treatment is in the patient's best interests

Facts

See 3.2 above.

Decision

See 3.2 above. Lord Goff stated: 'to fall within the principle [of necessity], not only (1) must there be a necessity to act when it is not practicable to communicate with the assisted person, but also (2) the action taken must be such as a reasonable person would in all the circumstances take, acting in the best interests of the assisted person.'

Re Y (Adult Patient) (Transplant: Bone Marrow) (1996): The patient's best interests should be interpreted broadly to include emotion, psychological and social factors

Facts

The plaintiff suffered from non-Hodgkin's lymphoma. She required a bone marrow transplantation. The defendant, Y, was one of the plaintiff's three sisters. She was a severely mentally retarded adult. The plaintiff sought a declaration that it would be lawful to perform blood tests and a bone marrow harvest despite Y being unable to give consent.

Decision

The High Court granted the declaration. The procedure would be lawful as in the patient's best interests. The family was particularly close and Y benefited from family visits. The plaintiff's death would adversely affect the health of Y's mother and may result in fewer visits or loss of contact with Y, which would be detrimental to her. There was no real long-term risk and the disadvantages, to Y, of the procedure were small. Therefore, the procedures would provide emotional, psychological and social benefits to Y and so would be in her best interests.

Connell J stated: 'if the transplant occurs, this is likely to improve the defendant's relationship with her mother who in her heart clearly wishes it to take place and also to improve her relationship with the plaintiff who will be eternally grateful to her.'

Comment
See also *R-B (A Patient) v Official Solicitor* (2000), in which the Court of Appeal held that best interests encompassed medical, emotional and all other welfare issues. In *Making Decisions*, the Lord Chancellor (1999) has indicated that the following factors will provide a statutory framework for determining the patient's best interests:

(1) the ascertainable past and present wishes of the person and the factors the person would consider if able to do so; (2) the need to permit and encourage the person to participate ... in any decision affecting him; (3) the views of other people whom it is appropriate and practical to consult; (4) whether the purpose ... can be as effectively achieved in a manner less restrictive of the person's freedom of action; (5) whether there is a reasonable expectation of the person recovering capacity ... in the reasonably foreseeable future; and (6) the need to be satisfied that the wishes of the person without capacity were not the result of undue influence.

This list has been included in the draft Bill and endorsed by the Joint Scrutiny Committee.

F v West Berkshire HA (1989): The doctrine of necessity cannot be used to override a competently made advance directive

Facts
See 3.2 above.

Decision
See 3.2 above. Lord Goff stated: 'I wish to observe that officious intervention cannot be justified by the principle of necessity ... nor can it be justified when it is contrary to the known wishes of the assisted person, to the extent that he is capable of rationally forming such a wish.'

Re H (Mental Patient: Diagnosis) (1993): The doctrine of necessity also applies to diagnostic procedures

Facts
The patient suffered from schizophrenia. She had recently developed epilepsy and there was the possibility of a brain tumour. One of the diagnostic procedures would require the injection of contrast and a brain scan while the patient was under a general anaesthetic. The Health Authority sought a declaration that the procedure was lawful as being in the patient's best interests.

Decision
The High Court dismissed the application for a declaration. No distinction should be drawn between therapeutic and diagnostic procedures. A declaration was not

necessary because the doctors could lawfully perform the procedure providing it was in the patient's best interests.

3.5 Non-therapeutic medical interventions and the role of the court

F v West Berkshire HA (1989): The court can grant a declaration that a proposed treatment is lawful

Facts
See 3.2 above.

Decision
See 3.2 above. Lord Goff stated:

I can see no procedural objection to the declaration granted by the judge, either as a matter of jurisdiction or as a matter of exercise of the discretion conferred by the relevant rule of the Supreme Court, Ord 15, r 16. Rule 16 provides: 'No action or other proceeding shall be open to objection on the ground that a merely declaratory judgment or order is sought thereby, and the court may make binding declarations of right whether or not any consequential relief is or could be obtained.'

Comment
Lord Goff argued that the following were required before a court would exercise its discretion: (1) a real question; (2) about present circumstances and not regarding future rights; (3) that the plaintiff has a proper interest in; and (4) where the declaration is sought with proper argument. The draft Mental Capacity Bill 2004 will confirm this power. However, it should be remembered that a declaration simply states what the court believes the law to be. It cannot make an unlawful act lawful and cannot bind a criminal court.

F v West Berkshire HA (1989): There is no legal requirement but in certain cases it would be good practice to seek the court's approval

Facts
See 3.2 above.

Decision
See 3.2 above. Lord Bridge drew a distinction between curative or prophylactic treatment, which does not require the court's approval, and non-therapeutic treatment.

Comment
Lord Brandon gave six reasons why it would be good practice to involve the court in cases of non-therapeutic sterilisation: (1) it is 'in most cases ... irreversible'; (2) it will deprive the woman of the 'fundamental ... right to bear children'; (3) deprivation of this right raises important moral and emotional considerations; (4) there is a greater risk of a wrong decision without the court's involvement; (5) there is a risk the operation may be performed 'for improper reasons or with improper motives'; and (6) the court's involvement will protect the doctors.

The House of Lords in *Airedale NHS Trust v Bland* (1993) (see 6.2 below) decided that it would be good practice to seek the court's approval before withdrawing nutrition and other life-preserving treatment from patients in PVS. The Official Solicitor has produced a Practice Note (*Declaratory Proceedings: Medical and Welfare Decisions for Adults who Lack Capacity*, May 2001) covering both sterilisation and PVS, which reiterates the requirement of the court's approval 'in virtually all cases', available on the Official Solicitor's website: www.offsol.demon.co.uk/sitemap.htm (accessed September 2003). Under the draft Mental Capacity Bill 2004, a person with lasting power of attorney would only be able to give or refuse consent to 'life-sustaining treatment' if such authorisation is specifically provided for in the instrument granting the power of attorney (clause 7(a)).

Re GF (Medical Treatment) (1992): Where there are therapeutic reasons for an operation, the court's approval is not necessary

Facts
GF was a severely mentally disabled adult who suffered from excessively heavy menstrual periods that she was unable to cope with. The recommended treatment was a hysterectomy but this would have the incidental effect of sterilising her.

Decision
The High Court held that no declaration was required where two medical practitioners were satisfied that: (1) the operation was necessary for therapeutic purposes; (2) the operation was in the best interests of the patient; and (3) there was no practicable, less intrusive means of treating the condition.

Comment
In *Re SG (Adult Mental Patient: Abortion)* (1991), the High Court held that an abortion was not a category of case that required the court's approval, especially as it was closely regulated by the Abortion Act 1967. In *An NHS Trust v D* (2003), Coleridge J – sitting in the High Court – held that 'where the issues of capacity and best interests are clear and beyond doubt, an application to the court is not necessary'. However, he was concerned that the ruling in *Re SG* left responsibility for all such decisions with the medical profession, which 'cannot be correct in all circumstances'. Therefore, where:

- there was dispute concerning capacity (or 'there is a realistic prospect that the patient will regain capacity ... within the period of her pregnancy or shortly thereafter');
- there is dispute between the medical professionals as to the patient's best interests;
- the Abortion Act 1967 procedures have not been followed;
- 'the patient, members of her immediate family, or the foetus' father have opposed, or expressed views inconsistent with, a termination of pregnancy'; or
- 'there are other exceptional circumstances (including where the termination may be the patient's last chance to bear a child)',

then the case should be brought before the court for approval. This guidance was approved by the President of the Family Division.

Re LC (Medical Treatment: Sterilisation) (1997): A treatment will not be declared lawful if, in all the circumstances, it is not in the patient's best interests

Facts

LC was moved to a small residential home with an excellent reputation after she had been sexually abused at her previous home. Her mother, worried in case LC was assaulted again, sought a declaration that a sterilisation would be lawful.

Decision

The High Court dismissed the application.

Comment

Where a treatment is proposed in order to avoid future risk of harm that risk should be a real possibility rather than speculative. Thorpe J stated: 'the present level of care and supervision at X House is of such an exceptionally high quality that it would not be in L's best interest to impose upon her a surgical procedure which is not without risks nor without painful consequences ... Of course, circumstances may change ... But ... leave could not be justified upon the basis of some vague and unsubstantiated fear that L in future will be exposed to risks from which she is presently protected.'

Re A (Male Sterilisation) (2000): It is the judge and not the doctor who decides what is in the patient's best interests

Facts

The mother of a 28-year-old male with Down's syndrome applied to the court for a declaration that a sterilisation operation would be lawful. The patient had indicated that he did not want the operation. At first instance the application was refused. His mother appealed.

Decision

The Court of Appeal dismissed the appeal. The declaration would not be granted. Butler-Sloss LJ distinguished the doctor's duty governed by the *Bolam* test as the professional standard of care and the doctor's duty to act in the best interests of the incompetent patient. In other words, the *Bolam* test applies to determining the range of appropriate treatment options but does not apply to determining the patient's best interests. She stated: 'in the case of an application for approval of a sterilisation operation, it is the judge, not the doctor, who makes the decision that it is in the best interests of the patient that the operation be performed.'

Comment

This only applies to cases that reach the courts. Obviously, healthcare professionals will make most best interest judgments in practice, but they should bear in mind that if their decision is challenged it is the court that will have the final word as to the patient's best interests.

Re S (Adult Patient: Sterilisation) (2000): There can only be one 'best option'

Facts

S was a 29-year-old woman with severe learning difficulties. She was distressed by her menstrual periods but had a phobia about hospitals. Her mother applied for an order that it would be lawful to perform a sterilisation operation or hysterectomy on S. At first instance the judge held that sterilisation was not in her best interests because, while it would protect her from pregnancy, it would not reduce her menstrual problems. The insertion of a contraceptive coil would achieve both of these ends but would have to be replaced every five years, which would require repeated general anaesthetics. A subtotal hysterectomy would achieve the same result without the need for further or repeated interventions and would be the best option. The doctors favoured the coil while the mother favoured the hysterectomy. The judge held that either would be lawful and left it to the mother to determine, with the doctors, which option should be chosen. An appeal was made on behalf of the patient.

Decision

The Court of Appeal allowed the appeal. While many different courses of action may be lawful, 'there could only logically be one best option and it was for the court to decide'. Once the doctors had proposed a range of acceptable options, the court should pick the one that was in the patient's best interests. In this case it would be the less invasive and less permanent option of the contraceptive coil.

Comment

On the relevance of the *Bolam* test Dame Butler-Sloss P stated:

I would suggest that the starting point of any medical decision would be the principles enunciated in the *Bolam* test and that a doctor ought not to make any decision about a patient that does not fall within the broad spectrum of the *Bolam* test. The duty to act in accordance with responsible and competent professional opinion may give the doctor more than one option since there may well be more than one acceptable medical opinion. When the doctor moves on to consider the best interests of the patient he/she has to choose the best option … the best interests test ought, logically, to give only one answer … the principle of best interest as applied by the court extends beyond the considerations set out in … *Bolam* … [and] will incorporate broader ethical, social, moral and welfare considerations.

Where a declaration is sought from the court then it is for the judge to make the decision as to the best option.

The Court of Appeal distinguished *Re ZM & OS (Sterilisation: Best Interests)* (2000) because in *Re S* medical opinion was unanimous while in *Re ZM* all four medical experts disagreed.

Simms v Simms (2003): Even if treatment is experimental and the potential benefit is only 'possible' rather than probable, it may still be in the patient's best interests to receive it

Facts

The case concerned two teenage patients suffering from variant Creutzfeldt-Jakob Disease (vCJD). Both patients showed signs of being aware and could communicate pleasure and displeasure. The court was asked to determine whether it would be lawful to use an experimental treatment that had not been tested on humans before. There was no other treatment available and the patients' parents supported the application. The medical experts were generally of the opinion that although there were risks associated with the treatment, 'the possibility of some benefit' could not be ruled out.

Decision

The High Court held that it would be in the best interests of the patients to receive the experimental treatment.

Comment

This case involved an 18-year-old and a 16-year-old. Under the draft Mental Capacity Bill, both would be treated as adults. Currently the parents of the 16-year-old could have given consent. However, the treatment of all incompetent individuals, whether adult or child, is governed by the best interests test and, therefore, the principle is equally applicable to children and incompetent adults.

CHAPTER 4

CHILDREN AND MEDICAL TREATMENT

As with adults, medical treatment needs to be justified. With competent adults the primary justification is the patient's consent. The child, however, may not have achieved competency and the patient's consent may therefore not be sufficient to justify treatment. In order to protect the patient, other safeguards have been established. Thus, for the incompetent child, the person with parental responsibility is permitted to give consent on behalf of the child. Because the child's interests are entrusted to the adult with parental responsibility, it is important to ensure that power is exercised responsibly. Thus, the decision-maker is not free to make whatever decision he or she pleases, but is restricted by the legal rules outlined below.

The situation is complicated because, as the child matures, so his or her autonomy will increase and he or she will, at some point, become competent to make his or her own decisions. As consent is predicated on autonomy, it might be thought rational to allow a competent child as much control over his or her treatment decisions as a competent adult. There is, however, a tension between the child's right to decide and the parents' duty to care for and nurture the child. Coupled with the lack of experience that might diminish the child's ability – even when rationally capable – this creates a guarded acknowledgment that the competent child should decide for him- or herself. The English courts have only reluctantly and incompletely ceded this power to the child. This incomplete transfer of power, which is perhaps not the case in Scotland (see in *Re Houston (applicant)* (1996)), has been the subject of much academic criticism and is evidenced in the cases discussed below.

The authority to include children as research subjects has been provided – for medicinal trials – by Part 4, Schedule 1 to the Medicines for Human Use (Clinical Trials) Regulations 2004. For other types of research the authority is still provided for by the common law and is thus subject to the best interests test. In one US Court of Appeal, the test was applied rigidly and the court held that the non-therapeutic research was unlawful irrespective of parental authorisation (*Grimes v Kennedy Krieger Institute* (2001)). There are no UK cases on this issue but some commentators have speculated that it would be lawful provided the research carried only minimal risk and was not contrary to the child's interests (Brazier, 2003).

4.1   Consent and children over the age of 16

In England and Wales, the Family Law Reform Act 1969 (s 8) creates a statutory presumption that children over the age of 16 are competent to give a legally effective consent (in Scotland, the equivalent provision is s 1(1)(b) of the Age of Legal Capacity (Sc) Act 1991). Although this applies to diagnostic and ancillary treatments, as well as more therapeutic measures, it probably does not include purely cosmetic surgery, research or organ donation (Montgomery, 2003). Although children over the age of

16 may consent to treatment, this does not, in England and Wales, negate the parental power of proxy consent (s 8(3)).

Re W (A Minor) (Medical Treatment) (1992): Parental consent can override a refusal of consent made by a competent child between the ages of 16 and 18

Facts
W was a 16-year-old girl with anorexia nervosa. She was under the care of the local authority in an adolescent residential unit. Because her condition had worsened, the local authority sought the court's approval to transfer her to a specialist unit. W refused consent and claimed that s 8 of the Family Law Reform Act 1969 gave her the same right as an adult to refuse treatment.

Decision
(Disregarding the question of W's competence – see 7.1 below.) The Court of Appeal held that s 8 of the Family Law Reform Act 1969 gave the child the right to give consent but did not take that right away from the person(s) exercising parental responsibility. Only one consent is necessary and that may be given by the child or the person with parental responsibility.

Comment
Lord Donaldson MR suggested that consent under this section could be seen as analogous to a:

... legal 'flak jacket' which protects the doctor from claims by the litigious whether he acquires it from his patient who may be a minor over the age of 16, or a 'Gillick competent' child under that age or from another person having parental responsibilities which include a right to consent to treatment of the minor. Anyone who gives him a flak jacket (that is, consent) may take it back, but the doctor only needs one and so long as he continues to have one he has the legal right to proceed.

This does not appear to be the case in Scotland (see 5.2 below).

4.2   Consent and children under the age of 16

Gillick v West Norfolk and Wisbech AHA (1986): Children under the age of 16 may give consent to a medical procedure providing they have sufficient maturity to understand all the implications

Facts
The Department of Health and Social Security issued guidance to Area Health Authorities concerning family planning provisions. The guidance included advice concerning children under 16. Although the advice stressed the importance of involving the child's parents, it added that in exceptional circumstances the doctor could prescribe contraceptives without informing the parents. Mrs Gillick sought a declaration that the guidance was unlawful. The application failed at first instance but succeeded in the Court of Appeal.

Decision

By a majority of 3:2, the House of Lords allowed the appeal and the declaration sought by Mrs Gillick was refused.

Lord Fraser laid down five requirements that should be satisfied before the doctor concludes that he may proceed without the parent's consent:

(1) that the girl (although under 16 years of age) will understand his advice;
(2) that he cannot persuade her to inform her parents or to allow him to inform the parents that she is seeking contraceptive advice;
(3) that she is very likely to begin or to continue having sexual intercourse with or without contraceptive treatment;
(4) that unless she receives contraceptive advice or treatment her physical or mental health or both are likely to suffer;
(5) that her best interests require him to give her contraceptive advice, treatment or both without parental consent.

Lord Scarman stated:

I would hold that as a matter of law the parental right to determine whether or not their minor child below the age of 16 will have medical treatment terminates if and when the child achieves sufficient understanding and intelligence to enable him or her to understand fully what is proposed. It will be a question of fact whether a child seeking advice has sufficient understanding and intelligence to enable him or her to understand fully what is proposed ... It is not enough that she should understand the nature of the advice which is being given: she must also have a sufficient maturity to understand what is involved. There are moral and family questions, especially her relationship with her parents; long term problems associated with the emotional impact of pregnancy and its termination; and there are risks to health of sexual intercourse at her age, risks which contraception may diminish but cannot eliminate.

Comment

In Scotland, s 2(4) of the Age of Legal Capacity (Sc) Act 1991 provides a statutory test for competence.

Re E (A Minor) (Wardship: Medical Treatment) (1993): The court will be slow to find the child Gillick competent where their decision puts their life in jeopardy

Facts

E was a 16-year-old boy Jehovah's Witness suffering from leukaemia. He required blood transfusions, which he refused. Both his parents were also Jehovah's Witnesses and supported his refusal. The hospital authority made him a ward of court and applied for the court's approval to the treatment.

Decision

The High Court granted a declaration approving the treatment. Ward J argued that although he was intelligent enough, he lacked sufficient understanding to be Gillick competent, stating: 'He may have some concept of the fact that he will die, but as to the manner of his death and the extent of his and his family's suffering I find he has not the ability to turn his mind to it.' He also stated that the court 'should be very slow to allow an infant to martyr himself'.

Comment

The *Gillick* requirements of competence are far more stringent than those required for adults. Many adults deemed competent would fail them. The *Re E* case had a sad outcome in that E waited until he was 18 and then refused any further consent to the blood transfusions and subsequently died.

Re R (A Minor) (Wardship: Consent to Treatment) (1991): Parental consent can override the refusal of consent by a *Gillick* competent child

Facts

R was a 15-year-old girl with a fluctuating mental disorder that varied between lucidity and 'florid psychotic behaviour'. She had been voluntarily placed in local authority care after a fight with her father but following violent and suicidal psychotic behaviour she was placed in an adolescent psychiatric unit. While taking medication she became clear, lucid and rational, but during these periods she refused consent to her medication. The local authority started wardship proceedings and applied for leave for the psychiatric unit to administer non-consensual medication.

Decision

The Court of Appeal held that, in exercising its wardship jurisdiction, the High Court had power to consent to medical treatment of a minor ward who was competent to consent but who had refused consent or was not asked.

Lord Donaldson MR argued that the *Gillick* decision did not remove the right of consent from the child's parents and stated that 'consent by itself creates no obligation to treat. It is merely a key which unlocks a door. Furthermore, whilst in the case of an adult of full capacity there will usually only be one keyholder, namely the patient, in the ordinary family unit where a young child is the patient there will be two keyholders, namely the parents, with several as well as a joint right to turn the key and unlock the door ... The parents can only have a right of determination if either the child has no right to consent, ie, is not a keyholder, or the parents hold a master key which could nullify the child's consent'. He concludes: 'There can be concurrent powers to consent. If more than one body or person has a power to consent, only a failure to, or refusal of, consent by all having the power will create a veto ... A "*Gillick* competent" child or one over the age of 16 will have a power to consent, but this will be concurrent with that of a parent or guardian.'

Comment

(1) This decision was heavily criticised and Lord Donaldson MR later regretted his keyholder analogy. He subsequently rejected it in favour of the legal flak jacket. See *Re W* (4.1 above).

(2) This does not appear to be the case in Scotland: see 5.2 below.

Re R (A Minor) (Wardship: Consent to Treatment) (1991): The person with parental responsibility cannot override the consent of a *Gillick* competent minor

Facts

See above.

Decision

See above. Lord Donaldson MR argued that the rights of the competent child and the parents were concurrent. This logically means that consent from any of the relevant parties will be sufficient and the decisions of the other parties become irrelevant. However, the child's wishes should always be borne in mind even where they are not determinative.

Comment

See also *Re P (A Minor)* (1982), in which a 15-year-old girl was allowed to have an abortion despite parental objections. However, P was a ward of court and the final decision was based on what would be in her best interests. Also, because the termination was under the Abortion Act 1967, the judge was unable to make the decision solely on the basis of what P wanted.

Re R (A Minor) (Wardship: Consent to Treatment) (1991): Even where the child is not competent, the doctor should take the child's views into account

Facts

See above.

Decision

See above. Lord Donaldson MR, commenting on the doctor's decision whether to treat a child, stated: 'In forming that judgment the views and wishes of the child are a factor whose importance increases with the increase in the child's intelligence and understanding.'

4.3   Limits to parental consent

Parents cannot give a legally valid consent to treatment that is contrary to public policy or outlawed by statute. This includes risky research procedures that hold no benefit for the child and, eg, female circumcision which is outlawed by the Female Genital Mutilation Act 2003.

Re J (A Minor) (Wardship: Medical Treatment) (1990): Parents have the power to give consent but no right to insist on treatment

Facts

J was a 'grossly handicapped' child who had been made a ward of court. The medical evidence suggested that he would develop spastic quadriplegia and would be deaf, blind and severely intellectually impaired. He would, however, be able to feel pain. Although he was not expected to survive into late adolescence he was not terminally ill. After two previous episodes requiring ventilation the 'medical prognosis was that any further collapse which required ventilation would be fatal'. The medical staff sought a court order as to whether he should be reventilated if the need arose. At first instance the judge made an order that J should be 'treated with antibiotics if he developed a chest infection but should not be reventilated if his breathing stopped unless the doctors caring for him deemed it appropriate given the prevailing clinical situation'.

Decision

The Court of Appeal dismissed the appeal. The doctors could lawfully withhold reventilation. Lord Donaldson MR stated, *obiter*:

No one can *dictate* the treatment to be given to the child, neither court, parents nor doctors. There are checks and balances. The doctors can recommend treatment A in preference to treatment B. They can also refuse to adopt treatment C on the grounds that it is medically contra-indicated or for some other reason is a treatment which they could not conscientiously administer. The court or parents for their part can refuse to consent to treatment A or B or both, but cannot insist on treatment C.

Comment

See also *Re J (A Minor) (Wardship: Medical Treatment)* (1992), in which the Court of Appeal held:

The court would not exercise its inherent jurisdiction over minors by ordering a medical practitioner to treat the minor in a manner contrary to the practitioner's clinical judgment since to do so would require the practitioner to act contrary to the fundamental duty which he owed to his patient, which ... was to treat the patient in accordance with his own best clinical judgment.

Re B (1987) (The Jeanette Case): Parental power of consent is limited to treatment that is in the best interests of the child

Facts

Jeanette was a 17-year-old voluntary patient in a local authority home. She suffered a moderate degree of mental handicap and had the intellectual capacity of a six-year-old. She was beginning to show signs of sexual awareness and a sexual drive. It was felt that she would be unable to cope with the demands of pregnancy, childbirth or child rearing. A court order was sought to allow Jeanette to be sterilised.

Decision

The House of Lords held that it would be in Jeanette's best interests and granted the order.

Comment

Lord Templeman suggested, *obiter*, that consent to the sterilisation of a minor was beyond the powers of the parent. He stated:

In my opinion sterilisation of a girl under 18 should be carried out with the leave of a High Court judge. A doctor performing a sterilisation operation with the consent of the parents might still be liable in criminal, civil or professional proceedings. A court exercising the wardship jurisdiction emanating from the Crown is the only authority which is empowered to authorise such a drastic step as sterilisation after a full and informed investigation.

This has been criticised as wrong in principle but it has been approved at first instance (*Re P* (1989)). In the Court of Appeal hearing of *F v W Berkshire HA sub nom Re F* (1989) Lord Donaldson suggested that, although it should be sought, a lack of court approval would not render the operation unlawful. In the same hearing, Butler-Sloss LJ argued that court approval was a requirement. Montgomery (2003) suggests that 'until further clarification emerges it would be safest to regard the sterilization of minors without court approval as unlawful'. This only applies to non-therapeutic sterilisations where the issue of the child's best interests is a complex balance best judged by the independent authority of the court.

S v McC; W v W (1972): Parental consent to treatment may be valid even if it is not in the child's best interests providing it is reasonable and not *contrary* to the child's best interests

Facts
Both cases involved the question of whether the court should grant an order authorising a blood test to determine the paternity of the child. The first of the two was an appeal against such an order; the second case was an appeal against the refusal of the lower courts to grant the order.

Decision
The House of Lords dismissed the first appeal and allowed the second appeal. The order for a paternity test was granted in both cases.

Lord Reid stated: 'even if one accepts the view that in ordering, directing or permitting a blood test the court should go no further than a reasonable parent would go, surely a reasonable parent would have some regard to the general public interest and would not refuse a blood test unless he thought that would clearly be against the interests of the child.'

Comment
This case was decided before the Family Law Reform Act 1969 came into force. In *Re O (A Minor) (Blood Tests; Constraint)* (2000), Wall J held that s 21 of that Act gave the person with parental responsibility the absolute right to give or refuse consent to blood sampling for the purposes of determining paternity (s 20). Wall J suggested, however, that: 'If Parliament does not implement reform, the law in this area will continue not to serve the best interests of children. In these circumstances I anticipate that reform may need to be achieved when the Human Rights Act 1998 comes into force by the point being taken that Part III of the Act of 1969 is not human rights compliant.' This case is incompatible with the decision in *Re R (A Minor) (Blood Test: Constraint)* (1998), which held that such an order could be made. In *Re H (A Minor) (Blood Tests: Parental Rights)* (1997), the Court of Appeal held that s 20(1) did not empower the court to order blood tests but merely permitted it to make a direction for the use of blood tests to determine paternity. This somewhat contradictory case law is made obsolete by s 82 of the Child Support, Pensions and Social Security Act 2000, which amends ss 20–23 of the Family Law Reform Act 1969 and covers blood and other bodily samples and gives the power to direct that such samples may be taken from a minor without the consent of the responsible carer.

Although treatment is justified by being in the best interests of the child, it may be lawful even where it is experimental and the benefit only a possibility: see *Simms v Simms* (2003) (see 3.5 above).

Re A (Children) (Conjoined Twins: Surgical Separation) (2000): A parental decision to refuse consent must be respected by the healthcare professional but may be challenged in court

Facts
See 4.5 below.

Decision
See 4.5 below. Ward LJ stated:

Since the parents are empowered at law, it seems to me that their decision must be respected and in my judgment the hospital would be no more entitled to disregard their refusal than they are to disregard an adult patient's refusal. To operate in the teeth of the parents' refusal would therefore, be an unlawful assault upon the child ... There is, however, this important safeguard to ensure that a child receives proper treatment. Because the parental rights and powers exist for the performance of their duties and responsibilities to the child and must be exercised in the best interests of the child, 'the common law has never treated such rights as sovereign or beyond review and control' [see *Gillick v West Norfolk and Wisbech AHA* (1986) *per* Lord Scarman].

Re J (A Minor) (Prohibited Steps Order: Circumcision) (2000): For certain important decisions, the court's approval should be sought where those with parental responsibility disagree

Facts
J's father, a Muslim, wanted to arrange a religious circumcision for J. The mother opposed this and was granted an order prohibiting the procedure. J's father appealed.

Decision
The Court of Appeal dismissed the appeal. Where there was an important decision and the parents could not agree, then, despite having parental responsibility under s 2(7) of the Children Act 1989, '[s]uch a decision ought not to be made without the specific approval of the court'.

Comment
In *Re J* (2000), the court included sterilisation in the decisions requiring court approval where the parents disagreed. In *Re C (A Child) (Immunisation: Parental Rights)* (2003), the Court of Appeal added immunisation to the list.

B v B (A Minor) (Residence Order) (1992): A person responsible for the care of a child may be able to give a valid consent to medical treatment

Facts
A grandmother (supported by the child's mother) applied for a residence order for her 11-year-old granddaughter. The justices refused the application under s 1(5) of the Children Act 1989, which required that the court only make an order if it was better for the child than making no order at all. The decision was based on the fact that the

child had been permanently resident with the grandmother for most of her life and there was little risk of her mother removing the child from her home. The grandmother appealed.

Decision
The High Court allowed the appeal. Although the magistrates had been correct in their application of s 1(5), there was a new ground that must be considered. Since the grandparent did not have parental responsibility, the education authority was reluctant to accept her authority, there may be problems with consent to medical treatment, and the child was anxious about her future. Johnson J noted the provisions of s 3(5) of the Children Act 1989 but argued that, although those provisions clearly allowed the grandmother to give consent for the child's medical treatment, the professionals involved may be reluctant to proceed on the basis of such authority. Since the order would give parental responsibility to the grandmother, this would make the child's position more certain and secure.

Comment
Section 3(5) of the Children Act 1989 states that where a person has care of a child, but lacks parental responsibility, that person may do 'what is reasonable in all the circumstances of the case for the purpose of safeguarding or promoting the child's welfare'.

4.4 The role of the court

Re B (A Minor) (Wardship: Medical Treatment) (1990): The court may override a parental refusal of consent if it would be in the child's best interests

Facts
B was born suffering from Down's syndrome and an intestinal blockage. The intestinal blockage could be cured by operation but, without the operation, she would die. Her parents refused consent because of her mental and physical handicaps. The local authority made her a ward of court and applied for the court's authorisation of the operation. At first instance the judge held that the parent's wishes should be respected and he refused the operation. The local authority appealed.

Decision
The Court of Appeal allowed the appeal and authorised the operation. Dunn LJ stated: 'although due weight must be given to the decision of the parents ... the fact of the matter is that this court now has to make this decision. It cannot hide behind the decision of the parents or the decision of the doctors; and in making the decision this court's paramount consideration is the welfare of this unhappy little baby.'

Comment
See also Re S (A Minor) (Medical Treatment) (1993), in which the court authorised blood transfusions for a child suffering from leukaemia against the parents' – who were Jehovah's Witnesses – wishes. Thorpe J stated: 'it is difficult to pursue the argument that the religious convictions of the parents should deny the child the

chance of treatment.' In *Glass v UK* (2004), the European Court of Human Rights held that where the doctors wished to provide treatment contrary to parental refusal of consent then they should seek the Court's authorisation. Without such authorisation the child's right to physical integrity under Article 8 of the European Convention on Human Rights would be breached. An exception might exist where the treatment was so urgently required that there was insufficient time to seek the Court's approval.

Re T (A Minor) (Wardship: Medical Treatment) (1997): In reaching a decision about the child's best interests, the wishes of the parents are important considerations

Facts
T had biliary atresia, a serious liver defect. Without a transplant he would not live for more than a couple of years. His mother (a healthcare professional) refused consent. At first instance the judge authorised the operation. T's mother appealed.

Decision
The Court of Appeal allowed the appeal and upheld the mother's refusal of consent. The Court of Appeal took account of the evidence of Dr P who stated that the mother's commitment would be crucial to the success of the procedure. Waite LJ stated:

... it is the duty of the judge to allow the court's own opinion to prevail in the perceived paramount interests of the child concerned, but ... in the last analysis the best interests of every child include an expectation that difficult decisions affecting the length and quality of its life will be taken for it by the parent to whom its care has been entrusted by nature.

Re C (A Child) (HIV Testing) (2000): The parents' views as to the child's best interests are presumed to be correct but this presumption may be rebutted

Facts
C might have contracted infection with HIV (Human Immunodeficiency Virus believed to be responsible for AIDS – Acquired Immune Deficiency Syndrome). Both parents refused consent to an HIV test as they did not believe the conventional theories regarding the link between HIV and AIDs. The local authority sought an order that an HIV test be performed.

Decision
The High Court granted the application. Although there was a presumption that parental views of the child's best interests were correct, this presumption could be rebutted, knowing the result could affect both the mother's decision to breast-feed and also the provision of sound medical advice and was therefore in the child's best interests.

Comment
The court argued that the rebuttable presumption in favour of the parents' views followed from s 1(5) of the Children Act 1989 which states that a court shall not make an order 'unless it considers that doing so would be better for the child than making no order at all'. This was supported by the decision in *Re T* (see above). Since making

no order at all would leave the decision-making responsibility with the parents, the court must be convinced that any order it was being asked to make must be sufficiently in the child's best interests to justify removing the decision-making responsibility from the parents.

Re R (A Minor) (Wardship: Consent to Treatment) (1991): The court may override the decision of a competent child if it would be in their best interests

Facts
See 4.2 above.

Decision
See 4.2 above.

Re K, W and H (Minors) (Medical Treatment) (1993): Where the parents have given consent to the treatment, there is no need to seek a court order

Facts
Some adolescents treated in a specialised hospital unit complained about the practices of the unit. Only one of the complaints related to the use of medication. Patients were only admitted if parental consent to the unit's regime was obtained. The Health Authority set up a committee to investigate the unit. The committee advised the unit that the law was complex and any doubt about the question of consent to treatment should be resolved by seeking a court order. The hospital subsequently submitted applications for three highly disturbed patients despite the fact that they had the parents' full co-operation and consent.

Decision
The High Court refused the applications. Where the professionals had obtained the parents' consent, there was no risk of criminal or civil proceedings irrespective of whether the child was *Gillick* competent or not.

Thorpe J stated: 'Where more than one person has the power to consent, only a refusal of all having that power will create a veto.' This is not the case for non-therapeutic procedures: see *Re J* (2000), 4.3 above.

Re W (A Minor) (Medical Treatment) (1992): The court will take the minor's views into account when deciding what treatment is in the child's best interests

Facts
See 4.1 above.

Decision
See 4.1 above. Balcombe LJ stated:

Undoubtedly the philosophy … is that, as children approach the age of majority, they are increasingly able to take their own decisions concerning their medical treatment … Accordingly the older the child concerned the greater the weight the court should give to its wishes, certainly in the field of medical treatment. In a sense this is merely one aspect of the application of the test that the welfare of the child is the paramount consideration.

Re W (A Minor) (Medical Treatment) (1992): The greater the threat to the child's life, the more likely the court will override a refusal of consent

Facts
See 4.1 above.

Decision
See 4.1 above. Balcombe LJ stated:

... if the court's powers are to be meaningful, there must come a point at which the court, while not disregarding the child's wishes, can override them in the child's own best interests, objectively considered. Clearly such a point will have come if the child is seeking to refuse treatment in circumstances which will in all probability lead to the death of the child or to severe permanent injury.

Comment
See also *Re M (Child: Refusal of Medical Treatment)* (1999) in which the High Court held that a 15-year-old girl was not competent to refuse consent to a life-saving heart transplant. Johnson J stated: 'Whilst I was very conscious of the great gravity of the decision I was making in overriding M's wish, it seemed to me that in seeking to achieve what was best for her required me on balance to give the authority that was asked.'

In *Re L (A Minor)* (1998), L was a 14-year-old Jehovah's Witness who, although 'mature', had led a sheltered life. Following an accident, she suffered severe burns. Without treatment her death would be 'agonising'. The court granted a declaration that she was not *Gillick* competent and that blood transfusions should be given in her best interests. Sir Stephen Brown P stated, *per curiam*, that: 'It is also my view, without any doubt at all, that it would be an appropriate order to make even if I were not justified in coming to the conclusion that she was not so-called *Gillick* competent. This is an extreme case and her position is grave indeed. It is vital, as I have already said, that she should receive this treatment.'

Re J (A Minor) (Wardship: Medical Treatment) (1990): The court will not dictate the treatment to the doctor

Facts
See 4.3 above.

Decision
See 4.3 above.

Comment
This was affirmed in *Re J (A Minor) (Wardship: Medical Treatment)* (1992); Balcombe LJ stated: 'I would also stress the absolute undesirability of the court making an order which may have the effect of compelling a doctor or Health Authority to make available scarce resources (both human and material) to a particular child, without knowing whether or not there are other patients to whom those resources might more advantageously be devoted.' See also *R v Cambridge DHA ex p B* (1995).

R v Portsmouth Hospitals NHS Trust ex p Carol Glass (1999): The court's reluctance to dictate treatment may be subject to the fact that the court must take decisions that are in the child's best interest

Facts

A 12-year-old boy with epilepsy, blindness and severe mental and physical handicaps developed a life-threatening infection following a tonsillectomy. The doctors decided not to actively treat with antibiotics and administered morphine to make the boy more settled. The mother was opposed to this course of action and was unaware that a do-not-resuscitate order had been entered into the child's notes. He survived and his mother sought judicial review of the doctor's decision. Leave to apply for judicial review was denied by the High Court. Mrs Glass appealed.

Decision

The Court of Appeal denied the appeal. Judicial review was too blunt a tool to consider difficult situations such as these and a High Court order sought at the time of the altercation would have been more appropriate.

Lord Woolf laid out a number of principles that the court should take into account:

(1) The sanctity of life.
(2) The non-interference by the courts in areas of clinical judgment in the treatment of patients ... where this can be avoided ...
(3) The refusal of the courts to dictate appropriate treatment to a medical practitioner ... subject to the power which the courts always have to take decisions in relation to the child's best interests. In doing so, the court takes fully into account the attitude of medical practitioners.
(4) That treatment without consent save in an emergency is trespass to the person.
(5) That the courts will interfere to protect the interests of a minor or a person under a disability.

He stated: 'The difficulty in this area is that there are conflicting principles involved. The principles of law are clearly established, but how you apply those principles to particular facts is often very difficult to anticipate.'

Comment

It is the third of Lord Woolf's principles that is a theoretically important reservation of the judicial right to order treatment. It is a notable modification of the statements in Re J (see above). However, notice the importance placed on the medical view. It is suggested that, despite Lord Woolf's reservation of the judicial right to order treatment, the court is likely to place such an emphasis on the medical view of the child's best interests that they will rarely – if ever – dictate the treatment that a doctor must provide. The High Court has subsequently reiterated the view that 'it is well established that there can be no question of the court directing a doctor to provide treatment which he or she is unwilling to give and which is contrary to the doctor's clinical judgment', per Cazalet J in NHS Trust v D (2000) (see also Royal Wolverhampton Hospitals NHS Trust v B (2000)).

4.5   Re A (Children) (Conjoined Twins: Surgical Separation) (2000): The case of conjoined (Siamese) twins

Facts

The twins, Jodie and Mary, were conjoined twins. Mary had non-functioning lungs and an abnormal heart capable of only 10% of its normal function. Mary was dependent on Jodie to supply her with oxygenated blood. The doctor's wanted to operate to separate the twins. It was accepted that without such an operation both twins would die, probably within three to six months. Following separation it was probable that Jodie would survive with a reasonably normal life expectancy and quality. It was unlikely that there would be any mental handicaps and the physical abnormalities were mostly correctable by surgical intervention. Mary, however, would inevitably die as a result of the operation and thus her life would be foreshortened by it. The parents refused consent to the operation for a number of reasons, both religious and practical, but their overriding reason was that they did not want one child to survive at the expense of the other, they could not choose between their children this way, and that their lives should be left in God's hands. The hospital applied to the court for a declaration that the operation would be lawful. At first instance, the judge granted the declaration since it would be in the best interests of both children: Jodie would survive and Mary would be spared the prolongation of a life, which – because she was attached in such a manner to her twin – would be hurtful and distressing to her. The parents appealed.

Decision

The Court of Appeal dismissed the appeal on the following grounds:

(1) Every life has inherent and equal value regardless of any disability or reduction in the person's ability to enjoy life. The person's quality of life should not be used to make judgments about the value of that person's life.

(2) The proposed operation was a positive act and could not be classified as an omission.

(3) Since it was not certain that Mary was in pain, the operation was in Jodie's but not Mary's best interests (Walker LJ dissented from this and argued that the operation was in Mary's best interests).

(4) There was a conflict between Jodie's and Mary's best interests, welfare and right to life. There was, therefore, a conflict in the court's duty to give paramount consideration to the welfare of each twin. As such, the court had to choose the lesser of two evils and adopt the least detrimental course. This involved a balancing exercise.

(5) Although both twins had the same right to life, the value to Jodie in operating was far greater than the value to Mary in not operating. Jodie could be helped by medical treatment, but Mary was beyond help. Therefore, the proposed operation was the least detrimental alternative.

(6) Although the operation was the best course of action, it must still be shown to be lawful. Because the benefit was to one person while the detriment fell on the

other, the doctrine of double effect was not applicable. The operation would kill Mary and, unless justified, would be murder. However, Mary was putting such a strain on Jodie's vital organs that she was, in effect, killing her. The doctor's were justified in coming to Jodie's defence. Thus the operation was justified by a plea of 'quasi self-defence' in the exceptional circumstances.

Comment

(1) It was also argued that the operation would be justified by necessity. Brooke LJ stated:

> According to Sir James Stephen, there are three necessary requirements for the application of the doctrine of necessity: (i) the act is needed to avoid inevitable and irreparable evil; (ii) no more should be done than is reasonably necessary for the purpose to be achieved; and (iii) the evil inflicted must not be disproportionate to the evil avoided ... Given that the principles of modern family law point irresistibly to the conclusion that the interests of Jodie must be preferred to the conflicting interests of Mary, I consider that all three of these requirements are satisfied in this case.

(2) The balancing act to find the least detrimental course is only appropriate where the conflict is between two legal duties. It does not apply where one of the duties is a moral duty only.

(3) The court also considered that conjoined twins were two legal persons. Walker LJ stated: 'They have two brains and two nearly complete bodies, despite the grave defects in Mary's brain and her heart and lungs. There are cases of incomplete (or heteropagus) twinning in which a child is born with abnormalities which can be regarded as no more than a parasitic attachment. But it ... could not be suggested that this case comes anywhere near that category.'

(4) The court held that 'intention' in Article 2 of the European Convention on Human Rights should be given its ordinary meaning rather than the meaning of 'intention' in the criminal law (which includes acts where death is foreseen as a virtually certain consequence of the act irrespective of the actor's desire or the purpose of the act: *R v Woollin* (1999) HL). As such, since the operation did not have the purpose of causing Mary's death, it would not be contrary to the Human Rights Act 1998.

(5) Ward LJ stated that the decision was restricted to 'unique circumstances'. The circumstances that must be satisfied for the decision to be used as an authority are: 'that it must be impossible to preserve the life of X without bringing about the death of Y, that Y by his or her continued existence will inevitably bring about the death of X within a short period of time, and that X is capable of living an independent life but Y is incapable under any circumstances (including all forms of medical intervention) of viable independent existence.'

4.6   Children and confidentiality

Children are entitled to confidentiality. For minors who do not possess *Gillick* competence, parents can determine when to consent to disclosure. The *Gillick* case has been interpreted as implying that a competent child is equally entitled to confidentiality. This is logical if one considers that one of Lord Fraser's justifications for allowing the minor to consent was 'that he [the doctor] cannot persuade her to inform her parents or to allow him to inform the parents that she is seeking contraceptive advice. This implies that she is entitled to the doctor's confidence otherwise he would not have to try and persuade her "to allow him to inform the parents"'.

Apart from the common law duty of confidence, there are statutory duties by virtue of s 4 and Schedule 1 to the Data Protection Act 1998 (DPA). Children in Scotland are specifically provided for by the Act. Section 66(1) states: 'Where a question falls to be determined in Scotland as to the legal capacity of a person under the age of sixteen years to exercise any right conferred by any provision of this Act, that person shall be taken to have that capacity where he has a general understanding of what it means to exercise that right.' Section 66(2) provides that 'a person of twelve years of age or more shall be presumed to be of sufficient age and maturity to have such understanding'. The capacity of children in England will be governed by s 8(1) of the Family Law Reform Act 1969 and the principles laid down in *Gillick*.

Re Z (1995): When a parent consents to disclosure of confidential information that is not in the child's best interests, the courts can prevent them from doing so

Facts
The mother of a handicapped child obtained an injunction *in rem*, to prevent the media from revealing the identity of the child or any school or other establishment in which she was residing, being educated or treated. The child began to receive treatment at a specialised foreign institution. A television company wanted to make a film about the work of the institute. The mother wanted to permit the filming in order to publicise the valuable work of the institution and thereby to enhance the child's welfare and self-esteem. She applied for the injunction to be discharged or varied to allow the filming. Her application was turned down at first instance and the mother appealed, contending that the court should never override the reasonable decision of a responsible parent and that freedom of publication should prevail.

Decision
The Court of Appeal dismissed the appeal:

(1) In accordance with s 1(1)(a) of the Children Act 1989, the child's welfare was the court's paramount consideration and prevailed over the interest in the freedom of publication. The court may not exercise its power if freedom of publication was in the prevailing interest *and* the material was only indirectly referable to the child.

(2) The disclosure of confidential information relating to a child was an exercise of parental responsibility within the meaning of s 3(1)(b) of the 1989 Act, which the court was empowered to restrain by means of a prohibited steps order under s 8 of the Act. The court could refuse to permit a parent's exercise of parental responsibility even though it was *bona fide* and reasonable if it was contrary to the child's best interests.

(3) In this instance the child's welfare would be harmed by the publicity from a television programme.

Comment

Under s 8 of the Children Act 1989, the court may make a number of orders subject to the provision under s 1(5) that 'doing so would be better for the child than making no order at all'.

Gillick v West Norfolk and Wisbech AHA (1986): The child's right to confidentiality mirrors the child's right to consent

Facts

See 4.2 above.

Decision

See 4.2 above.

Comment

Specifically, Lord Fraser's five conditions must allow a right of confidence. See discussion above.

4.7 Right of access to medical records

Under s 7 of the DPA, competent children have a statutory right to access their medical records. A competent child may also prevent the person with parental responsibility from having the right to access their notes: see the Data Protection (Subject Access Modification) (Health) Order 2000.

CHAPTER 5

REFUSAL OF TREATMENT

For competent adults, the right to refuse consent follows from the existence of a right to consent. If medical treatment is only lawful – as it is for competent adults (excluding public health and mental health (see 9.3 below) justifications) – when it is done with consent, then a refusal to give consent will make medical treatment unlawful (see Chapter 2). The right to refuse treatment is thus based on the principle of autonomy and the right to bodily integrity. Respecting the individual's right to refuse treatment also respects his dignity and this is important both ethically and legally (Article 3 of the European Convention on Human Rights prohibits inhuman or degrading treatment). However, the right to give or refuse consent is not absolute. Ethically, a number of liberty-limiting constraints operate when an individual's actions threaten to adversely affect other individuals. The most widely accepted of these is the 'harm theory' (Mill, 1991), which states that the only justification for restricting an individual's liberty is to prevent harm to others. Some commentators extend this to also prevent self-harm (Raz, 1989). The question for the law is whether and how these ethical constraints should be legally enforced.

The right to refuse treatment was most strongly threatened in the short spate of cases in which the court was asked to declare on the lawfulness of performing a non-consensual caesarean section. In *Re T (Adult: Refusal of Medical Treatment)* (1992) (see 2.1 above), Lord Donaldson MR stated, *obiter*:

An adult patient who, like Miss T, suffers from no mental incapacity has an absolute right to choose whether to consent to medical treatment, to refuse it or to choose one rather than another of the treatments being offered. The only possible qualification is a case in which the choice may lead to the death of a viable foetus. That is not the case and, if and when it arises, the court will be faced with a novel problem of considerable legal and ethical complexity.

This *dictum* was seized upon by Sir Stephen Brown P to justify a non-consensual caesarean in *Re S* (1992) in which the competent adult woman had refused the operation on religious grounds. That decision was heavily criticised (see Thomson, 1994) and was overruled by the Court of Appeal's judgment in *St George's Healthcare NHS Trust v S* (1998) (see 5.1 below). However, the flexibility of the test for competency may still allow judges to circumvent a refusal by finding the woman incompetent: in *Rochdale Healthcare (NHS) Trust v C* (1997) (see 3.1 above), Johnson J overruled the consultant obstetrician's opinion that the woman was competent and argued:

The patient was in the throes of labour with all that is involved in terms of pain and emotional stress ... a patient who could, in those circumstances, speak in terms which seemed to accept the inevitability of her own death, was not a patient who was able properly to weigh-up the consideration that arose so as to make any valid decision, about anything of even the most trivial kind, surely still less one which involved her own life.

Although the patient has the right to refuse medical treatment, it is arguable that no such right exists in relation to basic care. The justification for limiting the right would be based on public policy arguments, such as the effect that the refusal would have on other patients and on the carers looking after the patient. Arguments may also be raised concerning human dignity that might also justify non-consensual basic care. The Law Commission (1995, para 5.34) states: 'In the consultation paper we proposed that an advance directive should never be effective in refusing either pain relief or basic care. On consultation, there was general agreement to the proposition that a patient's right to self-determination could properly be limited by considerations based on public policy' (see also Law Commission, 1993, para 3.25). The draft Mental Capacity Bill 2004 (s 25) is silent on the issue despite the Joint Committee's (2002–03) recommendation, in the context of withdrawing treatment, that basic care is distinct from medical treatment and 'should always be available' (Recommendation 64). This, however, is of little assistance in anticipating whether the courts would currently protect a patient's right to refuse such care, which, therefore, remains uncertain.

5.1 A competent adult patient has the right to refuse medical treatment

Nancy B v Hotel-Dieu de Quebec (1992): This right exists even if it will result in the patient's death

Facts
Nancy B was a 25-year-old woman suffering from Guillain-Barre syndrome. This incurable neurological disorder meant that she was paralysed and, since she was unable to breathe without assistance, ventilator-dependent. She was mentally competent and sought an injunction to prevent the hospital from continuing to treat her with artificial ventilation.

Decision
The Quebec Superior Court granted the injunction. The hospital must stop treatment with the ventilator. The right of the individual to refuse treatment is almost absolute, being subject only to a corresponding right of others. The individual may not threaten the life or health of others.

Dufour J stated: 'The logical corollary of this doctrine of informed consent is that the patient generally has the right no to consent, that is the right to refuse treatment and to ask that it cease where it has already been begun.'

Comment
Although this is a Canadian case, the same principle has been explicated by the House of Lords in *Airedale NHS Trust v Bland* (1993) (see 6.2 below). Lord Goff stated:

… it is established that the principle of self-determination requires that respect must be given to the wishes of the patient, so that, if an adult patient of sound mind refuses, however unreasonably, to consent to treatment or care by which his life would or might be prolonged, the doctors responsible for his care must give effect to his wishes, even though they do not consider it to be in his best interests to do so. To this extent, the principle of the sanctity of life must yield to the principle of self-determination.

St George's Healthcare NHS Trust v S; R v Collins and Others, ex p S (1998): The right to refuse treatment exists even if the patient is pregnant with a viable fetus

Facts

S was a pregnant 28-year-old veterinary nurse who, at 36 weeks of gestation, was diagnosed with pre-eclampsia severe enough to require hospital admission and an induction of labour. S was advised as to the potentially life-threatening risks to her and her baby. It was accepted that she understood the risks but she rejected the advice because, as she later documented: 'I have always held very strong views with regard to medical and surgical treatments for myself, and particularly wish to allow nature to "take its course", without intervention.' She was compulsorily detained for assessment under s 2 of the Mental Health Act (MHA) 1983, justified by a previous diagnosis of moderate depression, her own admission that she was probably depressed and her GP's statement that her 'mental state may be compromising her ability to make decisions'. An ex p declaration that a non-consensual caesarean would be lawful was granted, the operation was performed and the baby safely delivered. S appealed.

Decision

The Court of Appeal held that, since S was competent, the non-consensual caesarean section was unlawful and a battery. The judgment stated:

... while pregnancy increases the personal responsibilities of a woman it does not diminish her entitlement to decide whether or not to undergo medical treatment. Although human, and protected by the law ... an unborn child is not a separate person from its mother. Its need for medical assistance does not prevail over her rights. She is entitled not to be forced to submit to an invasion of her body against her will, whether her own life or that of her unborn child depends on it. Her right is not reduced or diminished merely because her decision to exercise it may appear morally repugnant.

Comment

While upholding the pregnant woman's right to autonomy, the Court of Appeal strongly criticised the misuse of the MHA 1983 to protect the fetus, and the Trust's failure to inform S of its intentions to seek the declaration, which had meant that S was unrepresented at the High Court hearing. The Court of Appeal laid down guidelines for future practice.

Secretary of State for the Home Department v Robb (1995): Public policy might constrain the competent adult's right to refuse treatment

Facts

An adult prisoner was refusing all nutrition. He was found to be competent. The Home Secretary sought a declaration that it would be lawful for those looking after the prisoner to abide by his refusal.

Decision

The High Court granted the declaration that an adult of sound mind and capacity had a specific right of self-determination which entitled him to refuse nutrition and hydration. That right was not diminished just because he was a detained prisoner.

Thorpe J considered four state interests that might override a competent adult's refusal of consent. These were detailed in the US case *Thor v Superior Court* (1993):

(1) preserving life;
(2) preventing suicide;
(3) maintaining the integrity of the medical profession;
(4) protecting innocent third parties.

None of these applied in the case before him.

Comment

There will be very few circumstances when these might apply in the context of medical treatment. They do not apply under normal circumstances, nor do they apply when the life of a fetus is at risk. Regarding the third interest, Thorpe J stated: 'The third consideration of maintaining the integrity of the medical profession is one that I find hard to recognise as a distinct consideration.' Perhaps the main situation is in the justification of treating attempted suicides without their consent. This would not apply to the refusal of life-saving treatment (*Nancy B*) or nutrition (*Robb*).

F v West Berkshire HA (1989): The doctrine of necessity cannot be used to override a competent adult's decision

Facts

See 3.2 and 3.4 above.

Decision

See 3.2 and 3.4 above. Lord Goff stated: 'I wish to observe that officious intervention cannot be justified by the principle of necessity. So intervention cannot be justified … when it is contrary to the known wishes of the assisted person, to the extent that he is capable of rationally forming such a wish.'

Ms B v An NHS Hospital Trust (2002): Non-consensual treatment of a competent patient will be a battery and cannot be justified by the consequences of non-treatment

Facts

Ms B had suffered a bleed into her spinal cord and was left paralysed and dependent on assisted ventilation. Four months after becoming paralysed she instructed the hospital, via her solicitors, that she wished to be removed from the ventilator. She was initially assessed as competent but the psychiatrists subsequently amended their reports. An independent psychiatrist then assessed her and stated that she was competent. She was offered a 'one-way weaning' programme whereby the ventilatory support would be gradually removed. This she rejected because it would have taken three weeks and she would not be given pain relief. She also refused referral to a spinal rehabilitation unit or to a hospice that would not respect her wishes to have the ventilator withdrawn. She sought a declaration that treatment with artificial ventilation was an unlawful trespass.

Decision

The High Court held that Ms B was competent and the continued treatment had been unlawful.

Comment

In responding to the possibility that Ms B may be temporarily incompetent, Dame Butler-Sloss P stated:

Unless the gravity of the illness has affected the patient's capacity, a seriously disabled patient has the same rights as the fit person to respect for personal autonomy. There is a serious danger, exemplified in this case, of a benevolent paternalism which does not embrace recognition of the personal autonomy of the severely disabled patient. I do not consider that either the lack of experience in a spinal rehabilitation unit and thereafter in the community or the unusual situation of being in an ICU for a year has had the effect of eroding Ms B's mental capacity to any degree whatsoever.

5.2 The right to refuse is not absolute

F v West Berkshire HA (1989): Incompetent patients have no legal right to refuse consent

Facts

See 3.2 and 3.4 above.

Decision

See 3.2 and 3.4 above.

Comment

This naturally follows because incompetent patients are unable to give a legally valid consent. However, it is important to distinguish between patients with psychiatric disorders who may still be competent to refuse consent (*Re C (Adult: Refusal of Treatment)* (1994) (see 2.1 above)) and those patients who lack capacity (who may or may not have a psychiatric disorder). When an incompetent patient does refuse treatment, the healthcare professional may have a duty to treat the patient against their will. The patient's refusal is an important factor that will have to be added to the benefits/harm equation. If treatment is in the best interests of the incompetent patient, then treatment may be given despite the wishes of the patient (see Chapter 3).

Re R (A Minor) (Wardship: Consent to Treatment) (1991): A competent minor's refusal to give consent may be overridden by the court or any person with parental responsibility

Facts

See 4.2 above.

Decision

See 4.2 above.

Comment

(1) This also applies to children over the age of 16 who have a statutory right to consent under s 8 of the Family Law Reform Act 1969. In *Re W (A Minor) (Medical Treatment)* (1992) (see 4.1 above), which concerned the refusal of consent by a 16-year-old girl with anorexia, the Court of Appeal argued that s 8 gave the child the right to consent but did not take that right away from the parents. Lord Donaldson MR regretted his 'key holder' analogy and argued instead:

> I now prefer the analogy of the legal 'flak jacket' which protects the doctor from claims by the litigious whether he acquires it from his patient who may be a minor over the age of 16, or a '*Gillick* competent' child under that age or from another person having parental responsibilities which include the right to consent to treatment of the minor ... the doctor only needs one [flak jacket].

He concluded that:

> No minor of whatever age has power by refusing consent to treatment to override a consent to treatment by someone who has parental responsibility for the minor and *a fortiori* a consent by the court. Nevertheless such a refusal is a very important consideration in making clinical judgments and for parents and the court in deciding whether themselves to give consent. Its importance increases with the age and maturity of the minor.

(2) The situation may be different in Scotland. In *Re Houston (Applicant)* (1996), s 2(4) of the Age of Legal Capacity (Sc) Act 1991 was interpreted so that a capacity to consent entailed the capacity to refuse treatment.

CHAPTER 6

DEATH AND EUTHANASIA

Euthanasia refers to the practice of ending another person's life with the intention of ending their suffering. It is sometimes described as the practice of bringing about a 'good' or 'quiet' death. It can be classified as involuntary (against the wishes of a competent person); voluntary (with the wishes of a competent person); and non-voluntary (where the individual is incompetent). These categories may be sub-divided as active (a positive act that causes the death) or passive (an omission or failure to act). Euthanasia should be distinguished from physician assisted suicide, in which a mentally competent person is given help to enable him to commit suicide. The meanings of these terms were all considered by the House of Lords Select Committee on Medical Ethics and may be found in their Report (HL Paper 21-1, 1993–94). A final distinction worth bearing in mind when reading the case law is between an act and an omission. Although it may be open to criticism from a moral perspective, the law only holds a person responsible for an omission where there was a prior duty to act: the mother of a child may be criminally liable if she fails to feed her baby, but a stranger will not be even if it would be of minimal inconvenience.

In Holland, euthanasia has for some time been treated as a less serious offence than murder. In the 1970s, cases such as that of Dr Postma (1973), attracted lenient sentences. Although others received custodial sentences, Dr Postma was given a conditional sentence of one week and a year's probation. In 1981, the District Court in Rotterdam argued that assisted suicide was justifiable if the victim's suffering was enduringly unbearable, the victim voluntarily wanted to die, there was no other way of improving the situation and a doctor had been consulted (*The Wertheim Case* (1981)). Other cases followed and in 2001 the Dutch Parliament passed a bill (Termination of Life on Request and Assisted Suicide (Review Procedures) Act) to decriminalise euthanasia provided the doctor satisfies certain requirements: it must be a voluntary decision by the patient who faces unending suffering, the doctor must inform the patient and they must agree that there is no other reasonable solution, and the doctor must consult with an independent doctor.

6.1 Active euthanasia

R v Cox (1992): Active euthanasia is murder

Facts

Dr Cox was a consultant physician. One of his patients was a 70-year-old woman suffering from severe and extremely painful rheumatoid arthritis. It was uncertain how much longer she would have lived for but she could have died at any time. The pain she suffered was not controllable with analgesic drugs. After she asked Dr Cox to put her out of her misery he injected her with a lethal dose of potassium chloride.

Because she could have died at any time and hence pre-empted the effect of the potassium chloride, Dr Cox was charged only with attempted murder.

Decision

Dr Cox was found guilty of attempted murder by the jury. In directing the jury Ogden J stated:

... if it is proved that Dr Cox injected Lillian Boyes with potassium chloride in circumstances which make you sure that by that act he intended to kill her, then he is guilty of the offence of attempted murder ... You must understand, members of the jury, that in this highly emotional situation, neither the express wishes of the patient nor of her loving and devoted family can affect the position.

Comment

In *Airedale NHS Trust v Bland* (1993) (see 6.2 below), Lord Goff stated:

But it is not lawful for a doctor to administer a drug to his patient to bring about his death, even though that course is prompted by a humanitarian desire to end his suffering, however great that suffering may be ... So to act is to cross the Rubicon which runs between on the one hand the care of the living patient and on the other hand euthanasia – actively causing his death to avoid or to end his suffering. Euthanasia is not lawful at common law.

R v Bodkin Adams (1957): Where death is not 'intended', a positive act (for a lawful purpose) that also hastens the death of the patient is lawful

Facts

One of the accused's patients was an elderly patient who had suffered a stroke. Dr Bodkin Adams was a substantial beneficiary of the victim's will. He increased the dose of his patient's opiate analgesic. The victim subsequently died and Dr Bodkin Adams was charged with murder.

Decision

The jury found the accused not guilty of murder. In directing the jury Devlin J stated: 'If the first purpose of medicine, the restoration of health, can no longer be achieved there is still much for a doctor to do, and he is entitled to do all that is proper and necessary to relieve pain and suffering, even if the measures he takes may incidentally shorten life.'

Comment

The rationale behind this decision is the doctrine of double effect. The doctrine receives both academic support and criticism, but it has been accepted as a valid legal principle. Thus, in *R v Cox*, Ogden J explained: 'There can be no doubt that the use of drugs to reduce pain and suffering will often be fully justified notwithstanding that it will, in fact, hasten the moment of death. What can never be lawful is the use of drugs with the purpose of hastening the moment of death.' Montgomery (2003) suggests that three conditions must be satisfied:

(1)   the patient must be terminally ill;
(2)   the drugs given must be considered appropriate treatment by a responsible body of physicians; and

(3)   the motive must be to relieve suffering and not to shorten life.

In a criminal trial it seems that the test is whether the doctor subjectively believed he was acting properly (see *R v Moor* (1999) – case comment by Arlidge (2000)).

6.2   Passive euthanasia

Re T (Adult: Refusal of Medical Treatment) (1992): It is lawful to accede to a competent patient's wishes not to be treated

Facts
See 2.1 above.

Decision
See 2.1 above. Lord Donaldson MR stated: 'An adult patient who, like Miss T, suffers from no mental incapacity has an absolute right to choose whether to consent to medical treatment, to refuse it or to choose one rather than another of the treatments being offered.'

Comment
The legality of passive voluntary euthanasia is the corollary of the competent patient's right to refuse treatment. Once the patient has refused treatment, then, providing the patient is competent, the doctor is relieved of his duty to provide the treatment refused.

Airedale NHS Trust v Bland (1993): It is lawful to withdraw treatment from, or not to treat, an incompetent patient providing the treatment is not in the patient's 'best interests'

Facts
Anthony Bland suffered a severe crush injury in the Hillsborough disaster. He had been in a persistent vegetative state (PVS) for three and a half years. There was no hope of recovery. The Health Authority sought declarations that it would be lawful to withdraw and withhold life-preserving treatment.

Decision
The House of Lords held that it would be lawful to withhold life-preserving treatment if it was not in the patient's best interests that his life should be prolonged. Doctors were not under an absolute obligation to prolong life regardless of the circumstances or the patient's quality of life.

Comment
Although the judiciary generally refer to acting in the patient's best interests, it is clear that the test for withholding or withdrawing treatment is more accurately described as not being contrary to the best interests of the incompetent patient (see Lord Goff's judgment). As Lord Mustill stated:

Unlike the conscious patient he does not know what is happening to his body, and cannot be affronted by it ... The distressing truth which must not be shirked is that the proposed conduct is not in the best interest of Anthony Bland, for he has no best interests of any kind ... Although the termination of his life is not in the best interests of Anthony Bland, his best interests in being kept alive have also disappeared, taking with them the justification for the non-consensual regime and the correlative duty to keep it in being.

In *NHS Trust A v M; B v H* (2001), Dame Butler-Sloss P, sitting in the High Court, held that the decision in *Bland* conformed with the Human Rights Act (HRA) 1998 (for a criticism of this case, see Maclean, 2001).

Re R (Adult: Medical Treatment) (1996): Treatment may be withheld if the only life it could provide would be 'intolerable'

Facts

R was a 23-year-old man with severe mental and physical disabilities who existed in what was described as a 'low awareness state'. He had suffered five previous life-threatening episodes requiring hospital treatment. The Trust sought a declaration that it would be lawful to withhold cardio-pulmonary resuscitation. In the event of a life-threatening infection, the Trust also wanted to withhold antibiotics, but only if R's GP and one of his parents agreed.

Decision

The High Court granted the declaration in accordance with the experts' recommendations. Sir Stephen Brown P quoted with approval Taylor LJ, who stated: 'I consider the correct approach is for the court to judge the quality of life the child would have to endure if given the treatment, and decide whether in all the circumstances such a life would be so afflicted as to be intolerable to that child' (*Re J (A Minor) (Wardship: Medical Treatment)* (1990) CA (see 4.3 above)).

Re D (Medical Treatment) (1998): Artificial feeding may be withdrawn where there is no prospect of meaningful life even where the patient does not fulfil the guidelines for diagnosis of PVS

Facts

D was a young woman, totally dependent on artificial nutrition and hydration, who showed no signs of awareness. Her mother and all the expert witnesses agreed that it was in her best interests for the feeding and hydration to be withdrawn. Three consultant neurologists diagnosed that she was in an irreversible vegetative state. However, one of the paragraphs of the Royal College of Physicians' guidelines was not satisfied. The hospital applied for a declaration that it would be lawful to withdraw feeding and hydration. The Official Solicitor opposed the application on the grounds that she did not satisfy the guidelines and it could therefore not be said that it was futile to keep her alive.

Decision

The High Court granted the declaration. Where there was no awareness and no meaningful life and 'the patient was suffering a living death', it was not in her best interests to keep her alive regardless of whether she satisfied all the guidelines.

Sir Stephen Brown P drew attention to the present procedure that doctors are always advised to seek the court's declaration and stated: 'The court recognises that no declaration to permit or to sanction the taking of so extreme a step could possibly be granted where there was any real possibility of meaningful life continuing to exist ... In this case ... there is no evidence of any meaningful life whatsoever.'

Comment
This case extends the guidelines laid down in the Official Solicitor's Practice Note (see below) from patients in PVS to those with no real possibility of meaningful life. However, the patient was diagnosed as being in the vegetative state and therefore this extension may not apply to patients without a 'meaningful life' who are not in the vegetative state.

Airedale NHS Trust v Bland (1993): Withdrawal of treatment is an equivalent to an omission rather than a positive act

Facts
See above.

Decision
See above. Lord Goff stated:

I agree that the doctor's conduct in discontinuing life support can properly be categorised as an omission. It is true that it may be difficult to describe what the doctor actually does as omission, for example where he takes some positive step to bring the life support to an end. But discontinuation of life support is, for present purposes, no different from not initiating life support in the first place. In each case, the doctor is simply allowing his patient to die in the sense that he is desisting from taking a step which might, in certain circumstances, prevent his patient from dying as a result of his pre-existing condition; and as a matter of general principle an omission such as this will not be unlawful unless it constitutes a breach of duty to the patient.

Comment
This does not apply to oral feeding and hydration but solely to feeding and hydration by nasogastric, intravenous or percutaneous routes (eg, a feeding tube inserted directly into the stomach).

In *Bland*, artificial nutrition and hydration were considered to be forms of medical treatment that may be withheld or withdrawn where their provision was not in the patient's best interests. Lord Keith stated:

I am of the opinion that regard should be had to the whole regime, including the artificial feeding, which at present keeps Anthony Bland alive. That regime amounts to medical treatment and care, and it is incorrect to direct attention to the fact that nourishment is being provided. In any event, the administration of nourishment by the means adopted involves the application of a medical technique.

Note that the House of Lords held that it would be good practice to seek the court's approval before withdrawing artificial feeding and nutrition from patients in the vegetative state. This has been formally documented in the Official Solicitor's Practice Note, *Declaratory Proceedings: Medical and Welfare Decisions for Adults who Lack Capacity* (May 2001). It is available on the Official Solicitor's website: www.offsol.demon.co.uk/sitemap.htm.

Frenchay Healthcare NHS Trust v S (1994): When a decision as to continue artificial nutrition has to be taken urgently or as an emergency, it may not be necessary to follow the official guidelines

Facts
S suffered severe brain damage following a drug overdose. He was being fed by a gastrostomy inserted through his stomach wall. The tube became dislodged and there was no prospect of replacing it without a surgical operation. The consultant in charge of the patient felt that it was in S's best interests to be allowed to die. The hospital applied for an urgent declaration that it would be lawful not to replace the feeding tube. The declaration was granted. The Official Solicitor appealed because (i) he had not been given the opportunity to investigate the matter and ensure all the relevant material was available, and (ii) the judge had attached too much importance to the medical opinion of S's best interests.

Decision
The Court of Appeal dismissed the appeal:

Although the court had the ultimate power and duty to review the medical decision in the light of all the facts and should not necessarily accept medical opinion as to what was in the patient's best interests ... the court should be reluctant to place those treating the patient in a position of having to carry out treatment which they considered to be contrary to the patient's best interests unless the court had real doubt about the reliability, *bona fides* or correctness of the medical opinion.

Comment
As a *per curiam*:

Where a hospital seeks to discontinue treatment of a patient in a persistent vegetative state, as a general rule the hospital should apply to the court for and obtain a declaration that it was proper to do so, and such an application should be preceded by a full investigation with an opportunity for the Official Solicitor ... to explore the situation fully, to obtain independent medical opinions ... and to ensure that all the proper material was before the court. Nevertheless, emergency situations will arise in which an application to the court is not possible, or where, although an application to the court is possible, it will not be possible to present the application in the same leisurely way as in the case where there is no pressure of time.

6.3   Assisted suicide

Although suicide is not unlawful, assisting another to commit suicide remains a criminal offence by virtue of s 2(1) of the Suicide Act 1961, which states that: 'A person who aids, abets, counsels or procures the suicide of another, or an attempt by another to commit suicide, shall be liable on conviction on indictment to imprisonment for a term not exceeding 14 years.'

Attorney General v Able (1984): The offence requires that the accused had knowledge of and encouraged the suicide attempt

Facts

The Voluntary Euthanasia Society (VES) published a booklet which disapproved of hasty suicide decisions, but also provided descriptions of how to achieve successful 'self-deliverance'. The Attorney General, who had evidence that the book was associated with 15 suicides, sought a declaration that the book was unlawful under s 2 of the 1961 Act.

Decision

The High Court held that the book was not necessarily unlawful. A successful prosecution would have to show that:

(1)   the accused knew that suicide was being considered;
(2)   the accused approved of or assented to the decision; and
(3)   the accused encouraged the attempt.

R v McShane (1977): It is unlawful to attempt to assist another to commit suicide

Facts

The appellant had been left money that was held in trust. The trust provided that her mother should receive an income from the estate for life. Her mother was an elderly, infirm woman who had previously talked of committing suicide. The appellant, on a number of occasions, left fatal doses of pills with her mother. On the last occasion she was heard to say, 'Whisky with barbiturates is fatal'. She was convicted of an attempt to counsel or procure her mother's suicide. She appealed on the grounds that this was not an offence in law.

Decision

The Court of Appeal dismissed the appeal. An attempt to commit an offence (statute or common law) is a common law offence even where the crime 'is itself of the nature of an attempt'.

R (on the Application of Pretty) v DPP (2001): The prohibition of assisted suicide is not contrary to the HRA 1998

Facts

Mrs Pretty suffered from advanced motor neurone disease. Her husband was willing to assist her suicide in the final stages of the disease to allow her to avoid the associated suffering and indignity, provided the Director of Public Prosecutions (DPP) would grant him immunity from prosecution. The DPP refused and Mrs Pretty sought a judicial review arguing that the decision breached Articles 2, 3, and 8 of Schedule 1 to the HRA 1998.

Decision

The House of Lords dismissed the appeal and held that the DPP had no power to grant immunity to future acts, and the prohibition on assisted suicide did not breach the HRA.

Comment

The European Court of Human Rights confirmed the judgment in *Pretty v UK* (2002). Article 2 – the right to life – did not confer a right to die, nor did it grant a right to self-determination of life. Article 3 was not breached by the state's alleged failure to prevent her suffering. Article 8 may have been infringed but derogation was justified (legitimate and proportionate) to protect vulnerable terminally ill patients from potential abuse.

6.4   Death

Re A (1992): Legal death is the same as medical death

Facts

A was a 19-month-old child admitted to hospital with a head injury and absent heartbeat which his mother claimed arose from him having fallen from a table. The suspicion was of a non-accidental injury and A's left leg was still splinted from a previous admission. A few days following his resuscitation, A was diagnosed as brain-stem dead. The child had been the subject of an emergency protection order, which gave parental responsibility to the local authority. The parents subsequently applied and were granted an order that stated: 'No person with parental responsibility, namely the parents and the local authority, shall give consent to the switching off of a life support machine in respect of A without the consent of these others with parental responsibility and after consultation with the guardian *ad litem*.' An application was made for a declaratory order that it would be lawful to disconnect A from the ventilator.

Decision

The High Court granted the declaration. Johnson J accepted the doctor's submission that A was brain dead according to the recommendations of the Royal College of Physicians, the Royal College of Surgeons and the British Paediatric Association. He stated: 'I hold that I have the jurisdiction to make a declaration that A is now dead for all legal, as well as medical, purposes, and also to make a declaration that should the consultant or other medical consultants at Guy's Hospital consider it appropriate to disconnect A from the ventilator, in so doing they would not be acting contrary to law.'

Comment

In *R v Malcherek* (1981) CA, Lord Lane LCJ stated: 'Where a medical practitioner, using generally accepted methods, came to the conclusion that the patient was for all practical purposes dead and that such vital functions as remained were being maintained solely by mechanical means, and accordingly discontinued treatment, that did not break the chain of causation.'

CHAPTER 7

ORGAN TRANSPLANTATION, RETENTION AND OWNERSHIP

The need for human organs for transplantation is well known: the NHS-run UK Transplant website states that more than 5,500 people are currently on the waiting list (www.uktransplant.org.uk/how_to_become_a_donor/how_to_become_a_donor.htm). Currently, the primary source is to harvest organs from a deceased donor. This method of obtaining organs is presently regulated by the Human Tissue Act 1961. This much-criticised Act, which carries no sanction for a breach, allows the deceased to have indicated a request either orally (in front of two witnesses) or in writing (s 1(1)). This request may be documented by an organ donor card or by registering with the NHS Organ Donor Register. The final authorisation for use of cadaver organs must come from the person in lawful possession of the body, which is usually the hospital in which the person died. Legally the relatives have no right to veto the deceased's expressed wish. However, in practice, doctors will usually ask the next of kin for permission. A Department of Health circular stated: 'If a patient carries a signed donor card or has otherwise recorded his or her wishes, for example by inclusion in the NHS Donor Register, there is no legal requirement to establish lack of objection on the part of the relatives although it is good practice to take account of the views of close relatives' (DoH, 1998).

If the deceased has not indicated their wishes, then a reasonable enquiry must be made of their spouse and relatives. Any objection from a relative precludes authorisation and here the Act is again problematic because it makes no restriction on how closely related that person must be (s 1(2)).

Following the revelation, in July 1999, that the UK Transplant Support Service Authority (UKTSSA) had accepted an organ with racist preconditions, the Government set up a panel to consider the lawfulness and desirability of conditional donation (DoH, 2000c). The report concluded that the Human Tissue Act 1961 'does not envisage conditional agreement'. Racist preconditions would breach ss 20(1) and 31(1) of the Race Relations Act 1976 and would be unlawful. Organs should not be accepted with conditions relating to the recipient, but if an organ is accepted by mistake, then the conditions may be disregarded and the organ used for the most suitable recipient (para 5.3(iii)). (For a discussion of racist preconditions, see Maclean, 1999.)

Following the Bristol Royal Infirmary Inquiry (2001), and the Alder Hey Inquiry into organ retention (The Royal Liverpool Children's Inquiry 2001), the Government established the Retained Organs Commission (www.nhs.uk/retainedorgans) to deal with the issue of organ retention following post-mortem. The Commission publishes guidance to improve hospital practice, which is available on their website. Presently, the formal legal regulation resides, like cadaveric organ donation, in the Human Tissue Act 1961. Also relevant are the Anatomy Act 1984, the Corneal Tissue Act 1986, the

Coroners Rules 1984 and the Coroners Act 1988 (see Chief Medical Officer, 2001). Because of the public concern that followed those, and other related inquiries, the Government published the Human Tissue Bill on 4 December 2003 (www.parliament.the-stationery-office.co.uk/pa/cm200304/cmbills/009/2004009.htm), which will replace the Human Tissue Act 1961 as well as the Anatomy Act 1984, the Corneal Tissue Act 1986 and the Human Organ Transplants Act 1989.

The Bill (which has just had its second reading in the House of Lords), if passed, will establish a new regulatory body (The Human Tissue Authority), predicates control on the basis of 'appropriate consent' and creates a number of offences to sanction a breach of the Act. Post-mortems and anatomical examinations of cadavers will only be lawful if carried out under the authority of a licence, and it will establish Inspectorates of Anatomy and Pathology, and Organ and Tissue for Human Use. The Bill deals with tissue from both cadavers and live patients and prohibits live organ transplantation except where it is provided for in Regulations made by the Secretary of State and no reward is involved. Finally, the Bill also has provisions to regulate the analysis of DNA. With the exception of the provision concerning DNA analysis, the Bill does not apply to Scotland, which is currently producing its own legislation to regulate the use of human tissue and organs.

Live human organ transplantation is currently governed by both the common law and the Human Organ Transplants Act 1989 (but see above). Regenerative tissue, such as blood or bone marrow, falls under the common law, but other organs are regulated by the Act and subsequent regulations. All commercial transplant dealings of non-regenerative organs (both living and dead donors) are prohibited by the Act (s 1(1)). The use of non-human organs for transplantation is regulated by the UK Xenotransplantation Interim Regulatory Authority and, following directions to Health Authorities, all proposals for xenotransplantation must be submitted to the Authority for approval (www.advisorybodies.doh.gov.uk/ukxira/index.htm).

7.1 Live organ donation

Organ transplantation using organs from live donors is governed partly by the common law and partly by statute. The common law requires that both parties give consent and clearly the consent of the donor will be invalid if donation of the organ would result in death. Where the donor lacks the capacity to give a valid consent it may be still possible for donation to be lawful. Under the Human Organ Transplants Act 1989, live organ donation is subject to restrictions unless the donor and recipient are genetically related (s 2) and the relationship must be established by testing (including DNA testing) by a tester approved by the Secretary of State (the Human Organ Transplants (Establishment of Relationship) Regulations 1998). Under the Human Organ Transplants (Unrelated Persons) Regulations 1989, authority to regulate unrelated donation is vested in the Unrelated Live Transplant Regulatory Authority (ULTRA). Any unauthorised transplant would be an offence.

Re Y (Adult Patient) (Transplant: Bone Marrow) (1996): It will only be lawful to accept organ donation from an incompetent adult patient if the donation is in their best interests

Facts

Y, a 25-year-old woman with severe mental and physical disabilities, had an older sister who required a bone marrow transplant. A declaration was sought to determine if non-consensual blood tests and bone marrow extraction would be lawful.

Decision

The High Court granted the declaratory order, as it would be in Y's best interests to assist her sister. Connell J stated:

The test to be applied in a case such as this is to ask whether the evidence shows that it is in the best interest of the defendant for such procedures to take place. The fact that such a process would obviously benefit the plaintiff is not relevant unless, as a result of the defendant helping the plaintiff in that way, the best interests of the defendant are served.

He argued that the donation would be beneficial because the death of her sister would have a detrimental effect on Y's mother. By helping to preserve her sister's life, Y would improve her relationship with her mother and her sister. A successful transplantation would also allow Y's mother more time to spend with Y. This visiting time would be adversely affected if her sister's health deteriorated.

Comment

Bone marrow is regenerative. It might be much harder to demonstrate that donation is in the donor's best interests for non-regenerative organs. However, in the US, the Kentucky Court of Appeal sanctioned a kidney transplant from an incompetent adult to his brother: *Strunk v Strunk* (1969).

Re W (A Minor) (Medical Treatment) (1992): Even where a minor is *Gillick* competent, the parents' consent should be sought

Facts

W was a 16-year-old girl suffering from anorexia. She was refusing consent to all treatment despite her deteriorating health. An order was sought that it would be lawful to treat her non-consensually in a specialist unit.

Decision

The Court of Appeal granted the order. The anorexia destroyed her ability to make an informed choice. Lord Donaldson MR stated (*obiter*):

I doubt whether blood donation will create any problem as a '*Gillick* competent' minor of any age would be able to give consent under the common law ... Organ transplants are quite different and, as a matter of law, doctors would have to secure the consent of someone with the right to consent on behalf of a donor under the age of 18 or, if they relied upon the consent of the minor himself or herself, be satisfied that the minor was '*Gillick* competent' in the context of so serious a procedure which would not benefit the minor. This would be a highly improbable conclusion. But this is only to look at the question as a matter of law. Medical ethics also enter into the question. The doctor has a professional duty to act in the best interests of his patient and to advise accordingly. It is inconceivable that he should proceed in reliance solely upon the consent of an under-age patient, however 'Gillick competent', in the absence of supporting parental consent ... [he] may well be advised to apply to the court for guidance.

Comment

Lord Donaldson MR is not suggesting that a 'Gillick competent' minor could *never* give a valid consent. However, he is advising that, at the very least, the doctor should also seek the parent's consent. The safest course would be for the doctor to seek a declaratory order. Clearly, Lord Donaldson MR does believe that parental consent may be valid. For this to be so, the parents would need to consider both the benefits and detriments of the donation and make a 'reasonable' decision.

7.2 Cadaver organ transplantation

Cadaver organ donation is regulated by the Human Tissue Act 1961 (see above). There are no sanctions contained within the Act for breaching its requirements. In *R v Lennox Wright* (1973) the accused was charged with the common law offence of disobedience of a statute. However, in *R v Horseferry Road Justices ex p IBA* (1986), the Court of Appeal ruled that contravening a statute would not be a criminal offence unless the statute makes an express provision to cover that eventuality.

Re A (1992): A person is dead if their brainstem function is irreversibly lost – brainstem death

Facts

See 6.4 above.

Decision

See 6.4 above. Johnson J accepted the guidelines for the definition of death laid down by the Royal College of Surgeons, the Royal College of Physicians and a working party of the British Paediatric Association. See (1976) 2 BMJ 1187.

7.3 Post-mortems and organ retention

Post-mortems are regulated by the Coroners Act 1988 and the Human Tissue Act 1961. Because of the concerns regarding organ retention, the Human Tissue Act 1961 stands to be repealed by the Human Tissue Bill (see above). However, the Coroners Act 1988 remains unaffected and, under s 19, the coroner may require a post-mortem where the cause of death is unknown. (The Government has published a Position Paper (March 2004) that includes reform of the coroner's rules regarding post-mortem investigations.) Until the Human Tissue Bill is passed, hospital post-mortems are regulated by s 2(2) of the Human Tissue Act 1961. Pending the new legislation, the Department of Health has published interim guidance (2003a). While the Code acknowledges that the Human Tissue Act 1961 does not require the consent of the spouse or nearest relative, it suggests that good practice requires it.

7.3.1 Retention of body parts

There are a number of circumstances in which body parts may be lawfully retained. The Human Tissue Act 1961 allows organ retention for 'therapeutic purposes or for purposes of medical education or research' (s 1(1)). This power is under the same constraints as the power for post-mortem organ donation: that the person in lawful possession is unaware – following reasonable enquiry – of any objection made by the deceased or his relatives. The Anatomy Act 1984 makes similar provisions (s 4) regarding the retention of body parts for teaching, studying, or researching into morphology (s 1). Retention is also lawful following a post-mortem. Under r 9 of the Coroners Rules 1984, the coroner may direct the 'preservation of material which in his opinion bears upon the cause of death for such a period as the coroner sees fit'. For a post-mortem under the Human Tissue Act 1961, it is probably lawful to retain tissue providing the purpose of retaining the tissue can be implied into the authorisation obtained for the post-mortem. The forms recommended by the Department of Health as part of their interim guidelines (see above) require that a proposed retention be made explicit before authorisation is sought. A potential lacuna is where the tissue has been removed for a purpose that has since become frustrated or exhausted and the tissue is then put to some unauthorised use. Arguably, this is currently lawful providing the organ is used for some recognised medical use (see Maclean, 2000).

7.4   Ownership of body parts

Although English law does not traditionally allow a right of property in a corpse (*Williams v Williams* (1882)), there are circumstances in which rights in body parts may be claimed. Thus, it is possible to convict someone for theft of urine or blood (*R v Welsh* (1974); *R v Rothery* (1976)). There are also a number of statutory provisions (see above) that allow rights of possession in corpses and body parts (see also s 25 of the National Health Service Act 1977, which states that 'where the Secretary of State has acquired: (a) supplies of blood; or (b) any part of a human body; ... he may arrange to make such supplies or that part available ... to any person').

R v Kelly (1998): Once a body part has been lawfully altered in character the possessor gains the right to retain possession

Facts
A junior technician who worked at the Royal College of Surgeons removed some body parts. The parts were needed by an artist who wished to use them as moulds for his work. The defendants denied a charge of theft on the grounds that there was no property in a corpse.

Decision
The Court of Appeal held that the defendants were guilty of theft. It stated that: 'parts of a corpse are capable of being property ... if they have acquired different attributes by virtue of the application of skill, such as dissection or preservation techniques, for exhibition or teaching purposes.'

Comment
See also *Doodeward v Spence* (1908). In *Moore v Regents of the University of California* (1990), the defendants had patented a cell line developed from cells taken from the patient's excised spleen. The value of therapies developed from this cell line was in excess of $3 billion. The plaintiff claimed, amongst other things, that his property rights in the cells had been compromised. The Supreme Court of California decided

that it was inappropriate to recognise property in the body because it would hinder medical research and there was no precedent. However, as was pointed out by Broussard J, dissenting, the majority's argument rests not on a no property rule but 'on the proposition that a patient retains no ownership interest in a body part once the body part has been removed'. The plaintiff did succeed in negligence on the grounds that his consent had not been fully informed.

Dobson v North Tyneside HA (1996): The next of kin may have no right to have body parts returned for burial

Facts
The deceased's brain was removed and preserved in paraffin during a coroner's post-mortem. Once it was no longer required, the hospital disposed of the brain. The deceased's family required the brain for evidence in a medical negligence action against the hospital. They brought a claim in conversion against the hospital.

Decision
The Court of Appeal held that the hospital was not liable. The brain had not undergone any process that might have generated property rights (*Doodeward v Spence* approved). There was no right of possession vested in the relatives. Only the legal executor or administrator had any rights of possession and then only with a view to burial.

CHAPTER 8

ABORTION AND REPRODUCTIVE LAW

This is a particularly contentious area of law, with much of the discussion polarised into two camps: the pro-choice and the pro-life camps. Because advances in reproductive medicine are proceeding at a great pace, the law has struggled to keep up and this has allowed the development of possible lacunae in the legal regulation, which has allowed the pro-life campaigners to raise a number of legal challenges in the last few years. Apart from the common law, the main statutes relevant to reproductive law are the Abortion Act 1967, the Surrogacy Arrangements Act 1985 and the Human Fertilisation and Embryology Act 1990 (HFEA 1990). The Offences Against the Person Act 1861, the Infant Life (Preservation) Act 1921, the Congenital Disabilities (Civil Liability) Act 1976 and the Human Reproductive Cloning Act 2001 are also relevant. Most recent is the Human Fertilisation and Embryology (Deceased Fathers) Act 2003 (HFEA 2003), which allows a deceased sperm donor, providing certain conditions are satisfied, to be named on the birth certificate as the child's father.

A feature of this area of law, which is perhaps a reflection of a more general trend, is the establishment of regulatory bodies. The HFEA 1990 created the Human Fertilisation and Embryology Authority (s 5) (www.hfea.gov.uk). This body has the power to grant licences to allow clinics to provide assisted reproduction services that are regulated by the Act (ss 9–22). The Authority is required to keep a register of information (ss 31–35) and must also produce and maintain a Code of Practice (s 25). It should be noted that the Authority has no power to regulate self-insemination with fresh sperm or insemination using fresh sperm from the woman's partner, which are not covered by the Act. It also appears that, where the sperm is neither stored nor donated, the technique of gamete intra-fallopian transfer (GIFT) likewise falls outside the ambit of the Act and the Authority (for an excellent discussion of the Act, see Lee and Morgan, 2001). It is because of the incomplete coverage that certain unlicensed clinics were able to advertise sex selection services using, for example, sperm sorting techniques. The adverts were criticised for targeting vulnerable Asian communities and the Government instructed the Authority to investigate and report on the issue. Following a consultation exercise, the Authority has recommended that sex selection should be regulated and only licensed clinics should be permitted to offer it and only where there is medical justification, such as the risk of a sex linked disease (HFEA 2003).

Another important regulatory body is the Human Genetics Commission (HGC), which was established in 1999 to take over the responsibilities of the Advisory Committee on Genetic Testing, the Advisory Group on Scientific Advances in Genetics and the Human Genetics Advisory Commission (www.hgc.gov.uk/about_hgc.htm). The HGC co-ordinates the various different bodies and organisations involved in human genetics and also advises Government ministers on social and ethical issues arising from genetic advances. Given the lack of specific law in this area, the HGC has an important role to play. Issues that are covered by the Commission include genetics and employment, genetics and insurance (there is a moratorium on the use of genetic testing for insurance purposes, but this ends in 2006: www.hgc.gov.uk/business_ publications_statement_01may.htm), genetic databases, paternity testing and pre-implantation genetic testing. The Government White Paper, *Our Inheritance, Our Future – Realising the Potential of Genetics in the NHS* (2003), sets out the Government's plans for developing and regulating genetics (available at www.dh.gov.uk).

8.1 The legal status of the fetus

Attorney General's Reference (No 3 of 1994) (1998): The fetus is not a legal person

Facts

The accused stabbed a pregnant woman, causing the child to be born alive but prematurely. The child subsequently died because of its prematurity rather than through any direct injury from the stabbing.

Decision

The House of Lords held that, although a fetus was not a living person, the possibility of a dangerous act directed at a pregnant woman, causing harm to a child to whom she subsequently gave birth, made it permissible on public policy grounds to regard that child as within the scope of the defendant's *mens rea* when committing the unlawful act.

Lord Mustill stated: 'It is sufficient to say that it is established beyond doubt for the criminal law, as for the civil law (*Burton v Islington HA* (1993)), that the child *en ventre sa mère* does not have a distinct human personality whose extinguishment gives rise to any penalties or liabilities at common law.'

Comment

In *St George's Healthcare NHS Trust v S; R v Collins and Others ex p S* (1998) (see 5.1 above), the Court of Appeal stated: 'Although human, and protected by the law ... an unborn child is not a separate person from its mother. Its need for medical assistance does not prevail over her rights.' See also *Paton v British Pregnancy Advisory Service Trustees* (1979), 8.3 below. Sir George Baker said: 'The foetus cannot, in English law, in my view, have a right of its own at least until it is born and has a separate existence from its mother.'

Paton v UK (1980): The fetus is not protected by the European Convention on Human Rights

Facts

The plaintiff had failed in the English courts to gain an injunction to prevent his wife from having an abortion under the Abortion Act 1967. He subsequently claimed that the fetus had a right to life and an abortion would breach Article 2 (right to life) of the European Convention on Human Rights.

Decision

The European Commission on Human Rights denied that allowing the abortion of a fetus during the first half of pregnancy would be a breach of Article 2.

Comment

The Commission noted that the word 'everyone' was not defined in the Convention but 'both the general usage of the term "everyone" in the Convention and the context in which this term is employed in Article 2 tend to support the view that it does not include the unborn'. In *H v Norway* (1992) the Commission held that abortions on social grounds were not contrary to Article 2. This case involved a 14-week fetus so it may not be relevant to the rights of a viable fetus. It remains open whether a viable fetus has a limited right to life under the Convention, but it is suggested that in any conflict between the health or life of the pregnant woman and the fetus' right to life, the woman's rights will trump those of the fetus.

This case only applies to a non-viable fetus since the Commission declined to consider whether the fetus at any stage of pregnancy had a limited right to life. It did argue that an absolute right would be untenable because it 'would mean that the "unborn life" of the fetus would be regarded as being of a higher value than the life of the pregnant woman'. In *Vo v France* (2004), which concerned the negligent termination of pregnancy that the mother wished to carry to term, the European Court of Human Rights held that: 'the issue of when the right to life begins comes within the margin of appreciation which the Court generally considers that States should enjoy in this sphere.' It did, however, note that the fetus belonged to the 'human race' and so warranted some protection, but this could be provided through protection of the pregnant woman. It thus seems unlikely that the Court will afford even the viable fetus the right to life under the Convention.

8.2 The legal protection of the fetus

Despite not being recognised as a legal person, the fetus remains subject to the law's protection. Under s 58 of the Offences Against the Person Act 1861, the fetus is protected from abortions that are not lawful under the Abortion Act 1967 and an unlawful abortion may be punished by life imprisonment. Because of the way this section is worded, for a woman to be liable under this section, she must actually be pregnant; if a third party *attempts* to induce a miscarriage, the woman does not have to be pregnant. Also, the attempt to induce a miscarriage need not be successful. Further protection is provided by the Infant Life (Preservation) Act 1929, which makes it a criminal offence to intentionally destroy a child capable of being born alive (*prima facie*, this is set at 28 weeks' gestation). Again, the offender is liable to life imprisonment. The Act was drafted to cover the lacuna in the law that existed after the child had been born, but was not independent of the mother (before the umbilical cord had been cut), when destruction of the child was neither homicide nor an offence under the Offences Against the Persons Act 1861. However, the Act has a much wider effect than was intended, since it covers any fetus that is capable of being born alive. Note that omissions or reckless or negligent acts do not incur liability under the Act.

If the child is actually born alive then the law provides additional protection that relates to the period before birth. Under the Congenital Disabilities (Civil Liabilities) Act 1976, the child can bring a claim for harm resulting from a negligent act that occurred prior to the child's birth. The Act only covers children born after 22 July

1976, prior to which the common law allowed that negligent damage to a fetus could give rise to liability to the child once it is born alive (*Burton v Islington HA* (1993)). The action is derivative via a tort committed against either the mother or the father (s 1(3)). A mother cannot be liable to her own child except for negligent driving (s 2), but a father can be liable for any tort against the mother. Section 44(1) of the HFEA 1990 extends the Act by inserting s 1A to cover negligent acts that damage eggs, sperm or embryos prior to implantation during infertility treatment. The action for prenatal harm in Scotland remains governed by the common law.

C v S (1988): The meaning of 'capable of being born alive' is that the fetus can breathe independent of its mother

Facts
The plaintiff sought an injunction to prevent the mother of his 18–21 week fetus from aborting the child. One of the grounds for the injunction was that the child was capable of being born alive and so was protected by the Infant Life (Preservation) Act 1929.

Decision
The Court of Appeal refused to grant an injunction. Sir John Donaldson MR stated: 'We have no evidence of the state of the foetus being carried by the first defendant, but if it has reached the normal stage of development and so is incapable ever of breathing, it is not in our judgment "a child capable of being born alive" within the meaning of the Act.'

Comment
See also *Rance v Mid-Downs HA* (1991), 12.5 below. The child will still be capable of being born alive even if it is incapable of breathing without assistance from a ventilator.

Bagley v North Herts HA (1986): Even though there can be no liability to the child if it is stillborn, there may still be liability to the mother for the loss of the child

Facts
The negligent actions of the defendants in failing to carry out blood tests and deliver the child early by Caesarean section resulted in the birth of a stillborn child. The plaintiff sued for damages.

Decision
The High Court held that she was not entitled to damages for loss of the society of her stillborn son. However, damages were available for:

- the loss of satisfaction from a successful conclusion to her pregnancy;
- the physical loss of her child and the loss from being unable to complete her family by adding a second child to it;
- the physical illness brought on the plaintiff by her grave misfortune.

Re F (in Utero) (1988): A fetus cannot be made a ward of court

Facts

A pregnant woman with a history of psychiatric problems lived in a local authority residential home. She went missing from the home when she was in the 38th week of her pregnancy. The local authority sought an order to make her fetus a ward of court.

Decision

The Court of Appeal denied the request. Staughton LJ stated:

When the wardship jurisdiction of the High Court is exercised, the rights, duties and powers of the natural parents are taken over or superseded by the orders of the court. Until a child is delivered it is not, in my judgment, possible for that to happen ... The orders sought by the local authority ... are orders which seek directly to control the life of both mother and child. As was said by the European Commission of Human Rights in *Paton v UK* ... 'the "life" of the foetus is intimately connected with, and cannot be regarded in isolation from, the life of the pregnant woman ...'

Comment

Although the fetus cannot be made a ward of court, the House of Lords have held that the mother's behaviour while she was pregnant can be taken into account when making care orders after the child is born (see *Re D (A Minor)* (1986) HL).

8.3 Abortion

The legality of an abortion is determined by the terms of the Abortion Act 1967. Under s 1, an abortion may be lawful if 'the pregnancy has not exceeded its twenty-fourth week and that continuance of the pregnancy would involve risk greater than if the pregnancy were terminated, of injury to the physical or mental health of the pregnant woman or any existing children of her family ...'. Section 1 also requires that the abortion is sanctioned by two medical practitioners and a registered medical practitioner performs the abortion. Since s 1(2) of the Abortion Act 1967 allows the woman's 'actual or reasonably foreseeable environment' to be taken into account, the fetus – up to 24 weeks' gestation – may be aborted for relatively trivial reasons (social abortion). For an abortion after 24 weeks to be lawful it must be justified as necessary to protect the woman from serious harm or death (s 1(1)(b), (c)). Late termination is also permitted where the fetus is at substantial risk of serious handicap (s 1(1)(d)). Healthcare professionals are not obliged to participate in performing abortions unless it is necessary to prevent the woman from dying or suffering grave injury (the 'conscience clause': s 4).

Royal College of Nursing of UK v DHSS (1981): Nursing staff may administer drugs to induce an abortion providing the procedure is under the direction of a doctor

Facts

A Department of Health and Social Security (DHSS) circular authorised the practice of nurses administering prostaglandin to induce an abortion. The Royal College of Nursing sought a declaration that the circular was unlawful.

Decision

The House of Lords held (3:2 majority) that providing the nurse was acting on the instructions of the doctor who remained responsible for the procedure then the procedure would be within the wording of s 1(1) of the Abortion Act 1967.

R v Smith (1974): The doctor's opinion that the woman satisfies one of the statutory grounds must be formed in good faith

Facts

The defendant performed an abortion on a pregnant woman who subsequently became ill. It became apparent that the doctor had not obtained the necessary second opinion or satisfied himself that the woman was at greater risk from the pregnancy than from the abortion. The jury found him guilty of procuring a miscarriage contrary to s 58 of the Offences Against the Person Act 1861. The defendant appealed.

Decision

The Court of Appeal dismissed the appeal.

Janaway v Salford HA (1989): The conscientious objection clause does not apply to acts ancillary to the performance of an abortion

Facts

The plaintiff was a medical secretary. She was a practising Roman Catholic, and because of her religious views she refused to type a referral letter regarding an abortion. She was dismissed from her post. She subsequently brought an action for unfair dismissal on the grounds that s 4(1) of the Abortion Act 1967 protected her refusal.

Decision

The House of Lords held that typing the letter was an ancillary act and was not covered by s 4(1).

Paton v British Pregnancy Advisory Service Trustees (1979): The father of the fetus has no rights regarding a woman's decision to seek an abortion

Facts

The plaintiff sought an injunction to prevent his wife from terminating her pregnancy. She had obtained the necessary certificates from two medical practitioners but the plaintiff alleged that she was acting in bad faith.

Decision

The High Court refused the request for an injunction.

Comment

In *Paton v UK* (1980) the European Commission dismissed the claim that Mr Paton's right to respect for family life – protected by Article 8 of the European Convention on Human Rights – had been infringed. The lack of any paternal rights also holds in Scotland (see *Kelly v Kelly* (1997) Inner House).

8.4   Post-coital contraception

The types of contraception that work post-fertilisation but pre-implantation include the IUD (intra-uterine device) and post-coital emergency high dose oral contraceptives. The Attorney General stated that, in his opinion, preventing implantation is not procuring a miscarriage and so is not an offence under the Offences Against the Person Act 1861 (41 Official Report (6th series) col 239, 10 May 1983). In addition, since post-coital contraception has been effectively sanctioned by the Government, making provisions for the emergency contraceptive pill to be available without prescription to women over 16, it would be difficult to argue that it is unlawful (although such an attempt was made by the Society for the Protection of Unborn Children (SPUC) – see below). See also the Prescription Only Medicines (Human Use) Amendment (No 3) Order 2000.

R v Price (1969): A doctor who does not know or believe the woman is pregnant will not be committing an offence if he administers post-coital contraception to the woman

Facts

A woman told the defendant that she was pregnant and wanted an abortion. The doctor told her that he did not believe her to be pregnant and fitted her with an IUD. She miscarried two days later. She was seen by a police surgeon shortly before the miscarriage who stated that she was 'manifestly' pregnant. The accused was convicted of inducing a miscarriage under the Offences Against the Person Act 1861. The accused appealed.

Decision

The Court of Appeal quashed the conviction. The jury had been misdirected and there was insufficient evidence that the doctor believed the woman to be pregnant. Sachs LJ stated: 'The essential issue for the jury was, did the appellant ... know or believe that the patient was pregnant and, accordingly, introduce the instrument with intent to procure a miscarriage.'

Comment

In R v Dhingra (1991), a doctor fitted his secretary with an IUD 11 days after they had had intercourse. The judge withdrew the case from the jury after hearing evidence that implantation could not have occurred by this time.

R (John Smeaton on Behalf of SPUC) v Secretary of State for Health (2002): The use of post-coital contraception to prevent implantation of a fertilised egg is not unlawful

Facts

The applicant, acting on behalf of the SPUC, sought a declaration that the provision of the 'morning after pill' was a criminal offence under s 58 of the Offences Against the Persons Act 1861.

Decision

The High Court refused to grant the declaration. The court considered the meaning of miscarriage and decided that, since carriage (pregnancy) did not occur until the egg had implanted, contraception acting to prevent implantation fell outside the terms of the Act.

8.5 Infertility and assisted reproduction

The HFEA 1990 regulates assisted reproduction and *in-vitro* research on human embryos. The Act (s 5) establishes the Human Fertilisation and Embryology Authority (HFE Authority), which has the power to issue licenses to specified persons to store or use eggs, sperm and embryos for treatment or research in defined premises (ss 11–12). Under s 4(1) of the HFEA 1990 the use of third party gametes is only lawful if done under licence issued by the Authority and only with the donor's written consent (Schedule 3). The licences will only be issued if certain conditions are satisfied (ss 12–13). Perhaps the most controversial of these licence conditions is s 13(5), which states that: 'A woman shall not be provided with treatment services unless account has been taken of the welfare of any child who may be born as a result of the treatment (including the need of that child for a father), and of any other child who may be affected by the birth' (for a criticism of the welfare provision, see Jackson, 2002). The Act also requires the Authority to keep a Register of Information (s 31) and to publish a Code of Practice (s 25).

R v Human Fertilisation and Embryology Authority ex p Blood (1997): Gametes and embryos may only be stored and used with the donor's consent

Facts
Shortly before his death and while he was in a coma, sperm was extracted from Mr Blood and placed in storage. After his death, Mrs Blood wanted to be impregnated with the sperm but the HFE Authority refused to grant a licence because there was no written consent from Mr Blood to allow his sperm to be stored and used. Mrs Blood sought a judicial review of the Authority's decision.

Decision
The Court of Appeal held the storage of the sperm had been unlawful and the Authority was correct to refuse permission.

Comment
The requirement for written consent is contained in Schedule 3 to the HFEA 1990. The Court of Appeal held that, although she was not entitled to be treated in this country, the case was returned to the HFE Authority for reconsideration whether Mrs Blood was lawfully entitled to take the sperm and receive treatment in Belgium under Article 59 of the EC Treaty. The HFE Authority permitted exportation of the sperm under s 24 of the HFEA 1990 despite the fact that the original storage had been unlawful. Following the birth of her child and another child subsequently, Diane Blood challenged the law under the HFEA 1990, which refused to allow deceased fathers to be named on the birth certificate. Lawyers for the Health Secretary accepted that the HFEA 1990 was incompatible with the HRA 1998, and this has led to the HFEA 2003.

Evans v Amicus Healthcare Ltd (2004): If one member of a couple receiving treatment withdraws his/her consent to embryo storage or use then it will no longer be lawful to store or use the embryos

Facts

The case concerned two couples that had received IVF treatment and subsequently stored the resultant frozen embryos. After the couples split up, the men withdrew their consent. One of the women argued that her ex-partner had agreed the embryos would always be available to her and, since she had relied on this to her detriment, the equitable estoppel applied. The High Court held that the men's consents were for 'treatment together' and did not apply for sole use by the claimants. Also, Schedule 3, para 4(1) of the HFEA 1990 allowed either party an unconditional right to withdraw consent at any time and this provision was compatible with Article 8 (the right to private and family life), Schedule 1 to the HRA 1998. The claimants appealed.

Decision

The Court of Appeal upheld the judgment, as the policy of the HFEA 1990 was clear on the issue.

Re R (A Child) (Contact: Human Fertilisation and Embryology Act 1990) (No 2) (2003): To be the legal father of a child born by IVF using donated sperm, an unmarried male partner must be being 'treated', with the woman, at the time of embryo implantation

Facts

F attended for treatment with his partner M. M provided the eggs and the sperm was donated. The first implantation was unsuccessful, but some embryos were frozen. The couple split and M began a new relationship. She re-attended the clinic and underwent a successful embryo implantation without informing the clinic of her change of circumstance. F applied for an order declaring him to be the legal father under s 28(3) of the HFEA 1990, arguing that the second implantation was part of the course of treatment that had been initiated when he was M's partner. The judge granted the order and M appealed.

Decision

The Court of Appeal allowed the appeal. The relevant time was the second implantation and, at that point, F was not being treated with M. Because embryos could be stored for up to 10 years, the relevant time for determining paternity was at implantation not embryo creation.

Comment

Where the male partner is not married to the woman, s 28(3) applies. This states:

If no man is treated, by virtue of subsection (2) above, as the father of the child but –

(a) the embryo or the sperm and eggs were placed in the woman, or she was artificially inseminated, in the course of treatment services provided for her and a man together by a person to whom a licence applies; and

(b) the creation of the embryo carried by her was not brought about with the sperm of that man, then, subject to subsection (5) below, that man shall be treated as the father of the child.

Re B (Minors) (Parentage) (1996): Where the couple are not married, the biological father will be treated as the legal father if he expressly consented to treatment or if the couple received treatment together

Facts

An unmarried couple received IVF treatment together. However, the woman did not conceive until after the relationship had ended. She applied for financial support and the man raised the preliminary question of whether he was the legal father.

Decision

The Court held that the man was the legal father of the child. Under Schedule 3 to the HFEA 1990, if the biological father gives a valid consent to the use of his sperm, he will be treated as the legal father. If he receives treatment services as part of a couple with the woman then his consent will be implied unless expressly withdrawn.

L Teaching Hospitals NHS Trust v A (2003): Where the male partner is married to the woman, he will be treated as the father unless he has not consented to the treatment

Facts

Due to a mix-up, Mrs A was inseminated with Mr B's sperm. The Court was asked to determine the legal parentage of the twins born to Mrs A.

Decision

Dame Butler-Sloss P, sitting in the High Court, held that, because Mr A had not consented to the use of another man's sperm, s 28 of the HFEA 1990 did not apply and he was not the legal father. There was no breach of Article 8 (the right to private and family life), Schedule 1 to the HRA 1998, although there was a justified infringement of Mr and Mrs A's rights under that Article.

Comment

Under s 28, if the man is married to the woman he will be the legal father, 'unless it is shown that he did not consent to the placing in her of the embryo or the sperm and eggs or to her insemination' (s 28(2)). Mr B's application to be declared the legal father was adjourned.

R (Mellor) v Secretary of State for the Home Department (2001): There is no absolute right of access to assisted reproduction

Facts

A prisoner sentenced to life imprisonment due for release when he would be aged 35 and his wife 31 applied for permission to start a family using artificial insemination. The Secretary of State refused the application on the grounds that there was no medical need and out of concern for the long-term stability of the marriage. An application for judicial review was refused and the applicant appealed.

Decision

The Court of Appeal dismissed the appeal. Part of the purpose of imprisonment was to deprive the prisoner of certain liberties, including the right to found a family. Article 12 of the HRA 1998 – the right to marry and found a family – did not give a prisoner the right to access assisted reproductive services, except in exceptional circumstances.

R v Sheffield HA ex p Seale (1994): Access to assisted reproductive services may be restricted provided the decision is not irrational

Facts

The applicant was refused IVF treatment because, at 37, she was two years older than the age limit for treatment set by the Health Authority. The applicant claimed that this was unlawful as it breached the Secretary of State's duty, under s 3 of the National Health Service Act 1977, to provide services to meet all reasonable medical needs. She also claimed the decision was irrational as it failed to take into account individual circumstances. She applied for judicial review.

Decision

The High Court rejected the application. Since the Secretary of State had neither limited provision nor given any directions, the Authority had discretion and the refusal of treatment was not unlawful. The application also failed on the second ground. While treatment may be effective beyond the age of 35, the Authority's argument was that it became less effective. Although taking individual circumstances into account might make good clinical sense, the decision could not be described as irrational or *Wednesbury* unreasonable.

Comment

The *Wednesbury* test requires the decision to be so irrational that no reasonable authority could make such a decision. Under the HRA 1998, it is arguable that the test should be one of proportionality, which might be easier to show. However, the courts have traditionally been reluctant to challenge clinical discretion and it is perhaps easier to succeed on procedural rather than substantive grounds.

Seale was concerned with the effectiveness of treatment. Other applications have been made where the grounds for refusal were based on s 13(5) – the welfare provision – of the HFEA 1990. In *R v Ethical Committee of St Mary's Hospital ex p Harriott* (1988), an application for judicial review was refused where the woman, who had a criminal record for prostitution, had been refused treatment because she had been turned down by an adoption agency and she did not meet the hospital's criteria for being a satisfactory parent (see 11.1 below).

8.6   Surrogacy

Surrogacy arrangements are regulated by the Surrogacy Arrangements Act 1985, as amended by the HFEA 1990. The Act was passed following a wardship case that concerned a child born following a surrogacy arrangement (*Re C (A Minor)* (1985)). Section 1(2) of the Act defines a surrogate mother as:

... a woman who carries a child in pursuance of an arrangement –

(a) made before she began to carry the child, and
(b) made with a view to any child carried in pursuance of it being handed over to, and the parental rights being exercised (so far as practicable) by, another person or persons.

Note that arrangements made after a woman becomes pregnant are not covered by the Act. The Act makes it a criminal offence to negotiate or compile information about surrogacy arrangements (s 2(1)). However, this does not apply to either the commissioning couple or the surrogate mother (s 2(2)). Advertisements regarding surrogacy arrangements are also outlawed (s 3) and there is no exception for the surrogate mother or commissioning couple.

A v C (1985): Surrogacy arrangements are not legally enforceable

Facts
The plaintiff's partner was unable to bear the child that he wanted to father so they arranged for the friend of a prostitute to be a surrogate for a fee of £3,000. C was artificially impregnated with the plaintiff's sperm but she subsequently changed her mind and decided to keep the child. The plaintiff applied to the court. At first instance, custody was left with C but the plaintiff was given an order for access. C appealed.

Decision
The Court of Appeal granted the appeal. The order made would be withdrawn and the plaintiff would have no access rights to the child.

Comment
Although reported in 1985, this case was heard in 1978 and was prior to the Surrogacy Arrangements Act 1985. The lack of enforceability is given statutory force by s 1A of the Act. Where custody is disputed the courts will consider what is in the child's interests rather than those interests of the adult parties. In Re P (Minors) (1987), a surrogate mother was allowed to retain custody of twins who were made wards of court. Sir John Arnold P stated: 'In this, as in any other wardship dispute, the welfare of the children, or child, concerned is the first and paramount consideration which the court must, by statute, take into account ...' In that case, the fact that the children had bonded with the surrogate mother – who provided a satisfactory level of care – was determinative. See also W v H (Child Abduction: Surrogacy (No 2) (2002) in which the court held that, where the commissioning couple were from California, the case should be heard there because the Californian court might have a different approach to the child's welfare. Where it is in the child's best interests, then the court will grant an order allowing it to remain with the commissioning couple. Factors such as where the child has been living and which parent(s) would provide the most stable home were important in the Scottish case, C v S (1996).

Re Q (Parental Order) (1996): Where the commissioning couple provide one or both of the gametes, they may apply for a parental order

Facts
The commissioning couple, Mr and Mrs B, paid a surrogate £8,280 expenses for carrying an implanted embryo for them. After the child was born, the surrogate (Miss A) had some misgivings, and visited a solicitor with regard to securing the child's placement with her. On reflection, she subsequently agreed to the parental order.

Decision
The High Court granted the parental order. It was reasonable to pay Miss A £5,000 as compensation for loss of earnings and the £3,280 was a reasonable sum to cover the expenses of pregnancy and childcare provision for her other children while she was attending hospital, etc.

Comment
Under s 27 of the HFEA 1990, the default position is that the surrogate is the legal mother of the child. However, under s 30 of the HFEA 1990:

The court may make an order providing for a child to be treated in law as the child of the parties to a marriage ... if –

(a)   the child has been carried by a woman other than the wife as the result of placing in her of an embryo or sperm and eggs or her artificial insemination;

(b)   the gametes of the husband or the wife, or both, were used to bring about the creation of the embryo; and

(c)   the conditions in subsections (2)–(7) below are satisfied.

The authorisation for the expenses was given retrospectively following Re Adoption Application (Payment for Adoption) (1987). The court also held that, despite being the genetic father, Mr B was not the legal father of the child under s 28 of the HFEA 1990.

Re C (Surrogacy: Payments) (2002): Before the court will grant a parental order, it must authorise any expenses paid to the surrogate

Facts
The commissioning couple paid the surrogate more than could be accounted for as expenses. £12,000 was paid, but the surrogate was on income support.

Decision
Such payments would ordinarily not be authorised and the court could not make a parental order where unauthorised payments were involved. However, because it was in the child's best interests to be treated in law as the child of the commissioning couple, the court would retrospectively authorise the payment and grant the parental order.

8.7   Wrongful life and wrongful birth

McKay v Essex AHA (1982): Being born is not a legal harm for which a child may claim damages

Facts
The plaintiff was born with severe congenital disabilities after her mother had contracted rubella while pregnant. Her mother had been wrongly informed that she had not been infected and there was no need to consider an abortion. It was not disputed that the defendants were liable for causing her disabilities but she also claimed for the fact that she had been born at all 'into a life in which her injuries are highly debilitating'.

Decision
The Court of Appeal rejected the claim for 'wrongful life'. The proposition that there could be a duty to prevent a child from being born was contrary to the sanctity of life. Furthermore, the claim involved an impossible comparison between a disabled existence and non-existence.

McFarlane v Tayside HB (2000): An unwanted pregnancy is a legally recognised harm, but the birth of a healthy child is not

Facts
The claimants were husband (C1) and wife (C2). Following a vasectomy, C1 was advised that his sperm count was negative and he no longer needed to take contraceptive precautions. The claimants followed this advice and C2 became pregnant. At first instance, Lord Gill dismissed the claims. He decided that pregnancy and childbirth did not constitute a personal injury and 'the privilege of being a parent is immeasurable in money terms and that the benefits of parenthood transcend any patrimonial loss'. On appeal, the Inner House reversed the decision and held that the benefits of parenthood could not outweigh the damage caused by the unwanted pregnancy. The defendants appealed.

Decision
The House of Lords dismissed the appeal against damages for the unwanted pregnancy and the costs flowing. The appeal against the costs of raising the child was allowed.

Lord Steyn argued that the 'traveller on the Underground' would instinctively reply 'that the law of tort had no business to provide legal remedies consequent upon the birth of a healthy child, which all of us regard as a valuable and good thing'.

Comment
All of the judges applied the 'limited damages rule' (see Stewart, 1995) and denied the claim for the maintenance costs of a healthy child. There were a number of reasons which included: child maintenance is pure economic loss; the unjust enrichment that would result from compensating the parents for child maintenance costs; the moral intuition ascribed to the 'traveller on the Underground'; the potential scale of the damages; the incoherence of allowing a claim for wrongful birth but not wrongful life; judicial disquiet with the award of maintenance damages.

McFarlane was a wrongful pregnancy case, where the parents had tried to avoid both the pregnancy and birth of the child. These cases may also be called wrongful conception cases. Wrongful birth cases are where the parents sought to avoid the birth rather than the pregnancy. Typically, these cases arise where a healthy child is wanted but the child is born with a disability and the parents would have terminated had they not been negligently denied the opportunity. Confusingly, wrongful birth may also be used as a catch-all term to include both the wrongful pregnancy and the wrongful birth cases. There may, however, be good reason to distinguish them because the damage is different and, where the child is disabled, the proximity of the doctor is arguably greater in the wrongful birth case: in a wrongful conception case it is the pregnancy that is unwanted, but in a wrongful birth case it is the disabled child that the parents are seeking to avoid (see Mason, 2002).

Parkinson v St James and Seacroft University Hospital NHS Trust (2001): The extra costs, attributable to the disability, of raising an unwanted disabled child may still be recoverable

Facts
The claimant underwent a negligently performed sterilisation and she subsequently conceived and gave birth to a fifth child. Unfortunately the child was disabled.

Decision
The Court of Appeal held that, where a child was born with 'significant disability' as a result of the defendants' negligence, then 'damages were recoverable for the costs of providing for the child's special needs and care attributable to those disabilities, but not for the ordinary costs of his upbringing'.

Comment
For a wrongful birth case that also allowed recovery for the costs arising from the disability, see *Rand v East Dorset HA* (2000).

Rees v Darlington Memorial Hospital NHS Trust (2003): Extra costs attributable to parental disability are not recoverable

Facts
The mother was seriously visually impaired and sought to avoid children because she was concerned about her ability to look after them. She underwent a sterilisation, which failed due to the defendants' negligence. After giving birth to a healthy child she brought a claim against the Trust. The High Court decided against recovery of the additional costs. The Appeal, however, allowed the claimant to recover the extra costs attributable to her disability. The Trust appealed.

Decision
By a 4:3 majority, the House of Lords allowed the appeal. The majority followed Lord Millett's lead and adopted the solution he had first mooted in *McFarlane*: the real harm was to the claimant's reproductive autonomy, and general damages of £15,000 were awarded in recognition of the wrong rather than as compensation.

Comment

This is an important case: in the post-*McFarlane* cases, the courts had limited the harshness of the no recovery rule by limiting it to a healthy child. The thread tying the decisions together was the principle of distributive justice. In the Court of Appeal hearing of *Rees* (2002), the court relied on the principle – using 'need' as an endpoint in order to extend the rule to include disabled parents. The minority in the House of Lords also relied on distributive justice to support the Court of Appeal's decision. Despite strong criticism from the minority, the majority of the House of Lords have undermined all of those decisions by arguing that no maintenance costs at all should be recovered for a healthy child. The majority felt that their decision merely added a 'gloss' to *McFarlane* by allowing recovery for the harm done to parental autonomy, whilst the minority felt that the decision was far more than this. The decision also means that healthy parents of a healthy child can recover these general damages. However, because the decision discards all of the distributive justice arguments about need, it also throws into doubt the question of recovery for the additional costs associated with a disabled child (see Maclean, 2004).

Sabri-Tabrizi v Lothian HB (1998): Where the plaintiff is aware that a sterilisation has failed, there will be no liability for wrongful conception

Facts

Following a failed sterilisation the pursuer became pregnant. The pregnancy was terminated. She subsequently became pregnant (she claimed they were using condoms) for a second time but miscarried the pregnancy. As a preliminary point, the court was asked to decide whether the second pregnancy was caused by the failed sterilisation operation.

Decision

The court held that the use of a condom was irrelevant since there was a risk of pregnancy when using them. Acceptance of this risk was a *novus actus interveniens* that broke the chain of causation and relieved the defenders of liability.

Walkin v South Manchester HA (1995) CA: The limitation period for claims runs from the time of the injury and not from the child's birth

Facts

The plaintiff underwent a sterilisation operation. She subsequently became pregnant but did not start legal proceedings until four years later. At first instance, the court held that any claim was time barred.

Decision

The appeal was dismissed. The personal injury was the impairment of the plaintiff's physical condition by the unwanted pregnancy. This arose at the time of conception and not at the birth of the child.

8.8   Genetics

R (on the Application of Quintavalle) v Human Fertilisation and Embryology Authority (2003): The HFE Authority has the power to licence pre-implantation genetic diagnosis (PGD) for the purpose of tissue typing

Facts

The Hashmis had a child with beta thalassaemia major, which required regular blood transfusions and a cocktail of drugs. The condition might be cured by a bone marrow infusion with stem cells taken from the umbilical cord of a newborn child. After two failed attempts to conceive a child who was both disease-free and a tissue match, the Hashmis sought to use IVF and PGD tissue typing to select a suitable embryo. The HFE Authority announced that they would be prepared to grant a licence, but only where PGD was already necessary to avoid passing on a genetically inherited condition. A licence was issued and the Hashmis started the treatment process, which was then interrupted by a challenge to the HFE Authority's power to issue such a licence. There were two questions. First, was the genetic analysis of a cell taken from the embryo a 'use' of that embryo? Secondly, under s 2(1) '"treatment services" means medical, surgical or obstetric services ... for the purpose of assisting women to carry children'. Did that provision exclude PGD tissue typing? The High Court held that PGD was 'using' the embryo and therefore would be unlawful without a licence. Furthermore, the definition of 'treatment services' did exclude tissue typing. The Authority appealed.

Decision

The Court of Appeal allowed the appeal. Under Schedule 2, para 1(1)(d) of the HFEA 1990, a licence could be issued for treatment 'designed to secure that embryos are in a suitable condition to be placed in a woman or to determine whether embryos are suitable for that purpose'. The meaning of 'suitable' depended on the context, and if the purpose of treatment was to ensure a suitable source of stem cells, then tissue typing was treatment within the context of the provision.

Comment

For a discussion of the finer points of the HFE Authority's decision to grant a licence for the Hashmis but to refuse a licence for the similar case of the Whitakers, see Gavaghan (2003).

R (on the Application of Quintavalle) v Secretary of State for Health (2003): The production of a cloned human embryo by cell nuclear replacement is unlawful

Facts

The applicant, on behalf of the ProLife Alliance, applied for a judicial review contending that, since a cloned embryo was not created by fertilisation, it fell outside the definition of an embryo under s 1(1) and hence was not prohibited by the HFEA 1990. The High Court granted the application and the Secretary of State appealed. The Court of Appeal allowed the appeal and the applicant took the case to the House of Lords.

Decision

The House of Lords dismissed the appeal. Adopting a purposive approach to interpretation of the Act, the reference to fertilisation was not integral to the definition and embryo creation by cell nuclear replacement was therefore prohibited by the Act.

Comment

Following the High Court case, the Government took the precaution of passing the Human Reproductive Cloning Act 2001, which prohibits the placement of a cloned embryo into a woman.

CHAPTER 9

MENTAL HEALTH LAW

It is worth emphasising from the outset that, outside specific statutory provisions, the normal principles of medical law will apply. Thus, simply because someone suffers from a mental illness does not mean that he is automatically subject to different legal principles. Currently, statutory regulation of the care of the mentally ill is governed by the Mental Health Act (MHA) 1983 (see Jones, 2003). The Act is primarily concerned with three things: detention, compulsory treatment and safeguards that protect the patient's rights. Compulsory treatment is linked to detention, as is compulsory assessment, but the Act does allow a guardianship order or a supervised discharge order to assist the care of the patient in the community.

Although the MHA 1983 is currently in force, the Richardson Committee has reviewed it and a Government White Paper has proposed a number of changes (for an analysis of the proposals, see Laing, 2000). A draft Mental Health Bill is due to be published in September 2004 and its progress may be followed on the website of the Joint Committee on the draft Mental Health Bill (www.parliament.uk/ parliamentary_committees/jcdmhb.cfm).

The Council of Europe has also published a White Paper on mental health and human rights (CM(2000)23 Addendum) as a consultation exercise in advance of legislative proposals (www.cm.coe.int/reports.old/cmdocs/2000/2000cm23add.htm).

9.1   The definition of mental disorder

Section 1(2) of the MHA 1983 defines a 'mental disorder' as 'mental illness, arrested or incomplete development of mind, psychopathic disorder and any other disorder or disability of mind'. 'Mental impairment' is 'a state of arrested or incomplete development of mind (not amounting to severe mental impairment) which includes significant impairment of intelligence and social functioning and is associated with abnormally aggressive or seriously irresponsible conduct on the part of the person concerned'. 'Severe mental impairment' is similar but requires a 'severe' rather than 'significant' impairment. A 'psychopathic disorder' has no requirement for any 'impairment of intelligence'. Alcohol and drug dependency, promiscuity, sexual deviancy and immoral conduct are insufficient by themselves to count as a mental disorder. See *R v Mental Health Review Tribunal ex p Clatworthy* (1985) in which the court rejected the Tribunal's argument that sexual deviancy could have the features of mental disorder. The court held that sexual deviancy should be discounted as a mental disorder by virtue of s 1(3).

W v L (1974): The phrase 'mental illness' is not a term of art and should be given its ordinary meaning

Facts

A young man committed a number of cruel acts including hanging a puppy, cutting a cat's throat and putting another cat in a gas oven. After threatening his wife he was compulsorily admitted as an emergency under the MHA 1959. This order expired after 72 hours and an application was made, under s 27 of the MHA 1959, to the court to prolong the detention. Since the wife objected, the detention could not be prolonged unless it could be established that the man was suffering from a mental illness.

Decision

The Court of Appeal held that the detention could be prolonged as he was suffering from a mental illness. Lawton LJ stated:

> The words [mental illness] are ordinary words of the English language. They have no particular medical significance. They have no particular legal significance ... ordinary words of the English language should be construed in the way that ordinary sensible people would construe them ... what would the ordinary sensible person have said about the patient's condition in this case if he had been informed of his behaviour to the dogs, the cat and his wife? In my judgment such a person would have said: 'Well, the fellow is obviously mentally ill.'

R (on the Application of P) v Mental Health Review Tribunal (2001): The definition of 'psychopathic disorder' only requires that the patient be liable or capable of abnormally aggressive or seriously irresponsible conduct

Facts

P had been detained under ss 37 and 41 of the MHA 1983 following a violent homicide. The Mental Health Review Tribunal (MHRT) decided that he should remain detained because he continued to suffer from a psychopathic disorder. He sought a judicial review of the decision on the grounds that s 1(2) of the MHA 1983 required evidence of current 'aggressive or serious irresponsible conduct', which was not present in his recent behaviour.

Decision

The High Court refused the application and held that just because the medical treatment had successfully suppressed his anti-social behaviour did not mean that he should be discharged into the community. Suppression of symptoms was not the same as a cure and he retained the potential for aggressive behaviour if he ceased treatment or changed environment.

Re F (A Child) (Care Order: Sexual Abuse) sub nom In Re F (Mental Health Act: Guardianship) (2000): In determining that an individual has a mental impairment, the words 'seriously irresponsible conduct' should be interpreted restrictively

Facts

F was a 17-year-old girl with the mental age of a five to eight-year-old who had been placed on the Child Protection Register because of neglect and sexual abuse. Her younger siblings were also on the Register and had been made the subjects of care orders. F was too old to be subject to a care order but lived voluntarily in a residential home. Her parents expressed the wish that she should return home and her father withdrew his consent to her voluntary residence. The local authority sought a guardianship order under s 7 of the MHA 1983. Her father objected and the local authority sought an order under s 29 of the MHA 1983 to be allowed to carry out the functions of the nearest relative because of his 'unreasonable objection'. To be made the subject of the guardianship order, F had to fall within the statutory definition of mental impairment and it was disputed that, while she exhibited signs of 'a state of arrested or incomplete development of mind', this was not associated with 'seriously irresponsible conduct'. At first instance, the judge held that F's expressed wish to return home to an environment in which she was at risk of neglect and sexual exploitation was 'seriously irresponsible conduct'. The order was granted and F's father appealed.

Decision
The Court of Appeal allowed the appeal. The White Paper, *Review of the Mental Health Act 1959* (Cmnd 7320), supported a restrictive interpretation of 'seriously irresponsible conduct'. Given that the consequences of returning home (ie, the neglect and sexual abuse) were in dispute and would not be settled until a subsequent hearing, F's desire to return home could not be seen as seriously irresponsible.

Comment
The Court of Appeal noted that the Law Commission, in its report on mental incapacity, stated that 'the vast majority of those with a learning disability ... will be excluded from guardianship'. The Court of Appeal's view was that, while there was doubt as to the actual risk faced by F, it could not be unreasonable to return to the source of the alleged risk.

9.2 Compulsory admission to hospital

Under the MHA 1983, a patient may be detained for assessment (s 2) or treatment (s 3). The nearest relative or an approved social worker – who may be under a duty (s 13) – may make applications for admission (s 11), which also require the written recommendations of two doctors. Compulsory assessment is limited initially to 28 days, while treatment admissions last for six months but may be renewed for a further six months and then yearly. Emergency admissions (s 4) only require the recommendation of one doctor, but such admissions are limited to 72 hours. Patients who have already been admitted informally may be compulsorily detained under s 5. Under s 37 of the MHA 1983, the courts may order hospital admission (or guardianship), but this is only where the person has been convicted of 'an offence punishable with imprisonment' (see *R (on the Application of A) v Harrow Crown Court* (2003)).

R v Hallstrom ex p W; R v Gardner ex p L (1986): Section 3 of the MHA 1983 cannot be used to allow compulsory treatment in the community

Facts

L had been admitted under s 3 of the MHA 1983 for treatment. He was subsequently granted a leave of absence under s 17. The s 3 admission was due to expire and Dr Gardner examined L under s 20(4) in order to renew the detention. L had returned on one occasion to allow a second opinion to be obtained. One of the issues was whether the return to hospital terminated the initial leave of absence such that L was subsequently on a second leave of absence. If a leave of absence lasts longer than six months, then the patient is no longer under the control of the Act (s 17(5)). As the second period of leave approached the six-month deadline, L was asked to return to the hospital. L alleged that either his leave of absence had expired, or the recall was an abuse of law, with the single night return to the hospital being used as a device for keeping the leave of absence going.

Decision

The High Court held that although s 20 could be used to renew a s 3 admission, the renewal must be because the patient needs to be in hospital and not simply to allow repeated leaves of absence and compulsory treatment in the community. McCullough J stated:

It stretches the concept of 'admission for treatment' too far to say that it covers admission for only so long as it is necessary to enable a leave of absence to be granted after which the necessary treatment will begin ... the concept of 'admission for treatment' has no applicability to those whom it is intended to admit and detain for a purely nominal period, during which no necessary treatment will be given.

Comment

In *Barker v Barking Havering & Brentwood Community Healthcare NHS Trust* (1999), the Court of Appeal added a variation to this judgment. It held that it was lawful to renew a detention under s 20(4)(c) in order to cover any problems that might arise during a graduated discharge programme, despite the fact that the patient did not, at the time, need to be confined. Similarly, in *R (on the Application of DR) v Mersey Care NHS Trust* (2002), renewed detention was lawful where hospital treatment was a significant part of the care plan for a patient living at home.

Under the MHA 1983, a leave of absence could only last six months but this has been extended by the Mental Health (Patients in the Community) Act 1995 so that the leave can last up until the patient's section is due for renewal.

R v East London and the City Mental Health NHS Trust ex p von Brandenburg (2003): Even where the MHRT has ordered discharge, an approved social worker (ASW), if acting objectively and in good faith, may apply for compulsory readmission

Facts

The patient was detained in hospital under s 2 of the MHA 1983. He applied for discharge and this was ordered by the MHRT. The discharge was deferred for a week to allow suitable accommodation to be found and a care plan established. Before he was actually discharged, he was again compulsorily detained under s 3 of the MHA 1983. The appellant applied for a judicial review of the decision to apply for admission under s 3, which he claimed was unlawful 'unless there had been a relevant change of circumstances', which was not the case. The High Court and the Court of Appeal both rejected his application. The Court of Appeal held that, while it cannot be legally binding, a Tribunal decision could not be ignored. Sedley LJ stated: 'a recent mental health review Tribunal decision to discharge a patient, if the circumstances have not appreciably changed, must be accorded very great weight if the second decision is not to be perceived as an illicit overruling of the first ... there will have to be a convincing reason ... for readmission.' The appellant appealed.

Decision
The House of Lords dismissed the appeal. Following the Tribunal's decision to order discharge, the appellant had stopped taking his medication and his condition had deteriorated. Giving the House's judgment, Lord Bingham stated:

An ASW may not lawfully apply for the admission of a patient whose discharge has been ordered by the decision of a Mental Health Review Tribunal of which the ASW is aware unless the ASW has formed the reasonable and bona fide opinion that he has information not known to the Tribunal which puts a significantly different complexion on the case compared with that which was before the Tribunal.

Comment
Lord Bingham argued that the ASW is statute-bound to interview the patient and enquire into the patient's background and medical history, but this will not guarantee that he will be alerted to the MHRT's decision in all cases. Therefore, he rejected Sedley LJ's argument that the decision will be vitiated if he fails to take account of a Tribunal decision of which he is unaware. He also held that, if the MHRT decision is to be accorded due weight, then the ASW had a limited duty to provide 'reasons in general terms' to explain the decision to apply for readmission.

R v Cannons Park Mental Health Review Tribunal ex p A (1994): In the case of psychopathic disorder or mental illness, the 'treatability' requirement of s 3(2)(b) of the MHA 1983 would be satisfied simply if the treatment would prevent deterioration

Facts
A was suffering from a psychopathic disorder that might be treated by group therapy. The MHRT found that, as she was unco-operative, the group therapy was unlikely to be an effective treatment. She was therefore deemed untreatable but the MHRT detained her in the interests of her own health and safety and for the protection of others. A applied for judicial review and the Divisional Court held that, because the treatment would neither alleviate nor improve A's condition, the matter should be remitted to the Tribunal with a direction that they should discharge A. The MHRT appealed.

Decision

The Court of Appeal allowed the appeal. The Divisional Court had been in error and had taken too narrow a view of the treatability test, which would be satisfied provided that it prevents deterioration. A patient should not be considered untreatable because of their refusal to co-operate. Roch LJ defined the following principles:

First, if a Tribunal were to be satisfied that the patient's detention in hospital was simply an attempt to coerce the patient into participating in group therapy, then the Tribunal would be under a duty to direct discharge. Second, treatment in hospital will satisfy the treatability test although it is unlikely to alleviate the patient's condition, provided that it is likely to prevent a deterioration. Third, treatment in hospital will satisfy the treatability test although it will not immediately alleviate or prevent deterioration in the patient's condition provided that alleviation or stabilisation is likely in due course. Fourth, the treatability test can still be met although initially there may be some deterioration in the patient's condition due, for example, to the patient's initial anger at being detained. Fifth, it must be remembered that medical treatment in hospital covers nursing and also includes care, habilation and rehabilitation under medical supervision. Sixth, the treatability test is satisfied if nursing care, etc, is likely to lead to an alleviation of the patient's condition in that the patient is likely to gain an insight into his problem or cease to be unco-operative in his attitude towards treatment which would potentially have a lasting benefit.

Comment

Under the MHA 1983, s 3(2)(b) requires that 'in the case of psychopathic disorder or mental impairment, such treatment is likely to alleviate or prevent deterioration of his condition'.

9.3 Non-consensual treatment

Under s 63, patients detained under the MHA 1983 may be treated non-consensually for their mental disorder. This power does not apply to those treatments covered by ss 57–58. Section 57 applies to treatments that destroy brain tissue or function, and any treatments specified by the Secretary of State (the surgical implantation of hormones to reduce the male sex drive: r 16 of the Mental Health (Hospital, Guardianship and Consent to Treatment) Regulations 1983). Under s 58, treatment continued for more than three months, and treatment specified by the Secretary of State (electro-convulsive therapy (ECT) under r 16(2) of the Mental Health (Hospital, Guardianship and Consent to Treatment) Regulations 1983) requires the patient's consent or a second medical opinion. (However, note that these provisions do not apply to all mentally disordered patients: see s 56.) The constraints imposed by ss 57–58 will not apply if treatment is immediately necessary (s 63).

The common law applies to treatment for things other than the patient's mental disorder and thus must be justified either by the patient's consent or – where the patient is incapable of consenting – by the doctrine of necessity.

B v Croydon HA (1994): Treatment for the patient's mental disorder includes care ancillary to the core treatment

Facts

B was compulsorily detained under s 3 of the MHA 1983. She suffered from a psychopathic disorder and made various attempts to harm herself. When these were frustrated she refused to eat. The Health Authority decided to force feed her and B applied to the court for an injunction. The application was rejected at first instance. B appealed.

Decision

The Court of Appeal denied the appeal. Despite the 'treatability' requirement of s 3, not every act of treatment 'must in itself be likely to alleviate or prevent a deterioration of that disorder'. The definition of 'treatment' given in s 145(1) is wide and includes 'nursing, and also includes care, habilitation and rehabilitation under medical supervision'. This definition includes a range of acts ancillary to the core treatment for the mental disorder. Hoffmann LJ stated:

It would seem to me strange if a hospital could, without the patient's consent, give him treatment directed to alleviating a psychopathic disorder showing itself in suicidal tendencies, but not without such consent be able to treat the consequences of a suicide attempt. In my judgment the term 'medical treatment ... for the mental disorder' in s 63 includes such ancillary acts.

Comment

in *SW Hertfordshire HA v KB* (1994), Ewbank J considered the naso-gastric tube feeding of an patient with anorexia nervosa. He stated that 'relieving symptoms is just as much a part of treatment as relieving the underlying cause'. Hoffmann LJ approved this in *B v Croydon HA*. The concept of ancillary treatment was widened in *Thameside and Glossop Acute Services Trust v CH* (1996) to include a Caesarean section. Wall J argued that ensuring the delivery of a live baby by a Caesarean section was justified since: it would prevent a deterioration of the patient's mental state; a dead baby might make her schizophrenia less responsive to treatment; and her anti-psychotic medication was interrupted by pregnancy and could not be resumed until delivery. See also *R v Ashworth Hospital Authority ex p Brady* (2000).

R v Mental Health Act Commission ex p X (1988): Part IV provisions will apply to treatment for a condition even if it is not a mental disorder, provided it is 'inextricably linked with the mental disorder'

Facts

A compulsorily detained paedophile had been treated with standard anti-androgen therapy, which had failed to reduce his sex drive. His doctors decided to switch to 'Goserelin', a synthetic, relatively new and experimental drug, which acts to reduce testosterone levels. The drug was inserted under the skin by injection. The Commission withdrew its approval for certification of the treatment under s 57 and the patient applied for a judicial review. The issues before the court included whether the treatment qualified for s 57 certification.

Decision

The High Court quashed the Commission's decision as it was irrational and a s 57 certificate was not required:

(1) the drug was a synthetic 'hormone analogue' and was therefore not a 'hormone' under r 16 of the Mental Health (Hospital, Guardianship and Consent to Treatment) Regulations 1983;

(2) the drug was introduced by 'injection' and not by 'surgical implantation' as required by r 16.

Comment

Although it was dropped during the hearing, the applicant also raised the question of whether treatment for sexual deviancy is covered by s 57. Stuart-Smith LJ argued that treatment for sexual deviancy is not treatment for a mental disorder and is not covered by s 57; 'however, it seems likely that the sexual problem will be inextricably linked with the mental disorder, so that treatment for the one is treatment for the other, as in this case'. The 'Code of Practice' recommends that 'if there is any doubt as to whether it is a mental disorder which is being treated, independent legal and medical advice must be sought' (para 16.8).

R (on the Application of B) v Ashworth HA (2003): Compulsory detention on the basis of one mental disorder does not permit compulsory treatment of a different mental disorder

Facts

B had been found guilty of manslaughter and was detained for treatment of schizophrenia. His doctors at the hospital diagnosed that B also had a personality disorder and transferred him, against his wishes, to a personality disorder ward. The MHRT refused an application for discharge but did not reclassify his mental disorder. B sought a judicial review of the decision questioning whether s 63 of the MHA 1983 allowed compulsory treatment of any mental disorder, or only those specified by the court or MHRT.

Decision

The Court of Appeal allowed the appeal. Section 63 only allows compulsory treatment of the mental disorder for which the patient has been detained. Compulsory treatment of other mental disorders was unlawful unless sanctioned by an appropriate change in the classification of the patient's mental disorder by the MHRT under s 72(5).

R v Bournewood Community & Mental Health NHS Trust ex p L (1998): Voluntary patients, admitted informally under s 131 of the MHA 1983, who lack the capacity to consent, may be detained and treated non-consensually under the doctrine of necessity

Facts

L was a 48-year-old, severely mentally retarded, autistic man. Following more than 30 years of residential care he was discharged – on a trial basis – to paid carers, Mr and Mrs E, who treated him as one of the family. He subsequently became severely agitated while at a day centre and he was taken to hospital where a psychiatrist decided that he would benefit from in-patient care. Since L made no attempt to leave or resist, the consultant, Dr M, decided it was not necessary to admit him formally under the MHA 1983. Although correspondence with Mr and Mrs E explained that the plan for L was to return him to their care as soon as possible and that visits would be arranged, no programme of visits was achieved. Relations between Mr and Mrs E and the hospital broke down and they applied to the court for judicial review of the decision to detain L, a writ of habeas corpus and damages for false imprisonment and assault. The Court of Appeal allowed Mr and Mrs E's claims and awarded nominal damages of £1. The Trust appealed.

Decision
The House of Lords allowed the appeal. A hospital was entitled to admit and care for an incompetent patient informally under s 131 even though he was incapable of consenting. Although the statute was silent on the issue, this could be justified on the basis of the common law doctrine of necessity. The doctrine of necessity also justified L's detention.

Comment
This case allows non-consensual hospitalisation on the basis of assent or non-dissent without providing any of the protections afforded patients compulsorily detained under the MHA 1983.

R (on the Application of N) v Dr M (2002): Where the doctrine of necessity is relied on to administer non-consensual treatment to detained patients, that treatment must be 'shown convincingly' to be medically necessary

Facts
The patient refused consent to depot (slow release, prolonged action) anti-psychotic medication. Medical opinion was divided on the diagnosis of psychosis, the need for treatment and her capacity to consent. The court accepted that she was incompetent to consent and held that, despite the split opinion, it would be in her best interests to receive the treatment. N appealed.

Decision
The Court of Appeal held that, where a breach of Article 3 of the HRA 1998 was alleged, the appropriate test was that set out in *Herczegfalvy v Austria* (1992). This meant that the *Bolam* test, while necessary, was an insufficient test and the 'court cannot permit the forcible administering of medical treatment unless it is shown convincingly to be medically necessary'.

Comment
In *Herczegfalvy*, the European Court of Human Rights held that: 'as a general rule, a method which is a therapeutic necessity cannot be regarded as inhuman or degrading. The court must nevertheless satisfy itself that the medical necessity has been convincingly shown to exist.' Dyson LJ held that this was a single question, influenced by a number of factors, including: certainty of diagnosis; seriousness of disorder; risk to others; treatability of the disorder; and the adverse consequences of treatment. See

also *R (on the Application of Wilkinson) v Broadmoor Special Hospital Authority* (2002), in which the Court of Appeal held that to justify forcible treatment as a medical necessity under Article 3 of the HRA 1998 it must provide a 'substantial benefit'.

9.4   Protecting the mentally ill

The patient's health may be protected under the MHA 1983 through compulsory detention for assessment or treatment. If not subject to compulsory detention, then a patient over the age of 16 may be subject to a guardianship order (s 7). The guardian has the power to require the patient to reside at a specified place and to attend for treatment (s 8), but it does not allow non-consensual treatment. As an alternative, a supervised discharge order is an option available for compulsory in-patients to ensure they receive appropriate after-care (s 25A–25H of the MHA 1983, inserted by the Mental Health (Patients in the Community) Act 1995). In addition to the statutory provisions for guardianship, two non-statutory schemes exist to provide some protection within the community. One initiative is the 'Care Programme Approach' (CPA) implemented in 1991 to ensure co-operation between health services and social services so that the patient may be assessed to determine their needs and any risks they might pose to themselves or others. Each patient should be assigned a key worker and a programme of care should be agreed. The second initiative (NHS Executive, 1994) was to establish 'supervision registers' for those mentally ill persons at risk of committing serious violence, suicide or self-neglect. The CPA is currently under review and the suggestions include: creating a two-tiered system of 'standard' CPA and 'enhanced' CPA for those at particular risk; abolishing the Supervision Registers; and taking a greater account of the needs of the individual's family (DoH, 2000a).

Under the MHA 1983, the patient's nearest relative plays an important role and may apply for the patient's admission or guardianship and may make an order for discharge under s 23(2)(a). Currently the patient has no power to appoint the nearest relative. In *JT v UK* (2000), this was held to breach the European Convention on Human Rights and the case was settled before the Court on the understanding that the Government would amend the Act. The MHA 1983 currently remains incompatible with the HRA 1998 (see *R (on the Application of M) v Secretary of State for Health* (2003)).

One danger of the MHA 1983 is that concern with the patient's health, or the health of others, may result in an abuse of the patient's civil liberties. The MHA Code of Practice, published under s 118 of the MHA 1983, provides a degree of protection. This Code gives guidance to professionals in how the MHA 1983 should be applied. In the foreword to the Code, the Secretary of State writes: 'This revised Code puts a new emphasis on the patient as an individual ... Patients and their carers are entitled to expect professionals to use it' (see DoH, 1999).

Amongst other things, the Code requires (para 1.1) that people affected by the Act should:

- receive recognition of their basic human rights under the European Convention on Human Rights;
- be given respect for their qualities, abilities and diverse backgrounds as individuals ...;
- have their needs fully taken into account [within the limits of available resources];

- be given any necessary treatment or care in the least controlled and segregated facilities compatible with ensuring their own health or safety or the safety of others;
- be treated and cared for in such a way as to promote the greatest practicable degree of their self determination and personal responsibility, consistent with their own needs and wishes; [and]
- be discharged from detention or other powers provided by the Act as soon as it is clear that their application is no longer justified.

The Mental Health Act Commission and the MHRT provide further protection of liberty. These bodies are given powers by the MHA 1983 to oversee the conditions and duration of detention. There is also specific statutory protection for mentally impaired females. Under s 7 of the Sexual Offences Act 1956, it may be a criminal offence for a man to have sexual intercourse with a woman with severe mental impairment. Similarly, male members of staff, carers or guardians are prohibited from having sexual intercourse with female patients (MHA 1959, s 128). While the law looks to protect the mentally disordered, it should also be noted that the MHA 1983 grants criminal and civil law immunity to those acting under the Act unless 'done in bad faith or without reasonable care'. This latter criterion still permits liability for negligence. Any legal action that is brought must receive leave from the High Court or the Director of Public Prosecutions (MHA 1983, s 139). Leave is not required under s 139 to apply for judicial review: see *R v Hallstrom ex p W* (1985) CA.

R (on the Application of Munjaz) v Mersey Care NHS Trust (2003): Compliance with the MHA Code of Practice may prevent a practice from being an unjustified breach of a patient's human rights

Facts

The appellant was lawfully detained as a psychiatric patient and had been secluded within the hospital. He applied for a judicial review of his seclusion, which, he alleged, had not complied with the Code of Practice. His application was refused and he appealed.

Decision

The Court of Appeal allowed his appeal. Seclusion was a breach of Article 8, Schedule 1 of the HRA unless 'in accordance with the law' and, because the Code of Practice established predictability and transparency, hospitals must comply with it. Any departure from the Code must be justified by good reason. The unjustified seclusion could also amount to a breach of Article 3, but not Article 5.

Re F (Adult: Court's Jurisdiction) (2000): Where there is a gap in the protection offered by the MHA 1983, the courts could make a declaratory order in the best interests of the person justified by the doctrine of necessity

Facts

Following a judicial decision that F could not be made the subject of a guardianship order (see 9.1 above), her father died. Her mother wanted her to return home. The local authority applied to the court under its inherent jurisdiction for a declaratory order that the local authority could determine where F should reside. At a preliminary hearing, Johnson J held that the court did have jurisdiction under Ord 15, r 16 of the Supreme Court 1965 to make such a declaration but that it should be exercised conservatively. T's mother appealed and argued that such an order was coercive and would give the local authority the same power that they had failed to achieve under the guardianship application.

It was accepted for the purposes of the appeal that F lacked the capacity to decide where she should reside. The disputed allegation about the sexual abuse of F was also accepted for the purposes of the appeal only (these assumptions would be disputed at a substantive hearing).

Decision

The Court of Appeal dismissed the appeal. Although the local authority had no power to direct F's place of residence except under a guardianship order, the doctrine of necessity might apply and the court could grant a declaratory order. The reasons were:

(1) F lacked the mental capacity to determine what was a serious justiciable issue;
(2) the MHA 1983 did not exclude the use of a declaratory order in these circumstances;
(3) there was an obvious gap in the statutory protection and the court could act to fill the gap to prevent a vulnerable person, such as F, from being placed at risk.

A declaration is a flexible remedy that may be relevant in a range of circumstances.

The case was referred back to the High Court for the judge to consider the substantive issues.

Comment

See also *R v Bournewood Community and Mental Health NHS Trust ex p L* (1998), 9.3 above.

R v Mental Health Act Commission ex p Smith (1998): Protection for patients detained under the MHA 1983 is provided by the Mental Health Act Commission

Facts

The applicant's deceased brother had been compulsorily detained under the MHA 1983. Following his death she made complaints to the Mental Health Act Commission (MHC). The MHC accepted jurisdiction regarding complaints about the appropriateness and illegality of the detention and the dosage of drugs that had been given to the deceased, but held that it had no jurisdiction to consider complaints that the deceased had been inappropriately detained and cared for in a secure unit and that his risk of harming himself had been inadequately assessed.

Decision

The High Court quashed the decision of the Commission and ordered the MHC to fully consider the complaints. Management, control and treatment were all inseparable parts of compulsory detention and thus the MHC had the appropriate jurisdiction under s 120(1) to investigate such complaints. Complaints relating to things like bed linen or food would not be within the MHC's jurisdiction.

Comment

See s 120 of the MHA 1983. The Commission, which was established under s 11 of the National Health Service Act 1977 and is continued under s 121 of the MHA 1983, carries out these functions as well as reviewing treatment given under ss 57–58 of the MHA 1983 (s 61 of the MHA). The Commission may also examine and comment on conditions in hospitals.

R (on the Application of H) v Ashworth Hospital Authority (2002): The MHRT may determine whether a patient should be discharged or remain compulsorily detained, but must give reasons for any decision reached

Facts

The claimant had been granted an absolute discharge from hospital by the MHRT despite the fact that five of six doctors submitting medical reports were opposed. Even the one doctor favouring discharge recommended that he be supervised post-discharge. Ashworth HA readmitted the patient under ss 3 and 13 of the MHA 1983, applied for a judicial review and, pending that, was granted an order by the High Court to stay the discharge decision. The claimant appealed.

Decision

The Court of Appeal allowed the appeal that the judge had been wrong to find that the decision to readmit was lawful, as Ashworth HA was not entitled to overrule a discharge order unless they were, in good conscience, able to suppose that new circumstances would have caused the MHRT to reach a different decision. No such new circumstances existed. However, the court did have the power to grant a stay of the discharge decision. In addition, the MHRT's decision was *Wednesbury* unreasonable and it had failed to give adequate reasons for rejecting the overwhelming expert evidence against discharge. It was not enough to simply state a preference for one witness over another, as the reasons given should explain, in a way that is comprehensible to laypersons, why that preference was conclusive.

See also *Bone v Mental Health Review Tribunal* (1985), *R v MHRT ex p Clatworthy* (1985) and *R v MHRT ex p Pickering* (1986), which effectively require that the reasons must be sufficient and comprehensible. See also *Perkins v Bath DHA* (1990).

Comment

Patients, or their nearest relative, have a right to apply to a Tribunal once during every relevant period of detention as defined by the MHA 1983 (ss 66 and 77(2)). Every time the detention is renewed, the patient may re-apply (s 66). Under s 68, the hospital managers must make an application on behalf of any patient who has not exercised their right to appeal within the first six months, and for all those who have been detained for three years or more since their last review. Patients under a supervised after-care order may also apply for review once in the first six months and then annually. Under s 23 of the MHA 1983, the patient may also challenge their detention by an informal administrative mechanism. The power to make a discharge order under this section is given to the hospital's managers or the patient's nearest relative.

These 'managers' are the non-executive directors and any associate members appointed for this purpose. They are not healthcare professionals.

Patients subject to a restriction order (s 41) may apply to the MHRT for a discharge order under s 73. The burden of proof lies with the patient to prove that he no longer suffers from a mental disorder. However, in *R (on the Application of H) v MHRT North and East London Region* (2001), the Court of Appeal declared this section incompatible with the HRA 1998. This has been remedied by the Mental Health Act 1983 (Remedial) Order 2001, which places the onus on the Tribunal to be satisfied, or those opposing discharge to prove, that the patient suffers from a mental disorder.

R v MHRT for the South Thames Region ex p Smith (1998): When considering a discharge order, both the 'nature' and the 'degree' of the disorder are independently relevant

Facts
The applicant suffered from paranoid schizophrenia. He sought a conditional discharge, which was refused on the basis that, while the 'degree' of his disorder did not warrant detention, the 'nature' of his disorder did. S sought judicial review, arguing that under s 72(1)(b)(i) of the MHA 1983, 'nature' and 'degree' should be read conjunctively.

Decision
The High Court rejected the application and held that the phrase 'nature or degree' did not require those variables to be determined conjunctively.

Comment
Section 72 (1)(b)(i) requires the patient to be discharged if the MHRT is not satisfied 'that he is then suffering from mental illness, psychopathic disorder, severe mental impairment or mental impairment ... of a nature or degree which makes it appropriate for him to be liable to be detained in a hospital for medical treatment'. Bartlett and Sandland (2003) suggest this judgment 'is another example of protectionism overriding patients' rights' and they question whether it survives the HRA 1998.

Re S-C (Mental Patient: Habeas Corpus) (1996): Where there was no power to detain, the patient may challenge their detention by making an application for habeas corpus

Facts
The applicant had been compulsorily detained. The approved social worker making the application for his detention claimed that his nearest relative, his mother, had approved the application for detention under s 3 of the MHA 1983. The mother stated that she had not approved the application for detention. At first instance the application for habeas corpus was refused. The applicant appealed.

Decision
The Court of Appeal approved the application for habeas corpus as the appropriate procedure where the requirements for detention have not, in fact, been satisfied. Sir Thomas Bingham MR stated:

... the present case is one in which, in principle, an application for habeas corpus is appropriate. There is no attempt being made to overturn any administrative decision. The object is simply to show that there was never jurisdiction to detain the appellant in the first place, a fact which on agreed evidence appears to be plainly made out.

B v Barking Havering & Brentwood Community Healthcare NHS Trust (1999): Where the power to detain has been exercised inappropriately, then the patient may challenge his detention by judicial review

Facts

B had a long history of personality problems requiring frequent admissions to hospital. She was readmitted under s 3 of the MHA 1983 after she set fire to her own home. Towards the end of the six months' detention allowed under s 3, B was granted a succession of weekly periods of leave under s 17. At the end of the six months, B's psychiatrist sought an extension of her detention under s 20 of the MHA 1983. B was then granted leave renewed on a weekly basis. She applied for a writ of habeas corpus and judicial review of the hospital's procedures. She subsequently was readmitted after she took amphetamines and developed a drug-induced psychosis. She later caused herself serious injuries. She acknowledged that her present detention was justified under s 3 but maintained her dispute with the initial renewal of her detention. One of the issues for the court to determine was whether habeas corpus or judicial review was the appropriate application.

Decision

The Court of Appeal dismissed the appeal and rejected the application. Although B could not be criticised for making both applications, since the relationship between them needed clarification, judicial review was to be preferred since it had a wider range of remedies available. Application for habeas corpus should be discouraged unless it was clear that no other relief would be required. *Re S-C* was approved on the facts of the case (see above).

Comment

In order for judicial review, the decision must have been irrational (*Associated Provincial Picture Houses v Wednesbury Corp* (1948)). However, under the HRA 1998, the courts should apply the principle of proportionality. This requires the following: (1) a legitimate aim; (2) it could not be achieved by a means less invasive of individual rights; and (3) the importance of the objective justifies the degree of infringement of the individual rights.

R (on the Application of C) v MHRT (2001): Undue delay in scheduling a discharge hearing will breach Article 5, Schedule 1 to the HRA 1998

Facts

The applicant applied for a judicial review of the MHRT practice of listing hearings eight weeks after the applications were made. At first instance the application was refused. C appealed.

Decision

The Court of Appeal allowed the appeal. It held that, while eight weeks was not inconsistent with the HRA 1998, the practice was one of convenience not necessity and that where an earlier hearing was requested, there should be good reason for refusing such a request. However, a blanket practice, with no attempt to ensure individual applications were heard earlier, was incompatible with the approach taken by the European Court of Human Rights.

Comment

Bartlett and Sandland (2003) suggest that the eight-week delay is based on the decision in *E v Norway* (1990). Whether a delay is unreasonable will, quite reasonably, depend on the exact circumstances. For example, where the delay is caused by factors relating to the patient's case, such as the time taken to obtain a medical report, then it may not breach Article 5 (see *Cotterham v UK* (1999)). In *R (on the Application of KB and Others) v MHRT* (2002), the court held that where the delay was due to an excessive workload or staff shortages then the responsibility lay with central government.

R (on the Application of H) v Ashworth Hospital Authority (2002): Even where the decision has been made to order the patient's discharge, that discharge may be delayed to protect the patient or others at risk

Facts

H had been granted a discharge but the hospital applied to the court for a stay of discharge while it sought a judicial review of the decision. The High Court granted a stay on the discharge order. H appealed against that decision and the lawfulness of the hospital's decision to readmit and detain him in the interim.

Decision

See above. The Court of Appeal allowed the appeal in part but rejected the appeal against the court's right to grant a stay of the discharge order. Such an action would be lawful if there was strong evidence that the MHRT's decision was unlawful, there was evidence of risk and dangerousness and the validity of the decision was speedily determined.

Comment

It is also lawful for the MHRT to defer discharge to ensure that suitable after-care arrangements are in place if there is a risk to the patient or others: see also *R (on the Application of B) v Mental Health Review Tribunal* (2003).

R v Secretary of State for the Home Department ex p IH (2003): It will not be a breach of the HRA 1998 to continue to detain a patient if the conditions for conditional discharge cannot be met

Facts

IH was subject to a restriction order under ss 37 and 41 of the MHA 1983. The MHRT determined that he was no longer suffering from a mental illness of a nature or degree warranting detention and he should be discharged. However, because of the risk of recurrence, the discharge would be conditional on psychiatric supervision. The community psychiatrists were unwilling to provide such supervision and so – despite the best efforts of the Health Authority – the conditions of discharge were unmet and the patient remained under detention. The appellant claimed that continued detention breached Article 5, Schedule 1 to the HRA 1998.

Decision

The House of Lords held that continued detention did not breach Article 5 where a Health Authority had made every effort but failed to meet the conditions of discharge. It set aside the ruling in *R v Oxford Regional Mental Health Tribunal ex p Secretary of State for the Home Department* (1988), and endorsed the Court of Appeal's statement that: 'Tribunals should no longer proceed on the basis that they cannot reconsider a decision to direct a conditional discharge on specified conditions where, after deferral and before directing discharge, there is a material change of circumstance.' There was also no basis for a claim under s 117 of the MHA 1983 as the duty is not absolute and the Health Authority did everything possible (see 9.5 below).

Comment

The House of Lords distinguished *Johnson v UK* (1997) in which the Tribunal had determined that the patient no longer suffered from a mental disorder. In that case, a prolonged delay in discharge to ensure suitable conditions in the community was held to breach Article 5 of the European Convention on Human Rights by the European Court of Human Rights. Some delay would have been acceptable but, in the circumstances, the duration of the delay and the lack of safeguards to ensure release meant that the Convention had been breached.

9.5   Rights to services and treatment

(See also Chapter 11 for a consideration of patients' general rights to healthcare and medical treatment.) There is a duty – under s 117 of the MHA 1983 (as amended) – on the Health Authority and Social Services to provide the patient who has been compulsorily detained for treatment with after-care services.

R v Ealing DHA ex p Fox (1993): If a Health Authority is unable to provide the after-care service required, they should try to obtain it from another Health Authority or refer the matter to the Secretary of State

Facts

The MHRT directed that the applicant could be discharged on the condition that a consultant psychiatrist would agree to act as his responsible medical officer. The Health Authority's psychiatrists refused. The applicant applied for judicial review and sought: a declaration that the Health Authority had erred in law in refusing to provide the supervision in the community; an order of certiorari to quash the Health Authority's decision; and an order of mandamus to compel the Health Authority to provide the supervision.

Decision

The High Court granted the declaration and the order of certiorari. The order of mandamus was refused since the court was not prepared to order the doctors to act against their will 'where the doctor's refusal arises from an honestly held clinical judgment that the treatment is not in the patient's best interests or is not in the best interests of the community'. Otton J stated:

... the mere acceptance by the Health Authority of the doctors' opinions is not of itself a sufficient discharge of their obligations ... In my judgment, if the ... Health Authority's doctors do not agree with the conditions imposed by the Mental Health Review Tribunal and are disinclined to make the necessary arrangements ... [the] Health Authority cannot let the matter rest there ... [The] Health Authority is under a continuing obligation to make further endeavours to provide arrangements within its own resources or to obtain them from other Health Authorities who provide such services so as to put in place practical arrangements for enabling the applicant to comply with conditions imposed ... or at the very least, to make inquiries of other providers of such services. If the arrangements still cannot be made then the ... Health Authority should not permit an impasse to continue but refer the matter to the Secretary of State to enable him to consider exercising his power to refer the case back to the Mental Health Review Tribunal under s 71(1).

Comment

In *R (on the Application of K) v Camden and Islington HA* (2001), the Court of Appeal held that duty to provide after-care under s 117 of the MHA 1983 was not an absolute obligation since the provision of such service was subject to budgetary discretion. Provided the Health Authority had used 'all reasonable endeavours to comply' with the discharge conditions then continued detention would be lawful.

R v MHRT ex p Hall (2000): The MHRT has no power to police the provision of after-care services

Facts

The respondent was granted a conditional discharge that proved difficult to satisfy. The conditions were relaxed, but the Tribunal's decision was caused to lapse by a renewed application for discharge. The second Tribunal found that the respondent was not suffering from mental illness but should be liable for recall on the event of a relapse. The Tribunal granted a discharge with more stringent conditions than those imposed by the first Tribunal. The Health Authority and county council continued to fail to make the necessary arrangements for the respondent's release. The respondent sought a judicial review. At first instance, the judge quashed the decision of the Tribunal and declared that the Health Authority and county council had erred in law in failing to make the necessary arrangements.

Decision

The Court of Appeal allowed the appeal. Once the Tribunal has made its decision the burden is passed to the Health Authority and local authority. The lower court had erred in blaming the Tribunal for failing to police the work of those authorities, as the Tribunal had no such power. The non-compliance of the authorities would not change the lawful imposition of conditions into an unlawful decision. Providing the conditions were not irrational, they were not open to judicial review and, although it may be sensible for the Tribunal to have available a care plan of workable conditions, this was not a legal requirement before imposing conditions.

9.6 Reforming the Mental Health Act (2000) Cm 5016

This is a Government White Paper, which consists of two parts: 'The new legal framework' and 'High risk patients'. Mental disorder will be defined broadly as 'any disability or disorder of mind or brain, which results in an impairment or disturbance of mental functioning' (para 3.3). There will no longer be any requirement that the disorder be treatable, and personality disorders are covered (para 3.5). New safeguards will be legislated for to ensure that compulsory powers will only be used when the person is resisting care, and treatment is either in their own best interests or necessary because they pose a significant risk of serious harm to others. The procedure for compulsory detention is in three stages:

(1) Preliminary examination by two doctors and a social worker (or other suitably trained mental health professional) to determine if the patient needs further assessment or treatment by specialist mental health services without which he might be at risk of serious harm or pose a risk of serious harm to others.

(2) Formal assessment and initial treatment under compulsory powers. This will be limited to 28 days (para 3.38) and a formal preliminary care plan must be set out within three days (paras 3.15–17). Any further detention must be authorised by the new independent Mental Health Tribunal following inquisitorial procedure including representation from the patient (para 3.62) and advice from independent experts (paras 3.45–46).

(3) Care and treatment order (paras 3.49ff). The Tribunal will make an order which will authorise care and treatment specified in a care plan recommended by the clinical team, although it is unclear how far the Tribunal may amend the plan (para 3.50). The duration of the order must be specified but may be up to six months for the first two orders and subsequently for up to 12 months. The order must also state whether the patient is to be detained. If not detained, the compulsory elements of the plan and the consequences of non-compliance must be specified. (Note: under the MHA 1983, compulsory treatment orders only apply to patients detained in hospital. The new legislation will extend this power so that orders may also be made in respect of patients' care in the community.)

The White Paper includes the Government's proposals for dealing with persons with dangerous severe personality disorders. This is achieved by allowing compulsory detention of patients where treatment is necessary to obviate the serious risk of severe harm to others. To this end, the courts will also have the power to remand the person for assessment and treatment. The Government suggests that the main safeguard arises from the overseeing independent Tribunal. Additional safeguards include: free legal representation; access to independent specialist advocates; and specific provisions to cover non-consensual treatment.

Following the White Paper, a draft Mental Health Bill 2002 was published along with a consultation document. This consultation has now finished and a new draft

Bill is due to be published in September 2004. The history of this reform is detailed on the Department of Health's website (www.dh.gov.uk/PolicyAndGuidance/ HealthAndSocialCareTopics/MentalHealth/fs/en).

CHAPTER 10

CONFIDENTIALITY AND ACCESS TO PATIENT RECORDS

10.1 Confidentiality

Confidentiality is an important part of the doctor's relationship with his or her patient. Ethically, it is justified by both consequentialist and deontological arguments. One consequentialist argument is that the duty of confidentiality allows the patient to trust his doctor and so encourages more complete and honest disclosure, which in turn allows better healthcare. Conversely, an absence of any duty of confidentiality may prevent patients with certain conditions from seeking timely medical assistance. This argument is relevant both to the individual and to the wider public where the patient is suffering from an infectious or communicable disease. Deontological arguments derive from the patient's right to autonomy. Kluge (1994), for example, suggests we should treat personal information as a 'gnostic analogue' to the body. The power to control information concerning oneself may be just as important to our liberty to be self-directing as the power to control our own bodies, and it is certainly relevant to our ability to control the closeness of our personal relationships. Other arguments supporting a duty of confidentiality derive from the concept of trust. The duty of confidentiality, however, is not absolute. The most widely accepted limiting factor is to prevent harm to others, and this may allow claims to the information by the state or a state agency, by other members of the community and by family members or blood relatives. The right to freedom of speech also competes with the duty of confidentiality, allowing the press to make claims on the information in certain circumstances.

The duty of confidentiality is protected by both the common law and statute law. In England and Wales, the primary common law action is based in equity (see below), but claims may also be brought in negligence (*Furniss v Flitchett* (1958)) and contract (*W v Egdell* (1990) (see below)). Statutory protection comes from a number of sources, including the Abortion Regulations 1991, the NHS (Venereal Diseases) Regulations 1974 and the NHS Trusts and Primary Care Trusts (Sexually Transmitted Diseases) Directions 2000, amongst others. The main statutes relevant to the protection of patient confidentiality are the Data Protection Act 1998 and the Human Rights Act (HRA) 1998. Under Article 8(1), Schedule 1 to the HRA 1998, there is a right 'to respect for ... private and family life'. This creates a right to privacy (see *Peck v UK* (2003)), which is a wider claim than a right to confidentiality since it does not require a relationship of confidentiality to exist. In *Douglas v Hello!* (2001), Sedley LJ explained:

What a concept of privacy does ... is accord recognition to the fact that the law has to protect not only those people whose trust has been abused but those who simply find themselves subjected to an unwanted intrusion into their personal lives. The law no longer needs to construct an artificial relationship of confidentiality between intruder and victim: it can recognise privacy itself as a legal principle drawn from the fundamental value of personal autonomy.

However, despite the terms of Article 8, the courts have been reluctant to acknowledge breach of privacy as a distinct tort (*A v B plc* (2002)) and, in *Wainwright v Home Office* (2003), the House of Lords clearly denies the existence of a separate tort of breach of privacy.

Derogation from Article 8(1) is allowed under Article 8(2), providing it is 'in accordance with the law and is necessary in a democratic society in the interests of national security, public safety or the economic well-being of the country, for the prevention of disorder or crime, for the protection of health or morals, or for the protection of the rights and freedoms of others'. When considering claims in this context under Article 8(1), Article 10 – the right to freedom of expression – should be considered. This right includes 'freedom to ... receive and impart information and ideas without interference by public authority'. In *Campbell v Mirror Group Newspapers* (2004), the House of Lords balanced the parties' rights under these two Articles to conclude that the journalist's right to freedom of expression justified a story to set the record straight regarding Naomi Campbell's drug-taking. However, it was a breach of Ms Campbell's right to a private life under Article 8 to publish the photographs of her leaving a Narcotics Anonymous meeting.

The Data Protection Act (DPA) 1998, passed as a result of the Data Protection Directive 1995, adds to the protection provided by the common law but only relates to recorded data and not to verbal confidences. It may provide compensation (s 13) and breaches of the Act may amount to criminal offences, but there is no private right of action. Under s 4, the data controller has a duty to comply with the data protection principles (Schedule 1, Part 1) when processing personal data. Medical information is 'sensitive personal information' under the Act and is given additional safeguards by requiring that that processing satisfies one of the conditions detailed in Schedule 3. The Government's Information Commissioner maintains a website, which is a useful source of information concerning the DPA 1998 (www.informationcommissioner.gov.uk).

In addition to a legal duty of confidentiality, the doctor also has a professional duty. The GMC (2000) has issued guidance on this duty. It states that:

Patients have a right to expect that information about them will be held in confidence by their doctors. Confidentiality is central to trust between doctors and patients ... If you are asked to provide information about patients you should:

(a)　Seek patients' consent to disclosure of information wherever possible, whether or not you judge that patients can be identified from the disclosure.

(b)　Anonymise data where unidentifiable data will serve the purpose.

(c)　Keep disclosures to the minimum necessary.

You must always be prepared to justify your decisions in accordance with this guidance.

The Department of Health (2003b) has also recently published a Code of Practice on Confidentiality. In Scotland, the Confidentiality and Security Advisory Group for

Scotland has recently prepared a report (2002) for Scottish Ministers recommending, amongst other things, nine principles for dealing with patient information, a national awareness campaign for healthcare staff, patients and the public, and the urgent need for a code of practice.

As will be seen below, the legal duty is not absolute and, under certain circumstances, there may even be a duty to disclose confidential information. A recent statute that caused some controversy is the Health and Social Care Act 2001. Section 60 of the Act gives the Secretary of State fairly wide powers to pass regulations concerning prescribed patient information if it is in the interests of providing patient care or in the public interest. Under s 61 of the Act, a Patient Information Advisory Group has been established to advise the Secretary of State on proposed regulations under s 60. Under this power, the Secretary of State has passed the Health Service (Control of Information) Regulations 2002, which modifies the duty of confidentiality in relation to cancer information for cancer registries and the processing of information concerning communicable diseases and other public health risks. Also relevant is the duty to report certain notifiable diseases under ss 10 and 11 of the Public Health Act 1984 and the Public Health (Infectious Diseases) Regulations 1988.

Hunter v Mann (1974): There is a legal obligation to respect a patient's confidence

Facts

A police officer, acting under s 168(2)(b) of the Road Traffic Act 1972 asked the defendant for information which might have resulted in the identification of a person suspected of dangerous driving in a stolen car. The defendant was a doctor who had obtained the information solely by virtue of his professional relationship with the suspect. He refused to divulge the information on the grounds that it would be a breach of professional confidence. He was convicted in the magistrates' court and appealed.

Decision

The Divisional Court dismissed the appeal. The court accepted that the doctor owed his patient a duty of confidence but held that the duty was limited and in the circumstances the doctor's obligation of patient confidentiality was overridden by the statutory duty imposed by s 168(2)(b).

Lord Widgery CJ did suggest that 'A doctor giving evidence in court, who is asked a question which he finds embarrassing because it involves him talking about things which he would normally regard as confidential, can ask the judge, who has an overriding discretion, if it is necessary to answer'.

Comment

The strongest basis to support a legal duty of confidence is in equity. In *Fraser v Evans* (1969), Lord Denning MR stated: 'The jurisdiction [for confidentiality] is based not so much on property or on contract as on the duty to be of good faith. No person is permitted to divulge to the world information which he has received in confidence, unless he has just cause or excuse for doing so.' In *Stephens v Avery* (1988), Sir Nicolas Browne-Wilkinson VC stated: 'The basis of equitable intervention to protect confidentiality is that it is unconscionable for a person who has received information on the basis that it is confidential subsequently to reveal that information.' That this obligation may arise from the doctor-patient relationship is clearly stated in *Attorney General v Guardian Newspapers (No 2)* (1990) (see below), *per* Lord Keith: 'The law has long recognised that an obligation of confidence can arise out of particular relationships. Examples are the relationships of doctor and patient, priest and penitent, solicitor and client, bank and customer.'

Attorney General v Guardian Newspapers (No 2) (1990): Information already in the public domain is not confidential

Facts
The case concerned the publication of the *Spycatcher* book, which contained sensitive government information. The book was to be published in Australia and the US but, because of the author's contract of service from his time working for the Government, it could not be published in the UK. Extracts of the book were published in a newspaper and the Attorney General obtained interlocutory injunctions to prevent further publication. These were subsequently discharged by the High Court, and the Attorney General appealed.

Decision
The House of Lords dismissed the appeal. Although the pre-emptive publications were a breach of confidence, because of the worldwide publication of the book, future publications would not breach confidentiality.

Comment
Whether or not something is in the public domain is a matter of degree. It is also affected by the nature of the publication. In *D v L* (2003), Waller LJ argued that the impact of a photograph is very different to the impact of a description of the scene so that, even though the information may be in the public domain, publication of an 'improperly obtained' photograph may still be restrained by the court.

H (A Healthcare Worker) v Associated Newspapers Ltd (2002): Where it is the identity of an individual that is confidential, it may be a breach of confidentiality to publish information that would allow that individual to be identified even though the actual identity was not published

Facts
The claimant was an HIV positive healthcare worker who had obtained an injunction to prevent the solicitation and publication of information that might lead to his identification. The defendants published an article that might have been in breach of the injunction. The judge set aside the original orders and replaced them with a new order that did not prevent the naming of the Health Authority. H appealed.

Decision
The Court of Appeal allowed the appeal in part and varied the injunction. It held that if the Health Authority was named it would allow H to be identified. However, it

would be permissible to name H's speciality, as the much lower risk of identification from that information did not justify the infringement on freedom of expression.

Comment
The Court of Appeal noted that there was 'considerable public interest' in the story that the defendants wished to publish, given that the claimant was challenging Department of Health guidelines regarding a look-back exercise involving disclosure of his patients' medical records. This was countered by H's personal interest in confidentiality and the public interest in maintaining the confidentiality of HIV infected healthcare workers so that they are not discouraged from notifying their employers. Also relevant was the balance between the doctor's duty of confidentiality to his patients and whether disclosure of their records might be in their interests.

R v Department of Health ex p Source Informatics Ltd and Others (2000): The use of anonymous data will not be a breach of confidence

Facts
An American company wanted to gain information about doctors' prescribing habits, to sell on to drug companies. The scheme they proposed was to have pharmacists collect computerised data of prescriptions. The data was anonymous in that it would not include details of the patient. The Department of Health issued a policy document stating that this would involve a breach of patient confidentiality. The company challenged the view by instigating a judicial review. The challenge was dismissed at first instance. The company appealed.

Decision
The Court of Appeal allowed the appeal. The concern of the law here was to protect the confider's personal privacy. The patient had no proprietary claim to the prescription form or to the information it contained. In a case involving personal confidences the confidence was not breached where the confider's identity was protected.

Comment
Under the DPA 1998, the anonymisation of data might count as data processing. However, once anonymised the data could be freely used.

C v C (1946): The patient's consent relieves the doctor of his duty of confidence

Facts
As part of proceedings in which the petitioner was seeking a decree of nullity under the Matrimonial Causes Act 1937, the doctor treating the respondent was asked for details of the venereal disease from which she was suffering. Both petitioner and respondent signed the request for information and, had the doctor complied with the request, the respondent would have been able to make out a successful defence. The doctor refused to give the information but stated that he would if subpoenaed. This is in fact what ensued. The judge was asked to give a direction in order that a similar problem would not recur.

Decision

The High Court directed that the doctor is not justified in refusing to divulge confidential information when asked by the patient so to do.

W v Egdell (1990): The duty of confidence is not absolute and may be overridden by the public interest

Facts

The plaintiff was imprisoned in a secure hospital following conviction for killing and other violent crimes. He made an application to a tribunal for transfer to a regional unit as a step towards release into the community. His legal advisors sought the opinion of an independent psychiatrist, Dr Egdell. Dr Egdell felt that the patient was still a danger to the public. W's application was withdrawn. W's case then fell to be automatically reviewed under s 79(1) of the Mental Health Act 1983. Dr Egdell's report would not have been included in the reports reviewed by the tribunal under this process. Dr Egdell felt that his report should be considered and sent a copy to the medical director of the secure hospital and also to the Home Office. W bought an action for breach of confidence. At first instance the court found for the defendant, as the breach was justified as being in the public interest. W appealed.

Decision

The Court of Appeal dismissed the appeal. The public interest in ensuring that decisions that may place the public at risk are made on the basis of adequate information outweighs the duty of confidence. Bingham LJ stated:

The parties were agreed, as I think rightly, that the crucial question was how, on the special facts of the case, the balance should be struck between the public interest in maintaining professional confidences and the public interest in protecting the public against possible violence ... Only the most compelling circumstances could justify the doctor acting in a way which would injure the immediate interests of his patient, as the patient perceived them, without obtaining his consent.

Comment

Traditionally, the duty of confidentiality has been founded in the public interest (*per* Lord Goff in *Attorney General v Guardian Newspapers (No 2)* (1990)). It is arguable, however, that the HRA 1998 (Article 8) would require the court to consider the private interest in the doctor's duty of confidence. Derogation under Article 8(2) is allowed in the interest of public safety and it is suggested that this would support the judgment in *W v Egdell*. In *Egdell*, the breach was justified to protect the public as a whole. There may also be a public interest in the protection of identified individuals (or groups) that would justify a breach of confidence. *In the Matter of B (Children)* (2003), the Court of Appeal noted, without disapproval, that the consultant child psychiatrist had 'balanced ... her child protection obligations ... against her obligation to maintain ... confidentiality' where children remained at risk of being abused. (See also, for example, *Tarasoff v Regents of the University of California* (1976) which not only held that a breach would be justified but that it would be the doctor's duty to disclose; and *Reisner v Regents of the University of California* (1995), in which the doctor had a duty to disclose the facts to the partner of a patient who contracted HIV from infected blood.)

X v *Y* (1988): The public interest must be substantial to justify a breach of confidence

Facts
A Health Authority employee passed on to a newspaper the names of two practising doctors being treated for AIDS. The Health Authority sought an injunction to prevent publication of the doctors' details.

Decision
The High Court granted the injunction. Rose J stated:

I keep in the forefront of my mind the very important public interest in freedom of the press. And I accept that there is some public interest in knowing that which the defendants seek to publish ... But in my judgment those public interests are substantially outweighed when measured against the public interests in relation to loyalty and confidentiality both generally and with particular reference to AIDS patients' hospital records ... The deprivation of the public of the information sought to be published will be of minimal significance if the injunction is granted.

Comment
In *British Steel Corp v Granada Television Ltd* (1981), Lord Wilberforce emphasised that 'there is a wide difference between what is interesting to the public and what it is in the public interest to make known'.

Duncan v Medical Practitioners' Disciplinary Committee (1986): A breach of confidence will only be justified if the information is divulged to the proper authorities or persons who need to know

Facts
A bus driver underwent a triple coronary artery bypass graft operation. Although he was then certified fit to drive by his surgeon, his GP requested that his licence be withdrawn. The GP also warned the bus driver's passengers of the supposed danger they faced. The Medical Practitioners' Disciplinary Committee found the GP guilty of professional misconduct for a breach of confidence. The GP sought a judicial review of the decision.

Decision
The New Zealand High Court refused the application.

Comment
The court accepted that public interest might justify a breach of confidentiality but, as Jeffries J stated, 'a doctor who has decided to communicate should discriminate and ensure the recipient is a responsible authority'. Thus, informing the vehicle licensing authority, when it is known that the patient will not, is likely to be justified. The GMC has detailed guidelines on this issue in Appendix 2 of their booklet on confidentiality (2000). It is suggested that, if these guidelines were followed, the court would accept that the breach was justified unless it was made in bad faith.

Hunter v Mann (1974): If the information is required by law, then the disclosure will not breach any duty of confidence

Facts

See above.

Decision

See above.

Comment

Statute law requiring the disclosure of information includes: s 19 of the Terrorism Act 2000; r 5 of the Abortion Regulations 1991; the notification of notifiable diseases under the Public Health Act 1984; and the Misuse of Drugs (Notification of Supply to Addicts) Regulations 1973.

Hunter v Mann (1974): There will be no breach of confidence if the information is requested during court proceedings

Facts

See above.

Decision

See above.

Comment

Lord Widgery CJ discussed the duty of a doctor giving evidence in court. It is clear that the doctor must respond to a question, but:

... if a doctor, giving evidence in court, is asked a question ... which he would normally regard as confidential, he can seek the protection of the judge and ask the judge if it is necessary for him to answer. The judge, by virtue of his overriding discretion to control his court which all English Judges have, can, if he thinks fit, tell the doctor that he need not answer the question. Whether or not the judge would take that line, of course, depends largely on the importance of the potential answer to the issues being tried.

The doctor is prevented from liability for a breach of confidence because of the absolute immunity of the witness (*Watson v M'Ewan* (1905) HL). This immunity, however, would not extend to a request for information from a solicitor.

Nicholson v Halton General Hospital NHS Trust (1999): A right to confidentiality ceases when the patient brings a court action that necessarily requires disclosure

Facts

While in the defendants' employment, the claimant developed 'radial tunnel' syndrome, which required surgical treatment. She brought an action claiming it was a work-related condition. The defendants' medical expert argued that it was not work-related but stated that he would need to consult the claimant's surgeon to discover the operative findings so that he could perfect his report. The claimant was advised by her counsel to refuse consent. The defendants brought an action seeking an order that the claimant's action should be stayed if she did not consent within a week. The order was refused and the defendants appealed.

Decision

The Court of Appeal allowed the appeal. Whilst there was a right to confidentiality, and it was for the claimant to waive that right, the court could order the claimant's action to be stayed if she refused consent. Order granted that the action would be stayed if the claimant did not consent to disclosure within two weeks.

Comment

See also the Canadian case *Hay v University of Alberta* (1991).

Re C (Adult Patient: Publicity) (1996): The duty to respect a patient's confidence may persist after the patient's death

Facts

The court had granted an order that life support treatment could be withdrawn from a 27-year-old man in a persistent vegetative state. An order was granted to prevent identification of the patient and his family. The Official Solicitor sought guidance as to whether the order would persist after the patient's death.

Decision

The High Court held that the order was made under s 11 of the Contempt of Court Act 1981 and would persist for as long as there were valid reasons. These reasons included: the detrimental effect on the medical staff that might happen if the order was revoked; consideration of the patient's family; the issue of medical confidentiality; and the public interest in allowing applications for withdrawal of treatment orders to be made without fear of publicity.

Comment

(1) Although the case concerned a court order, the judge clearly states that the issue of medical confidentiality is at stake even after the death of the patient. Whether this would be enforceable under equity has not been tested. However, Article 8 of the HRA 1998 arguably requires that confidentiality should be maintained after death where a breach would affect the deceased's relatives' right to respect for family life.

(2) The GMC (2000) state: 'You still have an obligation to keep personal information confidential after a patient dies.' A breach may incur liability for serious professional misconduct.

(3) Clearly confidentiality after death is not absolute, however, and disclosure may be necessary to assist the coroner and complete the death certificate.

(4) The DPA 1998 does not apply after the death of the person.

10.2   Common law remedies

X v Y (1988): An injunction may be available to prevent a breach of confidentiality

Facts

See 10.1 above.

Decision

The High Court granted an injunction to prevent the publication of confidential information.

Cornelius v De Taranto (2000): Damages

Facts

The claimant contracted with the defendant doctor for a medico-legal report. Without her consent, the defendant sent copies of the report to the claimant's GP and to a consultant psychiatrist. The claimant brought an action for libel, breach of contract and breach of confidence.

Decision

The High Court held that there was no liability for defamation. The defendant was liable for breach of confidence. It would be a 'hollow protection of the right to respect for private and family life in Art 8 of the European Convention on Human Rights if the only remedy for disclosure of details about C's private and family life in breach of confidence was nominal damages'. Although it was a novel remedy, the court was entitled to award damages in contract for injury to feelings.

Comment

The Court of Appeal upheld the High Court's judgment (apart from the order for costs): see *Cornelius v De Taranto* (2001).

Although this was a case in contract, it is submitted that the same argument could be applied to a case brought in equity. In determining the level of damages to be awarded, the judge held that the material factors to be considered included: the nature and detail of the disclosure; the recipients; and the extent of disclosure together with the psychological make-up of the claimant as known to the defendant.

10.3   A duty to disclose

Palmer v Tees HA (1999): There may be a duty to disclose otherwise confidential information where there is a risk of harm to an identifiable third party

Facts

The claimant's daughter had been sexually assaulted and murdered by a man who had been under the psychiatric care of the defendants. The claimant alleged that the defendants had negligently failed to diagnose the risk that the man posed to children and had negligently failed to provide appropriate care and treatment to reduce the risk. The High Court held that, because the claimant's daughter would not have been identifiable in advance as a potential victim, there was insufficient proximity between the claimant and the defendant. The claimant appealed.

Decision

The Court of Appeal held that the defendants were not negligent. For there to be a duty of care, it was necessary for the potential victim to be identified or identifiable since the most effective protection would be by warning the victim's parents or social services to enable them to take some protective measures.

Comment

The question that this case leaves open is how small a group of persons must be identifiable for the duty of care to be established. In *Hill v Chief Constable of West Yorkshire* (1989), there was insufficient proximity as the victim was simply a female member of the public. In the classic US case, *Tarasoff v The Regents of the University of California* (1976), there was liability where the victim was identifiable even though she was not identified to the defendants. In other cases, the duty has been wider. In *Lipari v Sears, Roebuck and Co* (1980), the court held that the duty was owed to persons 'who might foreseeably be endangered'. These victims need not be identified, or identifiable, providing they were foreseeable. However, in *Lipari*, the duty was not restricted to warning and included a duty to detain. This places a different slant on the possibility of executing that duty, since you may need to be able to identify a victim to provide a warning, but you do not need to in order to detain the patient. This duty to warn has also been established in some US jurisdictions where the risk of harm is from a communicable (*Bradshaw v Daniel* (1993)) or genetic disease (*Safer v Estate of Pack* (1996)).

C v Dr Cairns (2003): Where the potential victim is the doctor's patient and a child, then there may be duty to breach confidentiality where it is in the child's best interests

Facts

The defendant was alerted, by the claimant's mother, that the claimant had been sexually abused by her stepfather when she was 12 years old. The doctor simply made a brief note of the incident without doing anything further as he accepted the mother's assertion that she was 'confident' that it would not be repeated. Unfortunately, the claimant did suffer further abuse. The claimant alleged that the defendant doctor had been negligent in failing to disclose an act of abuse by her stepfather. She claimed that, had other agencies been brought in, she would not have suffered years of further abuse.

Decision

The High Court dismissed the claim because, amongst other reasons, the doctor's 'decision accorded with that likely to have been reached by many responsible, caring colleagues'.

Comment

Despite the fact that the claim failed, this case supports the existence of a duty to protect a third party. The claim related to some 30 years ago, but the court accepted the unanimous expert opinion that even then the duty of confidentiality 'would have to give way to the "best interests" of the patient'. The judge noted that: 'In 1975 substantial stress was placed (much more so than now) on doctor/patient confidentiality' and that, today, the claim would be 'irresistible'. This suggests that if the same case occurred in 2003, the breach of duty would be made out.

It will be noted that, in this case, the victim was also the doctor's patient, although the duty of confidence was owed to the mother who had disclosed the abuse in a private consultation with the doctor. It therefore leaves open the question of whether such a duty exists where the victim is not also a patient. However, given *Palmer*, it is arguable that the duty would apply irrespective of whether the victim is the doctor's patient.

10.4   Patient access to personal information

Under s 7 of the DPA 1998, patients have a right to access personal data. The data controller is only obliged to comply where he can be sure of the identity of the person requesting the information (s 7(3)). Also, if complying with the request would result in disclosure of information relating to a third party, the data controller need not comply unless that third party consents or it is reasonable to comply without the third party's consent (s 7(4)). Furthermore, under Article 5(1) of the Data Protection (Subject Access Modification) (Health) Order 2000, the data controller need not comply with s 7 of the DPA 1998 if compliance would cause serious harm. This exemption only applies to information relating to the physical or mental health or condition of the patient (Article 3(1)) and only if the data controller is the health professional that currently or most recently was responsible for the patient, or after the data controller has consulted such a health professional (Article 5(2)). Under s 1 of the Access to Medical Reports Act 1988, there is a statutory right of access to employment or insurance medical reports. The DPA 1998 does not apply to patients after their death; however, a right of access persists under s 3 of the Access to Health Records Act 1990.

R v Mid-Glamorgan FHSA ex p Martin (1995): There is no absolute right of access to medical records

Facts

The applicant had repeatedly made requests for access to his health records. The records had all been made prior to 1991 and were therefore not subject to the statutory right of access under the Access to Health Records Act 1990 or the DPA 1984. Access was refused on the grounds that disclosure might be detrimental to the applicant who had a history of psychological problems, although they offered to disclose the records to the applicant's current medical adviser for him to consider whether the information might harm the applicant. At first instance, the judge held that there was no common law right of access nor was there any breach of Article 8 of the European Convention on Human Rights. The applicant appealed.

Decision

The Court of Appeal dismissed the appeal. A Health Authority could deny a patient access to his medical records if it was in the patient's best interests to do so. Nourse LJ stated:

... a doctor, likewise a Health Authority, as the owner of a patient's medical records, may deny the patient access to them if it is in his best interests to do so, for example, if their disclosure would be detrimental to his health ... the doctor's general duty, likewise the Health Authority's, is to act at all times in the best interests of the patient. Those interests would usually require that a patient's records should not be disclosed to third parties; conversely, that they should usually be handed on by one doctor to the next or made available to the patient's legal advisers if they are reasonably required for the purposes of legal proceedings in which he is involved.

Comment

In *Breen v Williams* (1995), the Australian Supreme Court of New South Wales held that there was no common law right of access to medical records and this included any claims to rights of access in equity. In addition, the Code of Practice on Openness in the NHS 1995 requires healthcare professionals to release a patient's record at their request even where they pre-date the code. This is, however, a non-statutory code but is enforceable by the Health Service Commissioner.

Comment

CHAPTER 11

PATIENTS' RIGHTS

There is no specific legal instrument that provides the patient with enforceable rights. The Patient's Charter has no legal force and it is better to see the document as setting the standards that the NHS should aspire towards. More importantly, although not specific to healthcare, the Human Rights Act (HRA) 1998 came into force on 2 October 2000. This provides that a number of rights, previously protected by the European Convention on Human Rights, will be incorporated directly into English law. While this is not a text on human rights, it is worth noting some of the main implications for healthcare law. The most important changes that the HRA 1998 brings are as follows:

(a) Individuals will now be able to challenge public bodies directly in the domestic court when their protected human rights have been breached. Individuals will no longer have to exhaust all the domestic provisions and then make the slow and expensive trip to Strasbourg in order to claim a breach of one of their rights.

(b) Human rights issues may be raised in all cases and not just those where a direct challenge is available.

(c) Judicial scrutiny of decisions made by public bodies will become more rigorous and the emphasis will shift away from the duty of the public body to the right of the individual. The change is succinctly summarised by the former Lord Chancellor, Lord Irvine (1998), who stated:

> The courts' decisions will be based on a more overtly principled, and perhaps moral, basis. The Court will look at the positive right. It will only accept an interference with that right where a justification, allowed under the Convention, is made out. The scrutiny will not be limited to seeing if the *words* of an exception can be satisfied. The Court will need to be satisfied that the *spirit* of this exception is made out. It will need to be satisfied that the interference with protected right *is* justified in the public interests in a free democratic society. Moreover, the courts will in this area have to apply the Convention's principle of proportionality. This means the Court will be looking substantively at that question. It will not be limited to a secondary review of the decision making process but at the primary question of the merits of the decision itself.

Proportionality will replace the previous test of *Wednesbury* 'unreasonableness' (see 11.1 below). It has three elements: (1) there must be a legitimate aim, eg, the protection of public health; (2) it must be necessary, ie, it could not be achieved by a means less invasive of individual rights; and (3) the degree of infringement of the individual's rights must be justified and no greater than is necessary to achieve the legitimate aim.

(d) Under s 3(1) of the HRA 1998, 'So far as it is possible to do so, primary legislation and subordinate legislation must be read and given effect in a way which is compatible with the Convention rights'.

For a fuller discussion of the HRA 1998, see the relevant references in the suggested Bibliography.

The issues of the treatment of persons with mental health disorders, confidentiality and the right to refuse treatment have already been dealt with. The other area in which patients' rights have been explored is in the provision of healthcare.

11.1   The provision of healthcare

Under Article 11 (the right to protection of health) of the European Social Charter 1961 (revised 1996), the Government has accepted a political obligation, which is not legally enforceable by an individual, to protect health and provide medical assistance. This Article states:

With a view to ensuring the effective exercise of the right to protection of health, the Contracting Parties undertake, either directly or in co-operation with public or private organisation, to take appropriate measures designed *inter alia*:

1   to remove as far as possible the causes of ill-health;
2   to provide advisory and educational facilities for the promotion of health and the encouragement of individual responsibility in matters of health;
3   to prevent as far as possible epidemic, endemic and other diseases, as well as accidents.

Under Article 13(1) (the right to social and medical assistance), the Government must undertake:

1   to ensure that any person who is without adequate resources and who is unable to secure such resources either by his own efforts or from other sources ... be granted ... in case of sickness, the care necessitated by his condition.

This political obligation is provided for by the National Health Service Act 1977, which obligates the Secretary of State to provide a comprehensive health service that can meet all reasonable requirements. This would be unlikely to create any duty of care to individual patients; however, individuals may seek a judicial review of decisions made by the Secretary of State under this Act.

Claims to treatment may also be brought under the HRA 1998. Articles 2 (the right to life), 3 (the right not to be subjected to torture, inhuman or degrading treatment), 8 (the right to private and family life), 9 (the right to freedom of thought, conscience and religion) and 14 (the right to enjoy the Convention rights without discrimination) may be particularly relevant. The European Court of Human Rights has held that, under Article 2, the state owes a positive obligation to protect a citizen's life if it is aware of an immediate risk (*Osman v UK* (2000)). However, there is no case law (but see below) directly on the subject and any such right would be constrained by resources (see *Osman v UK*), and would be negated if the treatment was likely to be futile (see *LCB v UK* (1998)). Given these factors and the judicial reluctance to direct a doctor to treat against his clinical judgment, the case for a right to life-saving treatment is strongest when the treatment is being withheld for reasons that unfairly discriminate against the individual, protected by Article 14. This article only comes into play if the application of one of the other protected rights discriminates against the applicant. This does not mean that there has to be an independent breach of one of the other protected rights, but, where the state has decided to provide some measure that falls within the scope of one of those rights, then Article 14 becomes relevant where access is subject to discrimination, even if a complete failure to provide the measure would not be a breach: see *Belgian Linguistic Case* (1968). Also, discrimination *on any* ground is prohibited.

R v Secretary of State for Social Services, West Midlands RHA and Birmingham AHA (Teaching) ex p Hincks (1987): The Secretary of State's duty is not absolute and is constrained by the resources available

Facts
The Secretary of State had previously approved plans for additional orthopaedic services. Because of a lack of money the plans were put on hold for 10 years. The applicants claimed that the provision of health services in their area was insufficient and the decision to shelve the plans was a breach of the Secretary of State's duty under s 3(1) of the National Health Service (NHS) Act 1977. This was refused at first instance and the applicants appealed.

Decision
The Court of Appeal held that s 3(1) does not impose an absolute duty. The Secretary of State is only obliged to do what he can with the resources available to him. His duty is to the country as a whole rather than to a particular hospital department. Bridge LJ stated:

... the limitation [on the Secretary of State's duty] must be determined in the light of current government economic policy. I think that it is quite clearly an implication which must be read into s 3(1) of the National Health Service Act 1977 if it is to be operated realistically ... I only hope that ... [the applicants] have not been encouraged to think that these proceedings offered any real prospects that this court could enhance the standards of the National Health Service, because any such encouragement would be based upon manifest illusion.

Comment
In *R v North and East Devon HA ex p Coughlan* (1999) (see below), Sedley LJ stated: 'The truth is that, while [the Secretary of State] has a duty to continue to promote a comprehensive free health service and he must never, in making a decision under section 3, disregard that duty, a comprehensive health service may never, for human, financial and other resource reasons, be achievable.'

R v Central Birmingham HA ex p Walker; R v Secretary of State for Social Services ex p Walker (1987): Patients may challenge the allocation of resources by judicial review

Facts
A premature baby required an operation to repair a 'hole in the heart'. The operation had been cancelled several times because of a shortage of nurses but the child's life was not in any immediate danger. The child's mother applied for a judicial review of the Health Authority's decision. At first instance the judge held that it was impossible to

say that there was any substantive or procedural illegality in the decision. The applicant appealed.

Decision

The Court of Appeal would not substitute its own judgment for the judgment of those responsible for the allocation of resources unless the allocation was *Wednesbury* unreasonable. The jurisdiction to intervene did exist but leave would be refused in this case.

Comment

(1) Sir John Donaldson, in *ex p Walker*, commented that the jurisdiction to review resource allocation should be 'used extremely sparingly'. The difficulty in challenging resource allocation is illustrated by *R v Cambridge DHA ex p B* (1995), in which the Court of Appeal held that a Health Authority's refusal to fund chemotherapy for a 10-year-old girl with leukaemia was lawful. Sir Thomas Bingham MR stated: 'Difficult and agonising judgments have to be made as to how a limited budget is best allocated to the maximum advantage of a maximum number of patients. This is not a judgment which the court can make.'

(2) Generally, a public body's decision does not have to be the best possible decision although it should be responsible. It may be challenged by judicial review where the decision is: (a) illegal; (b) procedurally flawed (see *R v Secretary of State for Health ex p Pfizer* (1999), in which the court held that, while the Secretary of State could make a policy decision to restrict prescription of Viagra, this should be done through the proper channels and not simply by issuing an advisory circular); or (c) irrational. Irrationality was defined in *Associated Provincial Picture Houses v Wednesbury Corp* (1948) as a decision 'so unreasonable that no reasonable authority could ever have come to it'. This was restated by Lord Diplock, in *Council of Civil Service Unions v Minister for the Civil Service* (1985), as 'so outrageous in its defiance of logic or of accepted moral standards that no sensible person who had applied his mind to the question to be decided could have arrived at it'. This is, in practice, such an insurmountable test that some authors have described resource-allocation as non-justiciable (see O'Sullivan, 1998). The test is likely to be changed to one of 'proportionality' by the HRA 1998 (see below).

R v Gloucestershire CC ex p Barry (1996): Where a public body has a statutory duty to meet the needs of particular individuals, it may not take resources into consideration

Facts

The council decided to give greater priority to the seriously disabled following the withdrawal of a Government grant. This applicant's needs were not reassessed in light of the decision and they were informed by a standard form letter. The applicant applied for judicial review. The first instance judgment split the process into two stages: the discretionary assessment stage in which resources might be considered; and the provision of arrangements based on the assessment in which resources were irrelevant. The applicant appealed against the High Court's decision that, in assessing or reassessing a disabled person's needs under s 2(1) of the Chronically Sick and Disabled Persons Act 1970, the council could take account of the resources available.

Decision
The Court of Appeal held that a local authority was not entitled to take resources into account when performing its duty (under s 2(1) of the Chronically Sick and Disabled Persons Act 1970) of determining whether it should make arrangements to meet the needs of a disabled person as set out in that section. Once the needs of a disabled person were identified, resources might be taken into account when considering how to meet those needs.

Comment
This decision is restricted to those duties to provide for an individual's *needs*. Where an arrangement is simply *desirable*, then resources may be considered when making the assessment. Swinton LJ used s 29 of the National Assistance Act 1948 and s 47(1) of the National Health Service and Community Care Act 1990 as examples of when it would be proper to take resources into account.

R v North Derbyshire HA ex p Fisher (1997): A Health Authority must take national policy into account when allocating resources

Facts
The applicant, who suffered from multiple sclerosis, was considered by a consultant neurologist to be suitable for a course of beta-interferon. The Trust responsible for his care declined to fund the treatment as their policy, because of a lack of resources, was only to fund those patients involved in a national clinical trial. This policy was contrary to an NHS circular, which stated: 'Where the treatment with beta-interferon is appropriate, it is suggested that treatment should be initiated and the drug prescribed by the specialist.' The applicant sought a judicial review of the Trust's decision.

Decision
The High Court held that the NHS circular was not mandatory but sought only to provide guidance. However, although it was not mandatory, the Trust should at least have taken the guidance into account. Since the Trust had entirely disregarded the circular, their policy was unlawful. The Trust was ordered to formulate and implement a new policy to take account of the circular.

Dyson J stated: '[The Trust] knew that their own policy amounted to a blanket ban on beta-interferon treatment. A blanket ban was the very antithesis of national policy, whose aim was to target the drug appropriately at patients who were most likely to benefit from treatment.'

R v North and East Devon HA ex p Coughlan (1999): Where an authority creates a legitimate expectation of substantial benefit, any decision that frustrates that expectation may be so unfair as to be an abuse of power

Facts
The appellant was tetraplegic and permanently resident in a purpose-built NHS facility, Mardon House. When she was originally transferred to the facility, it was on

the express promise that it would be her home for as long as she wished. The NHS drew a distinction between 'general' and 'specialist' nursing services. Following guidance from the Secretary of State, delineating the division of responsibility between the NHS and social services, the Health Authority reviewed the care options for the appellant and other patients. The review concluded that they did not meet the eligibility criteria for NHS care, and the Health Authority subsequently decided to close Mardon House without detailing any provisions for the provision of alternative care. The appellant applied for judicial review and the Health Authority's decision was quashed by the judge at first instance. The Health Authority appealed.

Decision

The Court of Appeal dismissed the appeal. Amongst other grounds, the Court of Appeal held that the appellant had a legitimate expectation that the Health Authority would provide for her care at Mardon House. A legitimate expectation arises from a lawful promise of an important benefit limited to a few individuals. Where a public body treats the individual contrary to this expectation there are three possible outcomes:

(a) The court may decide that the authority is only required to bear in mind its previous policy or representation, giving it the weight it thinks right. There the court is confined to review on *Wednesbury* grounds.

(b) The court may decide that the promise or practice induces a legitimate expectation of being consulted, and the court will require an opportunity for consultation to be given unless there is an overriding reason to resile from it, when the court itself will judge the adequacy of the reason advanced for the change in policy.

(c) Where the court decides that a lawful promise or practice has induced a legitimate expectation of a substantive benefit, the court will, in a proper case, decide whether it is an abuse of power to frustrate that expectation by adopting a new course of action.

In such circumstances the court is not restricted to reviewing the decision on *Wednesbury* grounds. In the present case, fairness required the Health Authority not to resile from their promise, since there was no overriding justification and the Health Authority's failure to weigh the conflicting interests correctly was unfair and an abuse of power.

North West Lancashire HA v A, D and G (1999): It is unlawful to operate a blanket ban that makes no allowance for the clinical need of the individual

Facts

The respondents were transsexuals seeking gender reassignment treatment and surgery. The Health Authority refused to fund the treatment based on its policy to assign a low priority for funding to a number of procedures it considered to be ineffective in producing a health gain. Gender reassignment surgery was one of the procedures listed for which – apart from general psychiatric and psychological services – the Authority would not provide a service apart from in exceptional circumstances or where there was an overriding clinical need. At first instance, an order was granted quashing the Health Authority's decision and its policy. The Authority appealed.

Decision

The Court of Appeal dismissed the appeal. In prioritising life-threatening and serious illness, the precise allocation of resources is a matter for the Health Authority and not the court. However, the Authority must 'accurately assess the nature and seriousness of each type of illness ... determine the effectiveness of various forms of treatment for it; and ... give proper effect to that assessment and that determination in the formulation and individual application of its policy'. The Authority's policy was flawed because it did not treat transsexualism as an illness and, because it did not believe in such a treatment for the condition, its policy effectively amounted to a blanket ban.

R v Ethical Committee of St Mary's Hospital (Manchester) ex p Harriott (1988): A decision will be unlawful if it discriminates against persons on grounds that are protected by law

Facts

The applicant sought judicial review of a decision that rejected her application for IVF treatment because she was unsuitable. She had a criminal record for prostitution and had already been rejected by the adoption agencies she had applied to.

Decision

The High Court refused the application. The Committee's policy would have been unlawful had it decided to 'refuse all such treatment to anyone who was a Jew or coloured'.

Comment

Policies that discriminate on the basis of colour or race will contravene the Race Relations Act 1976. Similarly, discrimination between the sexes or on the basis of marital status may contravene the Sex Discrimination Act 1975. The Disability Discrimination Act 1995 prohibits discrimination on the grounds of disability. Article 14, Schedule 1 to the HRA 1998 may also be relevant (see above).

Hurtado v Switzerland (1994): A failure to provide necessary medical care may breach the European Convention on Human Rights and the HRA 1998

Facts

The applicant had been arrested on a drugs charge. He had been made to wear soiled clothing and was denied immediate medical assistance – a stun grenade had been used during the arrest.

Decision

The European Commission, deciding on the merits of the case, held that the failure to provide necessary medical care could amount to inhuman or degrading treatment and breach Article 3 of the European Convention on Human Rights.

Comment

It may be difficult to succeed where the claim is for a particular treatment rather than medical care in general, and in *North West Lancashire HA v A, D and G* (see above), the court held that Article 3 did not impose an obligation to provide free treatment. The court also rejected a claim under Article 8: Auld LJ stated that 'Art 8 imposes no positive obligation to provide treatment'. This case may be contrasted with *Van Kuck v Germany* (2003), in which a transsexual claimed that the German state had breached Article 8 because the domestic courts had failed to order her insurance company to reimburse her for the cost of hormone treatment and gender reassignment surgery. The European Court noted that Article 8 may impose a positive obligation on the state, but the extent of the obligation was subject to a margin of appreciation. The court held that there had been a breach of Article 8 since the domestic courts had failed to achieve a fair balance between the rights of the insurance company and the applicant and because the burden placed on the applicant to show the medical necessity of the treatment was disproportionate.

Where the Health Authority has created a legitimate expectation for the provision of a resource then Article 8 may make it unlawful for the Authority to subsequently withdraw that resource. Thus, in *R v North and East Devon HA ex p Coughlan* (see above), withdrawing the provision of specialist nursing home accommodation without providing a suitable alternative was held to be a breach of Article 8. Whether this might apply to other resources, such as kidney dialysis, is not certain.

In *R (on the Application of Burke) v GMC* (2004), which involved a judicial review of GMC guidance on withdrawing and withholding treatment, the High Court held that a competent patient, whether contemporaneously or by advance directive, could dictate what was in his own best interests even if the doctor was unwilling to provide that treatment. While the court would still refrain from dictating to a doctor that he must provide a particular treatment, the doctor would remain under a duty to treat that person until finding another physician to provide it. Declaratory relief could be ordered against the doctor and a mandatory order could be made against the Trust or Health Authority. The right for the patient to determine which treatment is in his own best interests is protected by Article 8 and possibly Article 3 of the European Convention on Human Rights and the HRA 1998. The case is, however, likely to be appealed.

CHAPTER 12

MEDICAL NEGLIGENCE

Medical negligence costs for the financial year 1990–91 were around £50 Million. A recent analysis of the records from within one Health Authority has estimated that the rate of litigation increased from 0.46 to 0.81 closed claims per 1,000 completed consultant episodes. This represents an estimated cost to the NHS of £84 million (not including administrative and in-house legal costs), which is one quarter of 1% of the annual cost of the NHS (Fenn et al, 2000). In March 2000, the National Audit Office (NAO) reported that the outstanding claims against the NHS had a net value of £2.6 billion, with another £1.3 billion of claims waiting to be made. In 1999–2000 alone there were 10,000 new claims (NAO, 2001). In 2001–02, the cost to the NHS of medical negligence claims was £446 million (Chief Medical Officer (CMO), 2003). When considering these costs, it should be borne in mind that 'Untoward harmful consequences of healthcare are more common than has previously been recognised', with up to 1 in 10 hospital in-patient admissions resulting 'in some kind of adverse event' and almost 1 in 5 patients reporting that they were a 'victim of a medication error' within the last two years (CMO, 2003).

These claims were protracted, with 22% being over 10 years old, and expensive, with the administrative costs often exceeding the damages awarded. Furthermore, many patients were deterred from making claims because of the costs, ignorance that they could make a claim or a lack of a suitable remedy. The NAO noted that 'claimants often want a wider range of remedies than litigation is designed to provide, for example, an apology, an explanation or reassurance that it will not happen again'. The success rate of claims funded by legal aid was only 24%. However, for cases proceeding beyond the initial investigation, the success rate rose from 46% in 1996–97 to 61% in 1999–2000 (NAO, 2001).

In 2003, the CMO published a consultation document, *Making Amends*, with the aim of ensuring 'that resources are better targeted to meeting the needs of the harmed patient' (CMO, 2003). The CMO expressly denied it was a cost-cutting exercise. He bemoaned the antagonistic nature of medical negligence litigation and argued that, while the harmed patient should receive an apology, an explanation, 'and where appropriate, financial compensation', the 'primary aim must be to reduce the number of medical errors that occur'. The CMO suggested that there were a number of reasons why the system needs reform: its complexity; its unfairness, with different outcomes for similar cases; its slowness to achieve resolution; its cost, both in administrative expense and on clinical time and 'public confidence'; the limitation of remedy to damages with no provision for explanation, apology or 'reassurance that action has been taken to prevent repetition'; and the encouragement of secrecy and defensive medicine. The CMO rejected a comprehensive no-fault compensation scheme primarily because it was too expensive. A tribunal system was also rejected because it was 'likely to end up as a replica of the courts'. Instead, the CMO recommended 'The establishment of a new system of providing redress for patients who have been harmed as a result of serious substandard NHS hospital care ...' (the NHS Redress Scheme).

The Scheme would consist of four components: investigation; explanation; remedial care; and financial recompense for expenses and care that the NHS was unable to provide. This Scheme would not replace the right to take the case to court but, if the package of 'care and compensation under the NHS Redress Scheme' were accepted, the patient would have to waive the right to sue. For those cases not falling within the ambit of the scheme, the CMO recommended: an initial attempt at mediation; the use of periodic payments rather than a lump sum; that the damages should no longer reflect the cost of private healthcare; and that judges should be specially trained to handle medical negligence claims.

At present, unless the case is settled (95% of claims – CMO, 2003), it will proceed to court. As with ordinary negligence, the elements of medical negligence are duty of care, breach of duty and damage.

12.1   Duty of care

Pippin v Sheppard (1822): A doctor owes a duty of care to anyone he accepts as a patient

Facts

The defendant surgeon treated the injuries and wounds of the plaintiff. The treatment was careless and the plaintiff's wound became inflamed and more painful. Her life was also endangered and she had to undergo further treatment by other surgeons.

Decision

The court held it was not relevant who retained or employed the surgeon but was enough that he had treated the plaintiff. It was also unnecessary for the plaintiff's declaration to allege that the surgeon owed a duty or that he had undertaken to treat the plaintiff skilfully.

Comment

See also *Edgar v Lamont* (1914), in which the court held that the doctor owed a duty to the patient irrespective of who actually paid the bill. In *R v Bateman* (1925) – a manslaughter case – the court stated: 'If a doctor holds himself out as possessing special skill and knowledge, and he is consulted, as possessing such skill and knowledge, by or on behalf of the patient, he owes a duty to the patient to use caution in undertaking the treatment.'

F v West Berkshire HA (1989): The doctor is under no legal obligation to treat a person who is not his patient

Facts

See 3.2 and 3.4 above.

Decision

See 3.2 and 3.4 above. Lord Goff stated: 'The "doctor in the house" who volunteers to assist a lady in the audience who, overcome by the drama or by the heat in the theatre, has fainted away is impelled to act by no greater duty than that imposed by his own Hippocratic oath.'

Comment

There may be professional obligations to assist strangers involved in accidents; see GMC (2001), para 9, which states: 'In an emergency, you must offer anyone at risk the treatment you could reasonably be expected to provide.' See also NMC (2002), para 8.5. Also, under Schedule 2 to the National Health Service (General Medical Services) Regulations 1992, GPs are under a statutory duty to treat emergencies within their practice area. Paragraph 4(1) states:

By virtue of his contract with the FHSA a GP must assist:

...

(h) persons to whom he may be requested to give treatment which is immediately required owing to an accident or other emergency at any place in his practice area, provided that –
   (i) he is not, at the time of the request, relieved of liability to give treatment under para 5 (if the doctor is elderly or infirm); and
   (ii) he is not, at the time of the request, relieved under para 19(2) (if another doctor is already present), of his obligation to give treatment personally; and
   (iii) he is available to provide such treatment ...

Thake v Maurice (1986): A doctor may owe a duty of care to a third party who is not his patient if injury is reasonably foreseeable

Facts

The plaintiff husband underwent a vasectomy. The defendant failed to warn either of the plaintiffs (husband and wife) of the risk that the vasectomy would fail to sterilise Mr Thake. The plaintiff wife subsequently became pregnant. They sued the defendant in both negligence and contract.

Decision

The Court of Appeal held that the failure to warn of the risk of failure was a breach of the surgeon's duty of care that he owed to both the husband and his wife.

Comment

See also *Tredget v Bexley HA* (1994), in which the defendants were liable for negligently inflicted psychiatric harm to the parents of a child who died after a negligently performed delivery. The duty to third parties also encompasses a duty to breach the patient's confidence where an identified or identifiable third party is at risk (see 10.3 above). *PD v Dr Harvey and Others* (2003) is an interesting Australian case. PD and FH attended together for blood tests to ensure neither had HIV prior to their getting married. FH was HIV positive. The New South Wales Supreme Court held that the doctor owed PD a duty of care in relation to FH's HIV status. The duty was not to ensure that she did not become infected, '[h]owever the scope of the duty required the doctors to take all reasonable steps to protect the plaintiff from what ... was clearly a foreseeable danger to her'. The Public Health Act 1991 prevented direct disclosure to PD of FH's status. However, the doctor could have informed the Director General. This duty certainly existed while PD was a patient, but the court's statement, 'that while she remained a patient the doctors were in breach of their obligation to her', might imply that the duty does not exist in relation to non-patients. This would be debatable in this country (see 10.3 above).

Goodwill v British Pregnancy Advisory Service (1996): A doctor will not owe a duty of care to third parties if they are not identifiable at the time of the breach

Facts

M had a vasectomy performed by the defendants. He was informed that the operation had been successful and that he would no longer need to use contraception to avoid pregnancy. The plaintiff, who was not M's partner at the time of the operation, began a sexual relationship with M. She subsequently became pregnant and sued the defendants.

Decision

The Court of Appeal held that there was no liability. The relationship between the doctors and the future sexual partners of a man undergoing a vasectomy was not sufficiently close to establish a duty of care. Gibson LJ applied the principles established in *Hedley Byrne* and stated:

I cannot see that it can properly be said of the defendants that they voluntarily assumed responsibility to the plaintiff when giving advice to Mr MacKinlay. At that time they had no knowledge of her, she was not an existing sexual partner of Mr MacKinlay but was merely, like any other woman in the world, a potential future sexual partner of his, that is to say a member of an indeterminately large class of females who might have sexual relations with Mr MacKinlay during his lifetime.

Powell v Boldaz (1997): There is no doctor-patient relationship between a doctor and the relatives of his patient

Facts

A young boy in the care of the defendants died after the defendants failed to diagnose that the boy was suffering from Addison's disease. The action for negligence, in failing to diagnose the disease, and the claim for damages – for psychiatric illness suffered by the boy's mother as a result of his death – were settled. The plaintiffs, however, further alleged that, following R's death, the defendants had attempted to cover up their negligence and that this had caused the first plaintiff psychiatric injury and had exacerbated the second plaintiff's psychiatric complaints. They brought a claim for injury and economic loss based on the events after their son's death. The claims were struck out at first instance and the plaintiffs appealed.

Decision

The Court of Appeal denied the appeal. A doctor-patient relationship is not established between the doctor and his patient's relatives when the doctor tells his patient's relatives that the patient has died. There was no freestanding duty of candour, irrespective of the doctor-patient relationship. Smith LJ stated:

I do not think that a doctor who has been treating a patient who has died, who tells relatives what has happened, thereby undertakes the doctor-patient relationship towards the relatives. It is a situation that calls for sensitivity, tact and discretion, but the mere fact that the communicator is a doctor, does not, without more, mean that he undertakes the doctor-patient relationship.

12.2 Liability of hospitals

Collins v Hertfordshire County Council (1947): Hospitals will be vicariously liable for the negligence of their employees

Facts

The night before an operation to remove an extensive growth from the jaw of the plaintiff's husband, the house surgeon (a final year medical student) took an order over the phone from the visiting surgeon. The house surgeon misheard the order and obtained a solution of cocaine and adrenaline instead of procaine and adrenaline. The surgeon failed to check the label and administered a dose of the solution that killed the plaintiff's husband.

Decision

The High Court held that the hospital was vicariously liable for the actions of the house surgeon as their employee. The hospital was not liable for the negligence of the visiting surgeon.

Comment

See also the DoH guidance on vicarious liability: *NHS Indemnity* (DoH, 1996). This states:

NHS bodies are vicariously liable for the negligent act and omissions of their employees and should have arrangements for meeting this liability.

NHS Indemnity applies where:
(a) the negligent healthcare professional was:
      (i)   working under a contract of employment and the negligence occurred in the course of that employment;
      (ii) not working under a contract of employment but was contracted to an NHS body to provide services to persons to whom that NHS body owed a duty of care;
      (iii) neither of the above but otherwise owed a duty of care to the persons injured;
(b) persons, not employed under a contract of employment and who may or may not be a healthcare professional, who owe a duty of care to the persons injured. These include locums; medical academic staff with honorary contracts; students; those conducting clinical trials; charitable volunteers; persons undergoing further professional education, training and examinations; students and staff working on income generation projects.

Where these principles apply, NHS bodies should accept full financial liability where negligent harm has occurred, and not seek to recover their costs from the healthcare professional involved.

Bull v Devon AHA (1993): The hospital may also be directly liable for failing to provide a reasonable system of care

Facts

The plaintiff was a woman who had presented with a twin pregnancy. After the first twin was born, the junior doctor called for urgent assistance from a senior colleague. The hospital operated a split site and the other doctor was in the gynaecology department over a mile away from the obstetric unit. It took over an hour for him to arrive and the second twin was born with severe brain damage.

Decision

The Court of Appeal held that the Health Authority was negligent because of its failure to provide and implement an efficient system of care.

Comment

In *Cassidy v Ministry of Health* (1951) (see 12.5 below), Denning LJ stated:

In my opinion, authorities who run a hospital, be they local authorities, government boards, or any other corporation, are in law under the self-same duty as the humblest doctor. Whenever they accept a patient for treatment, they must use reasonable care and skill to cure him of his ailment.

See also Lord Greene MR's judgment in *Gold v Essex County Council* (1942):

... if the obligation is undertaken by a corporation, or a body of trustees or governors, they cannot escape liability for its breach, any more than an individual can; and it is no answer to say that the obligation is one which on the face of it they could never perform themselves ... I cannot myself see any sufficient ground for saying that the respondents do not undertake towards the patient the obligation of nursing him as distinct from the obligation of providing a skilful nurse.

Robertson v Nottingham HA (1997): The duty of a hospital to provide care is a non-delegable duty

Facts

The plaintiff sued for negligence after she had been born with cerebral palsy. She alleged that the defendants had negligently interpreted cardiotocographic (CTG) recordings and had failed to act promptly enough once the trace became abnormal.

Decision

The Court of Appeal held that the delay caused by the doctor's incompetence was no more than two hours. There was evidence that the catastrophic event that caused the plaintiff's condition had occurred before the mother had been admitted to hospital. Thus, the culpable delay had not contributed to the injury and there was no liability. Brooke LJ stated:

Although it is customary to say that a Health Authority is vicariously liable for a breach of duty if its responsible servants or agents fail to set up a safe system of operation in relation to what are essentially management as opposed to clinical matters, this formulation may tend to cloud the fact that in any event it has a non-delegable duty to establish a proper system of care just as much as it has a duty to engage competent staff and a duty to provide proper and safe equipment and safe premises.

Comment

Direct liability has been found for: unsafe drug procedures (*Collins v Hertfordshire County Council* (1947)); negligently drafted consent forms (*Worster v City & Hackney HA* (1987)); failure to provide sufficiently skilled staff (*Wilsher v Essex AHA* (1986) CA – judgment reversed by House of Lords on causation); inadequate supervision of staff (*Jones v Manchester Corp* (1952)); inadequate system for checking equipment (*Denton v South West Thames RHA* (1981)); and a failure to communicate up to date information to members of staff (*Blyth v Bloomsbury HA* (1993), see 2.4 above).

12.3   Liability of the ambulance service

Kent v Griffiths (2000): Once it has agreed to answer a 999 call the ambulance service owes a duty of care to the subject of the call

Facts
P suffered a respiratory arrest after an ambulance failed to arrive in a reasonable time. No satisfactory reason was given for the delay.

Decision
The Court of Appeal held that the ambulance service could owe a duty of care to a member of the public on whose behalf a 999 call had been made if, for no good reason, an ambulance it despatched failed to arrive within a reasonable time. Lord Woolf MR stated:

Here what was being provided was a health service ... Why should the position of the ambulance staff be different from that of doctors or nurses? In addition the arguments based on public policy are much weaker in the case of the ambulance service than they are in the case of the police or fire service. The police and fire services' primary obligation is to the public at large ... But in the case of the ambulance service in this particular case, the only member of the public who could be adversely affected was the claimant ... Having decided to provide an ambulance an explanation is required to justify a failure to attend within reasonable time.

Comment
Under similar circumstances, it is unlikely that the police or fire service would be held to owe a duty of care to the subject of a 999 call. See *Capital and Counties plc v Hampshire County Council* (1996) CA.

12.4   Standard of care

Bolam v Friern Hospital Management Committee (1957): A doctor will not be liable in negligence if he acts in accordance with a practice accepted as proper by a responsible body of doctors

Facts
The plaintiff, who suffered from depression, was treated with electro-convulsive therapy (ECT). This treatment induces convulsions (a 'fit') by passing an electrical current through the brain. The defendants failed to warn the plaintiff of the slight risk of bone fracture. In accordance with the hospital's normal practice the doctors did not administer a muscle relaxant or apply manual restraint. The plaintiff suffered bilateral hip fractures. The plaintiff alleged negligence in:

- failing to use a muscle relaxant;
- failing to provide sufficient manual restraint;
- failing to warn of the risks associated with the treatment.

Expert opinion was divided on the issues.

Decision

The jury in the High Court found the defendants not liable for negligence. In directing the jury, McNair J stated:

A doctor is not guilty of negligence if he has acted in accordance with a practice accepted as proper by a responsible body of medical men skilled in that particular art ... Putting it the other way round, a doctor is not negligent, if he is acting in accordance with such a practice, merely because there is a body of opinion that takes a contrary view.

Comment

The *Bolam* test has been accepted and applied in many cases including those before the House of Lords. Thus, it has been held to apply to diagnosis (*Maynard v West Midlands RHA* (1984) HL), treatment (*Whitehouse v Jordan* (1981) HL) and disclosure of information (*Sidaway v Board of Governors of the Bethlem Royal Hospital and the Maudsley Hospital* (1985) HL (see 2.4 above)). It has also been applied to the issue of causation (see *Bolitho v City and Hackney HA* (1997) HL, below).

Bolitho v City and Hackney HA (1997): The court reserves the right to decide that a responsible body of physicians would not accept the practice as proper

Facts

See 12.5 below.

Decision

See 12.5 below. Lord Browne-Wilkinson stated:

[I]n my view, the court is not bound to hold that a defendant doctor escapes liability for negligent treatment or diagnosis just because he leads evidence from a number of medical experts who are genuinely of the opinion that the defendant's treatment or diagnosis accorded with sound medical practice ... The use of these adjectives [in previous cases] – responsible, reasonable and respectable – all show that the court has to be satisfied that the exponents of the body of opinion relied upon can demonstrate that such opinion has a logical basis ... the judge, before accepting a body of opinion as being responsible, reasonable or respectable, will need to be satisfied that, in forming their views, the experts have directed their minds to the question of comparative risks and benefits and have reached a defensible conclusion on the matter.

However, he later added the caveat:

I emphasise that in my view it will very seldom be right for a judge to reach the conclusion that views genuinely held by a competent medical expert are unreasonable. The assessment of medical risks and benefits is a matter of clinical judgment which a judge would not normally be able to make without expert evidence ... It is only where a judge can be satisfied that the body of expert opinion cannot be logically supported at all that such opinion will not provide the benchmark by reference to which the defendant's conduct falls to be assessed.

Comment

The court's power to rule that a medical practice is negligent pre-existed *Bolitho*, but was used so sparingly that Lord Scarman was able to state, in *Sidaway*, that: 'The *Bolam* principle may be formulated as a rule that a doctor is not negligent if he acts in accordance with a practice accepted as proper by a responsible body of medical opinion even though other doctors adopt a different practice. In short, the law imposes the duty of care: but the standard of care is a matter of medical judgment.' *Bolitho* may be seen as either adding a caveat to the *Bolam* test or simply as clarifying the inherent ambiguity of the standard. In either case, the judgment is important and may be seen as a key case within the trend towards a less deferential approach to the medical profession: see Brazier and Miola (2000) and Lord Woolf (2001). For an analysis of the impact of *Bolitho* on subsequent cases, see Maclean (2002b). For notable examples of instances where the court has ruled against accepted medical practice prior to *Bolitho*, see *Hucks v Cole* (1994) CA (decided in 1968), *Newell and Newell v Goldenberg* (1995) (2.4 above) and *Smith v Tunbridge Wells HA* (1994) (2.4 above).

Despite *Bolitho*, the reluctance of the courts to rule a medical opinion as unreasonable remains and may be seen in the Court of Appeal's judgment in *Wisniewski v Central Manchester HA* (1998). The Court of Appeal overruled the High Court's decision that the expert witness's evidence could not be logically supported as representing a reasonable body of medical opinion. However, the defendant's appeal was still dismissed on other grounds. *Marriott v West Midlands HA* (1999) is a case that may be used to support a claim that *Bolitho* will make a difference; however, the case is open to different interpretations and not all analyses justify that claim (Compare Brazier and Miola, 2000 with Maclean, 2002b).

Maynard v West Midlands RHA (1985): The court will not choose between the different opinions of responsible bodies of physicians

Facts
The plaintiff underwent a diagnostic mediastinoscopy to determine whether tuberculosis or Hodgkin's disease caused her enlarged lymph nodes. During the operation her left recurrent laryngeal nerve was damaged, resulting in paralysis of her left vocal cord. The plaintiff sued the Health Authority alleging that the diagnosis of tuberculosis was certain enough to make the doctors negligent in requiring the further diagnostic procedure. The expert witnesses were divided as to whether the decision to operate was appropriate. At first instance the defendants were held to be negligent. The Court of Appeal overturned the decision and the plaintiff appealed.

Decision
The House of Lords denied the appeal. The defendants had not been negligent. Lord Scarman stated:

It is not enough to show that there is a body of competent professional opinion which considers theirs as a wrong decision, if there also exists a body of professional opinion, equally competent, which supports the decision as reasonable in the circumstances ... I do not think that the words of Lord President (Clyde) in *Hunter v Hanley* 1955 SLT 213, 217 can be bettered: 'In the realm of diagnosis and treatment there is ample scope for genuine difference of opinion and one man is not negligent merely because his conclusion differs from that of other medical men ... The true test for establishing negligence in diagnosis or treatment on the part of a doctor is whether he has been proved to be guilty of such failure as no doctor of ordinary skill would be guilty of if acting with ordinary care.'

Comment

Under Part 35, r 35.7 of the Civil Procedure Rules 1998, the court has the power to direct that a single joint expert is appointed rather than each party having their own expert. However, where differing schools of thought exist, the choice of a single expert might prevent any challenge to that expert's view and would cause the court to choose that a particular school of thought be default. In those cases, the Court of Appeal has held that the court should exercise its discretion and allow the appointment of separate experts: see *Oxley v Penwarden* (2001).

DeFreitas v O'Brien (1995): The body of responsible medical opinion does not have to be substantial

Facts

The plaintiff suffered from chronic back and neck pain. An initial operation was unsuccessful and the plaintiff developed further pain and a swelling in the small of her back. Despite a myelogram indicating that there was no evidence of nerve root compression, she underwent a second operation during which the surgeon noted that there was severe compression of the L4-S1 nerve roots. After the operation she developed further pain in her back and legs that was relieved by epidural injections. The back wound became infected and her condition deteriorated. Eventually she underwent an operation to close a fistula that had been leaking cerebrospinal fluid (CSF) (the fluid that bathes the brain and spinal cord). She was left with an indwelling shunt and chronic arachnoiditis (inflammation of one of the layers of tissue that contains the CSF). The plaintiff claimed that the operations and management of the CSF leak were negligent. The evidence was that within the 1,000+ doctors who comprised the specialities of orthopaedics and neurosurgery there were only 11 who would be called 'spinal surgeons'. It was only this small sub-specialised group who would have countenanced surgery in this case. At first instance the judge found the defendant not liable. The plaintiff appealed.

Decision

The Court of Appeal dismissed the appeal.

Otton LJ stated: 'I do not consider the learned judge fell into an error in not considering whether the body of spinal surgeons had to be substantial. It was sufficient if he was satisfied that there was a responsible body.'

Comment

This decision has been criticised for licensing risk-taking. In one sense the Court of Appeal was correct in noting that the appropriate test is 'responsible' but the issue of the number of doctors required to constitute a body of opinion is important. As Khan and Robson (1995) have noted, 'Numbers must play a part in determining whether the practice is accepted and therefore responsible'.

Wilsher v Essex AHA (1988): The standard of care depends on the post occupied by the doctor and not on the level of training the doctor has received

Facts
See 12.5 below.

Decision
See 12.5 below.

Comment
In the Court of Appeal hearing of the case (1986), the majority held that the standard of care required of a doctor is assessed in relation to the post he holds rather than the training he has received. In rejecting the individualised standard, Mustill LJ stated, 'this notion of a duty tailored to the actor, rather than to the act which he elects to perform, has no place in the law of tort'. The House of Lords did not consider this point as the issue before them was solely one of causation.

Roe v Ministry of Health (1954): The standard of care is to be judged against the knowledge available at the time of the incident and not at the time of the trial

Facts
The two plaintiffs were each given a spinal anaesthetic. The anaesthetic administered had been stored in phenol that had seeped through microscopic cracks in the glass ampoules and contaminated the anaesthetic. Both plaintiffs were left permanently paralysed. The risk that this might occur was first drawn attention to in a book published in 1951, four years after the plaintiffs had received the fateful anaesthetics.

Decision
The Court of Appeal denied the appeal. There was no liability. The standard of care was to be judged against the knowledge that prevailed at the time of the incident.

Lord Denning stated: 'It is so easy to be wise after the event ... we must not look at the 1947 accident with 1954 spectacles.'

Crawford v Board of Governors of Charing Cross Hospital (1953): The standard of current knowledge will not be based on the publication of isolated articles in medical journals

Facts
The plaintiff underwent a bladder operation during which his left arm was positioned in such a way that it damaged the nerves, resulting in permanent weakness. The position was a standard one but, six months prior to the operation, an article had appeared in *The Lancet* warning of the potential dangers of the position. The anaesthetist looking after the patient had not read the article. At first instance the judge held that the anaesthetist was negligent in failing to keep up to date. The defendants appealed.

Decision

The Court of Appeal allowed the appeal. There was no evidence of negligence. Lord Denning stated:

... it would, I think, be putting too high a burden on a medical man to say that he has to read every article appearing in the current medical press; and it would be quite wrong to suggest that a medical man is negligent because he does not at once put into operation the suggestions which some contributor or other might make in a medical journal. The time may come in a particular case when a new recommendation may be so well proved and so well known, and so well accepted that it should be adopted, but that was not so in this case.

Hunter v Hanley (1955): Departure from accepted practice does not automatically constitute negligence

Facts

The plaintiff suffered from chronic bronchitis for which the defendant was treating her by a course of intra-muscular injections of an antibiotic. On the final injection the needle broke and the tip remained embedded in the plaintiff's buttock. The plaintiff alleged the defendant was negligent in the choice of needle he used. At first instance the defendant was found not liable. The plaintiff appealed.

Decision

The Inner House of the Scottish Court of Session held that the judge's direction to the jury was inaccurate. A new trial was ordered. Lord President Clyde stated that:

... a deviation [from ordinary professional practice] is not necessarily evidence of negligence. Indeed it would be disastrous if this were so, for all inducement to progress in medical science would then be destroyed. Even a substantial deviation from normal practice may be warranted by the particular circumstances. To establish liability by a doctor where deviation from normal practice is alleged, three facts require to be established. First of all it must be proved that there is a usual and normal practice; secondly it must be proved that the defender has not adopted that practice; and thirdly (and this is of crucial importance) it must be established that the course the doctor adopted is one which no professional man of ordinary skill would have taken if he had been acting with ordinary care.

Wilsher v Essex AHA (1988): The standard of care required may be lower in an emergency

Facts

See 12.5 below.

Decision

See 12.5 below.

Comment

In the Court of Appeal hearing of the case (1986), Mustill LJ stated: 'An emergency may overburden the available resources, and, if an individual is forced by circumstances to do many things at once, the fact that he does one of them incorrectly should not lightly be taken as negligence.' This point was not considered by the House of Lords. Further support comes from *Powell v Boldaz* (1997) (see 12.1 above), in which Smith LJ stated: 'a doctor who goes to the assistance of a stranger injured in an accident ... does not as a rule undertake the doctor-patient relationship so as to make him liable for lack of care, but only a duty not to make the condition of the victim worse.' This mirrors his statement in *Capital and Counties v Hampshire County Council* (1997):

... a doctor who happened to witness a road accident will very likely go to the assistance of anyone injured, but he is not under any legal obligation to do so (save in certain limited circumstances ...) and the relationship of the doctor and patient does not arise. If he volunteer his assistance, his only duty as a matter of law is not to make the victim's condition worse.

This suggested standard is analogous to that expected of public bodies exercising a statutory power (see *Stovin v Wise* (1996)). However, Smith LJ's comments are *obiter* and in these circumstances the doctor is not acting as an agent for a public body but as a private individual with the special skills of a doctor. Once he has stopped to offer assistance the doctor has voluntarily assumed responsibility and thus a duty of care should exist. It is suggested that the *Bolam* standard – which allows the difficulty of the circumstances to be taken into account – would apply.

12.5 Breach of duty and causation

Ashcroft v Mersey RHA (1983): The burden of proof lies with the plaintiff to prove that, on the balance of probabilities, the defendant was negligent

Facts
The plaintiff underwent an operation on her left ear to remove some granulation tissue on her eardrum. During the operation the surgeon damaged the plaintiff's facial nerve resulting in a partial paralysis of the left side of her face. The plaintiff's expert witness testified that the injury could only have occurred through negligence. The defendant, supported by the evidence of an eminent ear surgeon, denied the claim.

Decision
The High Court held that the plaintiff had failed to establish, on the balance of probabilities, that the surgeon had fallen below the requisite standard of care.

Comment
In *Bolitho*, Lord Brown-Wilkinson stated: 'Where, as in the present case, a breach of a duty of care is proved or admitted, the burden still lies on the plaintiff to prove that such breach caused the injury suffered.'

Barnett v Chelsea and Kensington Hospital Management Committee (1969): The plaintiffs must prove that the damage would not have occurred but for the negligence of the defendants

Facts
The plaintiff's husband, along with two other night watchmen, went to the Accident and Emergency Department of the defendant's hospital. They complained to the duty nurse that they had been vomiting continuously since drinking some tea. The nurse informed the on-duty doctor who replied that they should go home to bed and call in their own doctors. The plaintiff's husband died a few hours later from arsenic poisoning. The plaintiff sued.

Decision

The High Court held that the doctor had breached his duty of care but the plaintiff's husband would have died whatever the doctor had done. The defendants' lack of care had not caused Mr Barnett's death.

Bolitho v City and Hackney HA (1997): Where the doctor has breached his duty of care by an omission, the *Bolam* test may be applied in determining whether the omission has caused the plaintiff's damage

Facts

The plaintiff was a two-year-old boy who was admitted to hospital suffering from the respiratory infection, croup. His condition fluctuated and the doctors were asked to see him but failed to do so. The plaintiff deteriorated again and, while the nurse was trying to 'bleep' one of the doctors, the nurse with the plaintiff set off the emergency buzzer. The plaintiff suffered a cardiac arrest and was left with severe brain damage. The plaintiff's experts claimed that the disastrous outcome could have been avoided if the plaintiff had been intubated. The defendants acknowledged that the doctor had breached her duty of care by failing to attend the plaintiff when asked to by the nurse but claimed that she would not have intubated the plaintiff even if she had attended. The defendant's experts testified that, on the evidence, intubating the plaintiff would not have been the desirable or necessary course of action. At first instance, faced with a division of expert opinion, the judge held that negligence had not been proved. The plaintiff appealed, first to the Court of Appeal and then to the House of Lords.

Decision

The House of Lords turned down the appeal. Causation had not been proven. Lord Browne-Wilkinson stated:

There were ... two questions for the judge to decide on causation: (1) 'What would Dr Horn have done, or authorised to be done, if she had attended Patrick?' And: (2) 'If she would not have intubated, would that have been negligent?' The *Bolam* test has no relevance to the first of those questions but is central to the second.

Wilsher v Essex AHA (1988): Where the defendant's negligence is just one of many possible causes of the plaintiff's damage, it is for the plaintiff to prove – on the balance of probabilities – that, but for the defendant's negligence, the damage would not have occurred

Facts

The plaintiff was a baby born three months prematurely. He had breathing problems and needed supplemental oxygen. In order to monitor treatment, a catheter was inserted. Unfortunately it was inserted into a vein rather than an artery, which meant that the oxygen levels measured appeared to be lower than they actually were. The line was removed and replaced but was again misplaced into a vein. X-rays were taken to inspect the position of the catheter but the misplacement was not picked up. Because the oxygen readings appeared low, increased amounts of oxygen were given. The plaintiff developed retrolental fibroplasia and was left nearly blind. He sued the Health Authority alleging that this resulted from the excess oxygen he was given.

Decision

The House of Lords held that there were five other possible causes of the retrolental fibroplasia and the plaintiff had failed to establish causation.

Comment

In *McGhee v National Coal Board* (1973) HL, the plaintiff alleged that the dermatitis he developed was caused by the defendants' failure to provide washing facilities in the brick kilns where he worked. He was unable to prove that he would not have developed the dermatitis if the facilities had been available. However, there was evidence to suggest that the lack of facilities materially increased the risk of the dermatitis, thus there was a material contribution to the injury and the defendants were liable. The case was distinguished in *Wilsher* because in *McGhee* there was only one possible 'agent' – the brick dust – while in *Wilsher* there were five.

Lord Bridge commented: '*McGhee* ... laid down no new principle of law ... Adopting a robust and pragmatic approach to the undisputed primary facts of the case, the majority concluded that it was a legitimate inference of fact that the defendants' negligence had materially contributed to the pursuer's injury.'

Fairchild v Glenhaven Funeral Services Ltd (2002): Where the claimant's injury may have been caused by the negligence of several parties and it is impossible to determine which party was responsible, those parties will be jointly or independently liable for the full damage

Facts

The case concerned three appeals in which the claimants had been negligently exposed to asbestos by more than one of their employers. The claimants all developed mesothelioma (a lung tumour caused by exposure to asbestos) but were unable to show which of the exposures was responsible.

Decision

The House of Lords held that, where different defendants had negligently exposed the claimant to a risk of harm and that harm materialised then, even though it was impossible to prove which of the exposures had caused the harm, all or any of the defendants could be held liable.

Lord Hoffmann suggested that for a material contribution to the risk of harm to be sufficient proof of causation, five factors must be satisfied:

(1) that there is a particular duty to protect against the risk;
(2) the duty is 'intended to create a civil right to compensation';
(3) the greater the exposure the greater the risk;
(4) medical science cannot establish which of the different exposures was responsible; and
(5) the harm materialises.

Comment

Policy played its part in the decision since the House of Lords felt it important that the financial burden should be met by one of the parties that had breached their duty of care, rather than by the innocent victim. In the US case of *Sindell v Abbott Labs* (1980), the court took an interesting approach to the problem of attribution. The case concerned a class action for causing cancer by pre-natal exposure to DES (Diethylstilboestrol). There were many manufacturers of the drug and the claimants were unable to show which manufacturer was responsible. The court held that the manufacturers should be liable in proportion to market share.

Hotson v East Berkshire HA (1987): Where the defendant's negligence has deprived the plaintiff of the possibility of successful treatment, the plaintiff must show that, on a balance of probabilities, the delay or failure to treat was at least a material contributory cause of the damage

Facts

A schoolboy fell out of a tree and injured his hip. The defendant failed to X-ray the hip and the true extent of his injury went undiscovered for several days. He was left with a permanent disability. The medical evidence was that in 75% of cases the injury was such that even if the injury had been diagnosed immediately he would still have been left with the disability. The plaintiff sued, not on the basis of the disability but for the loss of the 25% chance of recovery. The trial judge awarded damages at 25% of the amount that would have been awarded for his disability. The Court of Appeal affirmed this. The Health Authority appealed.

Decision

The House of Lords allowed the appeal. If the plaintiff could show on the balance of probabilities that he would have recovered if given proper treatment then he was entitled to full damages. If he could not then he was not entitled to recover damages at all.

Comment

The House of Lords left it open whether it would ever be possible to claim damages for a loss of chance. Lord Bridge's speech suggests that if the probability of recovery had been 51% then he might have been entitled to damages since, on the balance of probabilities, treatment would have been successful. This argument – that a plaintiff was entitled to damages if the chance of recovery was greater than 50% – had been previously applied in *Kenyon v Bell* (1953). The plaintiff in that case was a girl who lost the sight in one eye following negligent treatment. However, the court held there was no liability because even if the medical treatment had been of the requisite standard, she would still have had a less than 50% chance of retaining the sight in her eye. In *Allied Maples Group Ltd v Simmons* (1995), the Court of Appeal held that if the lost chance represented a real and substantial possibility rather than just a speculative chance, then recovery would be allowed. In cases where loss of chance has succeeded, the common factor has been the uncertainty of a third party's behaviour. Where, as in medical cases, the chance has been based on epidemiological statistics, the claimants have yet to win. The chance of such a claim being successful, while not yet extinguished, was dealt another body blow by the Court of Appeal's decision in *Gregg v Scott* (2002).

Cassidy v Ministry of Health (1951): Where damage has occurred and the negligent event cannot be clearly identified, the plaintiff may raise *res ipsa loquitur* – the thing (damage) speaks for itself: under *res ipsa loquitur* it is for the defendants to rebut the evidential presumption of negligence that the principle establishes

Facts

The plaintiff underwent an operation for a contraction deformity of the third and fourth fingers of his left hand. The operation made his situation worse by causing his two unaffected fingers to become stiff, thus making his hand almost completely useless.

Decision

The Court of Appeal held that the defendants were liable for negligence. Lord Denning stated:

If the plaintiff had to prove that some particular doctor or nurse was negligent, he would not be able to do it. But he was not put to that impossible task: he says: 'I went into the hospital to be cured of two stiff fingers. I have come out with four stiff fingers, and my hand is useless. That should not have happened if due care had been used. Explain it if you can.'

Comment

The courts are reluctant to apply the doctrine in medical negligence cases, especially where the procedure in question carried a high risk. See *Whitehouse v Jordan* (1981) in which Lord Denning MR stated: 'the first sentence suggests that, because the baby suffered damage, therefore Mr Jordan was at fault. In other words *res ipsa loquitur*. That would be an error. In a high-risk case, damage during birth is quite possible, even though all care is used. No inference of negligence should be drawn from it.'

The requirements that must be satisfied before the principle can apply were laid down in *Scott v London and St Katherine Docks Co* (1865):

- whatever causes the damage must be under the management of the defendant or his servants;
- if proper care had been used, the accident is such that it would not normally happen;
- the defendants are unable to provide an explanation for the accident.

Thus, all the doctrine does is to satisfy the plaintiff's burden of proof, which is rebuttable if the defendants can provide a reasonable explanation. It does not shift the burden of proof to the defendants.

Saunders v Leeds Western HA (1985): For *res ipsa loquitur* to be rebutted the defendants' explanation must be reasonable

Facts

The plaintiff, a four-year-old girl, suffered a heart attack during an operation to correct a congenitally dislocated hip. She was left with permanent brain damage. She claimed that the heart of a fit child did not arrest under anaesthesia without negligence – *res ipsa loquitur*. The defendants' explanation was that a paradoxical air embolism had travelled from the operation site to the patient's heart where it had blocked a coronary artery.

Decision
The High Court held that liability was established. The defendants' explanation was rejected as they would have been forewarned of any problems if they had employed a proper system of monitoring.

Comment
See also *Glass v Cambridge HA* (1995).

Clark v MacLennan (1983): If the defendant's practice deviates from the accepted standard, he must be able to justify his actions

Facts
The plaintiff developed stress incontinence after giving birth. To treat the condition an anterior colporrhaphy was performed four weeks after the birth. The operation was a failure and two subsequent operations also failed. The plaintiff alleged negligence because the standard practice was to wait three months post-delivery in order to avoid the very complications the plaintiff suffered.

Decision
The High Court held that the defendants had not justified their departure from standard practice and were thus liable for negligence. Pain J stated:

Where ... there is but one orthodox course of treatment and the doctor chooses to depart from that ... it is not enough for him to say as to his decision simply that it was based on his clinical judgment. One has to inquire whether he took all the proper factors into account which he knew or should have known, and whether his departure from the orthodox course can be justified on the basis of these factors.

Comment
In *Wilsher v Essex AHA* (1986) CA, Mustill LJ argued that this case could only be properly understood as creating a presumption of negligence that the defendant must rebut by justifying his actions. As with *res ipsa loquitur*, the burden of proof is *not* shifted to the defendant.

Rance v Mid-Downs HA (1991): The chain of causation can be broken by an intervening act (*novus actus interveniens*), which relieves the defendant of liability

Facts
The plaintiff alleged that the defendants negligently failed to diagnose that her fetus had spina bifida, leaving her with a disabled child. At the time she was 26 weeks pregnant and abortion law – as drafted at the time – would have made it unlawful to terminate the pregnancy.

Decision

The High Court held that she would not have been able to lawfully terminate her pregnancy anyway and thus the provisions of the law broke the chain of causation.

Emeh v Kensington and Chelsea and Westminster AHA (1985): For the plaintiff's own act to constitute a *novus actus interveniens*, it must have been unreasonable

Facts

The plaintiff alleged that a sterilisation performed at the same time as an abortion had been carried out negligently. The plaintiff did not discover the subsequent pregnancy until she was 20 weeks into her gestation. She decided to keep the child, which was born with congenital abnormalities. She claimed damages for the pregnancy, birth and costs of raising a handicapped child. At first instance the judge held that her decision not to have a termination was a *novus actus interveniens*.

Decision

The Court of Appeal allowed the appeal. Damages would be awarded for the full extent of the consequences of the defendants' negligence. Slade LJ stated: 'Save in the most exceptional circumstances, I cannot think it right that the court should ever declare it unreasonable for a woman to decline to have an abortion.'

Comment

The House of Lords have held that damages are not available for the costs of raising a normal child following a 'wrongful birth', but they have been allowed for the cost incurred where the child is disabled: see 8.7 above.

Hepworth v Kerr (1995): The damage must not be too remote – the type of harm must be reasonably foreseeable

Facts

The defendant anaesthetised the plaintiff using the experimental anaesthetic technique of induced hypotension. The plaintiff subsequently suffered a spinal stroke (damage to the spinal cord caused by a reduced blood supply). It was known that there was a risk of cerebral stroke but there was no knowledge of the risk of spinal stroke.

Decision

The High Court held that the defendant was liable. Although the spinal stroke was not foreseeable, injury from under-perfusion of a major organ was foreseeable. The damage was of this type and thus it was not too remote.

12.6 Damages

There are no special rules applied to damages awarded in cases of medical negligence. The general aim is to return the claimant, as far as possible, to their position before the tort occurred. The damages are calculated to compensate for their losses and generally not to punish the defendant. There are three main components to damages awards:

(1) Financial loss – eg, loss of earnings. Usually the loss must be consequential on the physical harm. However, under certain limited circumstances, pure economic

loss may be recoverable. For a discussion of the difference between pure and consequential economic loss, see *Spartan Steel & Alloys v Martin & Co* (1972).

(2) Expenses – medical expenses, etc.

(3) General damages – pain, suffering, loss of amenity.

Heil v Rankin (2000): The court may set guidelines on the level of general damages

Facts

In a joint hearing of several appeals, the Court of Appeal considered the issue of the quantum of damages for pain, suffering and loss of amenity in light of the Law Commission's Report No 257 (1999). The defendants argued that it was inappropriate for the judiciary to alter the levels of damages as this should properly be done by Parliament.

Decision

The Court of Appeal held that it was part of its duty to consider the level of damages and it could not wait for Parliament to intervene. It was inappropriate to increase the damages to the degree recommended by the Law Commission. The Court of Appeal set guidelines on the level of damages for pain, suffering and loss of amenity in personal injury and clinical negligence claims worth above £10,000. The awards would be graduated, the rate of increase being proportionate to the size of the award, up to a maximum increase of one-third on awards at the highest level. Damages of £150,000 were to be increased by 33%; those of £110,000 by 25%; those of £80,000 by 20%; and awards of £40,000 by 10%.

Briody v St Helens and Knowsley AHA (2001): Only reasonable damages will be recoverable

Facts

Through the defendants' negligence, the claimant had been deprived of her womb and the opportunity to have children. She sought damages to cover the costs of arranging surrogacy. Initially the surrogacy was to be carried out in California. The claimant sought to adduce, on appeal, the new evidence that her surrogacy could now be carried out in England.

Decision

The Court of Appeal held that the costs were not reasonable because of the slim chances of a successful pregnancy ensuing, and it would be unreasonable to expect the defendants to meet the costs of international treatment. The application to introduce new evidence was rejected – any such case should be properly tested in court and not brought in on appeal. The Court of Appeal also rejected the possibility of any right to be provided with a child under Schedule 1, Article 8 of the Human Rights Act 1998.

12.7 Defences

The defences available include *volenti non fit injuria*, contributory negligence, and *ex turpi causa non oritur actio*. *Volenti* arises when the plaintiff agrees to run the risk of the defendant's tortious act. There have been no medical cases and it is difficult to think of this defence ever being applicable in this field. *Ex turpi* is the rule that the courts will not give assistance to a claimant whose injury arose because they were engaged in criminal activities. The most likely defence to arise is contributory negligence.

Crossmann v Stewart (1977): The liability of the defendant will be reduced if the plaintiff has contributed to the extent of the damage – contributory negligence

Facts
The plaintiff suffered from a skin disorder and was prescribed treatment (chloroquine) for this by the defendant. She was employed as a medical receptionist and when her supply ran out she obtained the drug without prescription from the salesman who supplied her employer with the drugs he needed for his practice. The defendant was unaware of this. The defendant became aware of evidence that suggested that long-term use of the drug might cause blindness. He contacted the plaintiff and referred her to an eye specialist. The eye specialist diagnosed '[b]ilateral superficial keratopathy ... which suggests a sequelae of chloroquine therapy'. The plaintiff was informed that the specialist's report was negative and she continued to take the drug without the defendant's knowledge. She subsequently consulted him and he continued her on the treatment for a further six months. Over the next six years, the plaintiff's sight progressively deteriorated. She sued the defendant.

Decision
The Supreme Court of British Columbia held that the defendant was liable for negligence for failing to properly consider the eye specialist's report. The plaintiff was guilty of contributory negligence in obtaining the prescription drugs without her doctor's knowledge. The plaintiff was two-thirds responsible for her damage and thus could only recover one-third from the defendant.

Comment
The defence of contributory negligence was given a statutory basis by the Law Reform (Contributory Negligence) Act 1945. Section 1 states:

Where any person suffers damage as the result partly of his own fault and partly of the fault of any other person or persons, a claim in respect of that damage shall not be defeated by reason of the fault of the person suffering the damage, but the damages recoverable in respect thereof shall be reduced to such extent as the court thinks just and equitable having regard to the claimant's share in the responsibility for the damage ...

Bernier v Sisters of Service (1948): A plaintiff will not be contributorily negligent if her acts or omissions are reasonable

Facts
The plaintiff was admitted for an appendicectomy. She had previously suffered frostbite of her feet, which she did not volunteer. She was given a spinal anaesthetic (which would reduce or block sensation from her feet) for the appendicectomy. Nurses placed two hot water bottles inside the foot of her bed and then left the ward. Over the next 20 minutes the plaintiff began to moan. The bottles were removed some

10 minutes later but the plaintiff had suffered third degree burns to both heels. She sued the hospital, which alleged contributory negligence.

Decision
The Alberta Supreme Court held that the hospital staff had been negligent in failing to test the hot water bottles with a thermometer, placing them directly against her feet and not having a nurse in attendance. The plaintiff was not guilty of contributory negligence. She had no reason to think that the frostbite was relevant. The allegation that she had failed to communicate the pain was irrelevant because the damage was done before the sensation returned to her feet.

Comment
This is simply applying the 'reasonable person' standard to the claimant as well as the defendant. It would be unjust to expect the claimant to achieve a higher standard of care than the defendant.

12.8 Time limitations on actions for personal injury

Under s 11 of the Limitation Act 1980, the limitation period for personal injury actions is three years, which starts to run from when the claimant knows of the cause of damage.

Davis v City and Hackney HA (1991): Knowledge of the cause of the damage includes both actual and constructive knowledge

Facts
The plaintiff was born with severe physical disabilities. When he was 17 he questioned his mother about the cause of his disability. She suggested that it might have been a mishandled delivery. She was reluctant for him to make any claim for damages. After he had left home he met a law student – when he was 22 – who thought that he might have a possible claim. He then consulted a solicitor. Just over one year later they received a medical report. Five months later they issued a writ which alleged that his disabilities were due to an injection of Ovametrin administered to his mother. The defendants pleaded that the case was time barred.

Decision
The High Court held that the claim was not statute barred. The plaintiff's knowledge (s 11(4)(b) of the Limitation Act 1980) arose at the time that the contents of the medical report were communicated to him. The plaintiff's disabilities meant that he had not been unreasonable in failing to seek legal advice any earlier. He could not be fixed with constructive knowledge at any earlier date under s 14(3).

Jowitt J stated: 'I turn now to section 14(3). The test is an objective one ... but it is an objective test applied to the kind of plaintiff I am here dealing with, with his disability, and looking at his age and his circumstances and the difficulties he has faced.'

Comment
Section 14(3) of the Limitation Act 1980 states:

For the purposes of this section, a person's knowledge includes knowledge which he might reasonably have been expected to acquire:

(a) from facts observable or ascertainable by him; or
(b) from facts ascertainable by him with the help of medical or other appropriate expert advice which it is reasonable for him to seek; but a person shall not be fixed under this subsection with knowledge of a fact ascertainable only with the help of expert advice so long as he has taken all reasonable steps to obtain (and, where appropriate, act on) that advice.

Headford v Bristol and District HA (1995): The three-year time limit does not start to run if the plaintiff is not legally competent

Facts
The plaintiff brought a claim in negligence against the defendants for personal injury resulting from an operation performed 28 years previously that had left the plaintiff severely mentally disabled. At first instance the judge held that the delay, caused by the plaintiff's carers, was unreasonable, prejudicial to the defendants and an abuse of process. The plaintiff appealed.

Decision
The Court of Appeal allowed the appeal. Section 28 of the Limitation Act 1980 makes no reference to 'prejudice' and contained no provision to restrict the time limit for a plaintiff who remained disabled. Since the plaintiff remained disabled and s 28 conferred a right in general to bring proceedings in negligence at any time during the period of continuing disability, the plaintiff was not time barred.

Comment
Section 28 of the Limitation Act 1980 states:

(1) Subject to the following provisions of this section, if on the date when any right of action accrued for which a period of limitation is prescribed by this Act, the person to whom it accrued was under a disability, the action may be brought at any time before the expiration of six years from the date when he ceased to be under a disability or died (whichever first occurred) notwithstanding that the period of limitation has expired.
     ...
(6) If the action is one to which section 11 or 12(2) of this Act applies, subsection (1) above shall have effect as if for the words 'six years' there were substituted the words 'three years'.

Section 38(2) states: 'For the purposes of this Act a person shall be treated as under a disability while he is an infant, or of unsound mind.'

Mold v Hayton and Newson (2000): The court has the discretion to allow time barred claims if it is equitable

Facts
The plaintiff alleged that, had she been examined vaginally in late 1979 or early 1980, the cervical cancer from which she suffered would have been detected earlier than it was. This would have meant that she could have had lower doses of radiotherapy and would have avoided the side effects she suffered. Her claim was not made until 1998. At first instance, the judge held that she had knowledge of the facts from September 1980, when she was diagnosed with the cervical cancer. However, he exercised his discretion under s 33 of the Limitation Act 1980 and extended the time limit to allow

her to bring the claim. The defendants appealed. The plaintiff cross-appealed against the judge's finding of the date of her knowledge.

Decision

The Court of Appeal held that: (1) dismissing the cross-appeal, the damage was the failure to diagnose the cancer and not the development of the side effects. Thus, the judge was correct in construing knowledge from the date of the actual diagnosis; and (2) allowing the appeal, the delay of 18 years was a huge delay and as such the judge was under a duty to give reasons for allowing the extension. He had failed to do this. Also, the claimant had been unable to cite any precedents for such a long extension and the defendants were not responsible for the delay in bringing the proceedings. It was not reasonable for them to be sued so many years after the events.

Comment

Under s 33(3) of the Limitation Act 1980, the court should pay particular regard to:

(a) the length of, and the reasons for the delay on the part of the plaintiff;

(b) the extent to which ... the evidence ... is likely to be less cogent than if the action had been bought within the time allowed ...;

(c) the conduct of the defendant after the cause of action arose ...;

(d) the duration of any disability of the plaintiff arising after the date of the accrual of the cause of action;

(e) the extent to which the plaintiff acted promptly and reasonably once he knew whether or not the act or omission of the defendant, to which the injury was attributable, might be capable at that time of giving rise to an action for damages;

(f) the steps, if any, taken by the plaintiff to obtain medical, legal or other expert advice and the nature of any such advice he may have received.

CHAPTER 13

LIABILITY FOR DEFECTIVE PRODUCTS

A common law liability for defective products has long existed as part of negligence law. However, because of the difficulties facing consumers in bringing a successful claim, and following the European Directive 85/374 on product liability, the Government passed the Consumer Protection Act 1987 (CPA). The CPA introduces strict liability where injury is caused by a defect, even where the defect was not caused by anyone's carelessness. Under s 2(2), this liability applies to the producer, anyone who 'by putting his name on the product or using a trademark or other distinguishing mark in relation to the product, has held himself out to be the producer of the product', and any person who supplies the product from outside the EU. Suppliers acting totally within the EU may be liable under s 2(3) if they fail, when asked, to identify any person who may be responsible for the product under s 2(2).

Under s 3, a 'defect' is present if the product is unsafe for its intended purpose, which takes into account anything that 'might reasonably be expected to be done with or in relation to the product' and any instructions or warnings that are included. Any risk inherent in the normal use of the product will not attract liability. Thus, an explanatory note from the Department of Trade and Industry (DTI) stated: 'A medicine used to treat a life-threatening condition is likely to be much more powerful than a medicine used in the treatment of a less serious condition, and the safety that one is reasonably entitled to expect of such a medicine may therefore be correspondingly lower' (DTI, 1985).

Although liability is strict, it is not absolute and s 4 provides for a number of defences. The most specifically relevant, and one of the more controversial of these is the developments risk defence. Section 4(1)(e) states: 'that the state of scientific and technical knowledge at the relevant time was not such that a producer of products of the same description as the product in question might be expected to have discovered the defect if it had existed in his products while they were under his control.'

Apart from the CPA, patients who have purchased a product may have a contractual remedy under s 14 of the Sale of Goods Act 1979. Section 14(2) provides that: 'Where the seller sells goods in the course of a business, there is an implied term that the goods supplied under the contract are of a satisfactory quality.' This is further explained by s 14(2A), which states that 'goods are of a satisfactory quality if they meet the standard that a reasonable person would regard as satisfactory, taking account of any description of the goods, the price (if relevant) and all the other relevant circumstances'.

For damage caused by vaccines, no-fault compensation has been provided by the Vaccine Damage Payments Act 1979. The Act provides for a statutory sum (currently £100,000: see the Vaccine Damage Payments Act 1979 Statutory Sum Order 2000) that may be awarded by the Secretary of State if he is satisfied 'that a person is, or was immediately before his death, severely disabled as a result of vaccination' (s 1(1)(a)). The Act only applies to the list of diseases detailed in s 2 and is limited in its effect to those who are severely disabled, which means 'if he suffers disablement to the extent of 80 per cent or more'. Under s 3(5) the claimant must prove on the balance of probabilities that the vaccine caused the damage. Section 3(4) allows the right of appeal from the decision of the Secretary of State to an independent medical tribunal.

13.1 Common law liability

Donoghue v Stevenson (1932): The 'manufacturer' of a product owes a duty of care not to injure the 'consumer'

Facts

The plaintiff went to a café with a friend who purchased a bottle of ginger beer (the bottle was opaque which made it impossible to inspect the contents). The plaintiff drank some of the ginger beer and then her friend poured the remainder of the bottle into the glass. It was alleged that the remains of a decomposed snail were poured out with the ginger beer. The plaintiff claimed that she subsequently became ill with gastro-enteritis and sued the manufacturers of the ginger beer for negligence. The manufacturers claimed that there could be no liability since there was no contract with the plaintiff.

Decision

The House of Lords held that liability could exist. A manufacturer owed a duty of care to the consumer irrespective of any contract. Lord Atkin stated:

… a manufacturer of products, which he sells in such a form as to show that he intends them to reach the ultimate consumer in the form in which they left him with no reasonable possibility of intermediate examination and with the knowledge that the absence of reasonable care in the preparation or putting up of the products will result in an injury to the consumer's life or property, owes a duty to the consumer to take reasonable care.

Comment

Liability in ordinary negligence requires that the claimant show that the manufacturer had failed to take reasonable care and that the defect produced by the manufacturer's carelessness caused the damage. It may be very difficult to show that the medical product (eg, a drug), rather than the patient's pre-existing illness, caused the damage. Thus, in *Loveday v Renton* (1990), the plaintiff was unable to show that the pertussis (whooping cough) vaccine was even capable of causing the damage suffered (compensation was, however, subsequently paid under the Vaccine Damage Payments Act 1979). The common law action has not been extinguished under the CPA.

13.2 Statutory liability

A and Others v National Blood Authority (No 1) (2001): A 'product' may include natural substances such as blood or organs for transplantation

Facts

The claimants had all been infected with Hepatitis C following transfusions with contaminated blood. The trial was to generically determine liability and quantum of damages under ss 3 and 4(1)(e) of the CPA. The issues were considered in terms of

Articles 6 and 7(e) of the the Council Directive 85/874/EEC ('the Product Liability Directive').

Decision

The High Court held that the Directive was passed with the purpose of achieving a high level of consumer protection and the public had a legitimate expectation that blood would be safe (although not 100% safe). The defence under Article 7(e) – the state of knowledge defence – would only be effective once if the problem causing a defect was unknown. Once the problem had occurred and was known, the defence would no longer be available. Thus, blood contaminated with the Hepatitis C virus was defective within the meaning of the Directive (and hence the CPA).

Comment

Under s 1(2) of the CPA, 'abstracting' a product is equivalent to manufacturing. Since blood is 'abstracted' it is logical that the CPA would cover its supply and use. This is also true for other body parts such as kidneys: see *Veedfald v Arhus Amtskommune* (2001), below.

Sam B and Others v McDonald's Restaurants Ltd (2002): A dangerous product is not defective if sufficient precautions are taken to meet the legitimate expectations of the general consumer

Facts

The trial was to consider a number of preliminary generic issues arising from a group of cases in which the claimants were injured by hot drinks served by the defendants. One of the issues was whether a hot drink was defective because of the danger it posed.

Decision

The High Court held that, since the members of staff were sufficiently well trained, the cups were of a suitable design and quality, and the majority of customers would be aware that hot drinks could burn, the hot drinks served by the defendants were not defective.

Comment

Under s 3(1) of the CPA, 'there is a defect in a product ... if the safety of the product is not such as persons generally are entitled to expect'. Some products are unavoidably dangerous and therefore the safety of the product must be determined in the context of the purpose of the product and any other measures that may limit the danger. In this case, Field J suggested that 'products that are obviously dangerous (such as a knife) are not defective: the consumer has a free choice whether to expose himself to the risk, but that choice must be an informed choice'. For medical products, provided the patient is reasonably well informed of the risks and side effects, then the product should not be classed as defective *simply* because it has associated dangers.

Veedfald v Arhus Amtskommune (2001): Under the EU Directive, liability for defective medical products exists even where the patient does not pay for it

Facts

The Supreme Court of Denmark referred a question to the European Court of Justice on interpretation of Articles 7 and 9 of the EU Directive 85/374. The claimant had received a defective kidney, damaged by the perfusion fluid used to prepare the organ. The defendant argued that it was exempt from liability because the product had neither been put into circulation nor manufactured for an economic purpose.

Decision

The European Court of Justice held that any product used in the provision of medical care was put into circulation. The exemption from liability where the activity had no economic or business purpose (Article 7(c)) did not cover publicly funded medical care.

Comment

The case concerned interpretation of the Directive. Under s 4(c) of the CPA it is a defence if the following conditions are satisfied:

(i)   that the only supply of the product ... was otherwise than in the course of a business of that person; and

(ii) that s 2(2) above does not apply to that person or applies to him by virtue only of things done otherwise than with a view to a profit.

Since both of these conditions must be satisfied, the fact that the NHS is not a profit-making business will not afford it a defence. This is confirmed by *A and Others v National Blood Authority (No 1)*.

CHAPTER 14

LIABILITY IN CRIMINAL LAW

The majority of medical practice is regulated by the civil law; however, there are some circumstances that raise the possibility of criminal liability. For example, a doctor may be guilty of an offence if he performs an abortion that falls outside the terms of the Abortion Act 1967. Under s 59 of the Offences against the Persons Act 1861 it remains unlawful to cause, or attempt to cause, a miscarriage where it has not been made lawful by the Abortion Act 1967. Where the child is 'capable of being born alive', then there may also be an offence under s 1 of the Infant Life Preservation Act 1929. Another example of possible criminal liability arises under the Data Protection Act 1998.

14.1 Assault and battery

Theoretically, a doctor who operates on a patient without their consent could be liable for battery or for the more serious offences covered by ss 18 and 20 of the Offences Against the Person Act 1861. Liability would only arise where the doctor failed to get any consent at all, operated on the wrong part of the body, or exceeded the scope of the consent without the justification of necessity. The same principles regarding the validity of a real consent – discussed in Chapter 2 – relating to the tort of battery will apply to the criminal offence.

R v Richardson (1998): The doctrine of informed consent has no place in criminal law

Facts
See 2.3 above.

Decision
See 2.3 above. Otton LJ stated:

The general proposition which underlies this area of the law [of battery] is that the human body is inviolate, but there are circumstances which the law recognises where consent may operate to prevent conduct which would otherwise be classified as an assault from being so treated. Reasonable surgical interference is clearly such an exception.

Later he stated:

It was suggested in argument that we might be assisted by the civil law of consent, where such expressions as 'real' or 'informed' consent prevail. In this regard, the criminal and civil law do not run along the same track. The concept of informed consent has no place in the criminal law. It would also be a mistake, in our view, to introduce the concept of a duty to communicate information to a patient about the risk of an activity before consent to an act can be treated as valid.

Comment

Otton LJ's argument suggests that 'informed consent' is part of the civil law. This is misleading as the doctrine was rejected in *Sidaway* (see 2.4 above). In both criminal and civil law, consent can be vitiated by a mistake (whether fraudulently induced or not) only as to the identity of the actor or the nature or character of the act (see *R v Clarence* (1888) and *Papadimitropoulos v R* (1957)).

14.2   Negligent manslaughter

R v Adomoko (1994): A doctor may be liable for manslaughter if a patient dies as a result of the doctor's negligence

Facts

The accused was an anaesthetist. During an operation the tube carrying the oxygen to the patient became disconnected. The accused did not notice the disconnection and the patient subsequently suffered a heart attack and died. The accused was charged with manslaughter by gross negligence. He was convicted of the charge and appealed.

Decision

The House of Lords turned down the appeal. The accused was guilty of manslaughter by gross negligence. Lord Mackay stated: 'The essence of the matter, which is supremely a jury question, is whether, having regard to the risk of death involved, the conduct of the defendant was so bad in all the circumstances as to amount in their judgment to a criminal act or omission.' Lord Mackay also quoted Lord Hewitt CJ – with approval – from *R v Bateman* (1925), who stated: 'the facts must be such that, in the opinion of the jury, the negligence of the accused went beyond a mere matter of compensation between subjects and showed such disregard for the life and safety of others as to amount to a crime against the State and conduct deserving punishment.'

14.3   Liability for euthanasia

R v Cox (1992): Actively ending life, even at the patient's request, is murder

Facts

Dr Cox was a consultant physician. One of his patients was a 70-year-old woman suffering from severe and extremely painful rheumatoid arthritis. It was uncertain how much longer she would have lived for but she could have died at any time. The pain she suffered was not controllable with analgesic drugs. After she asked Dr Cox to put her out of her misery he injected her with a lethal dose of potassium chloride. Because she could have died at any time and hence pre-empted the effect of the potassium chloride, Dr Cox was charged only with attempted murder.

Decision

The jury found Dr Cox guilty of attempted murder.

Comment

Criminal liability may also arise for assisting a patient to commit suicide (physician assisted suicide: see Chapter 6).

CHAPTER 15

PROFESSIONAL REGULATION

In addition to the law, healthcare professionals are also subject to regulation by their employers and the professional bodies. The Government has also established a new Special Health Authority – the National Clinical Assessment Authority (NCAA) (www.ncaa.nhs.uk) – that currently monitors the professional performance of doctors and dentists. Where the employer has doubts or concerns about the doctor's clinical performance the matter may be (but does not have to be) referred to the Authority. The Authority, acting as an advisory body, will investigate and make recommendations to the employer. The responsibility for resolving the problem always remains with the employer. The doctor may self-refer to the NCAA if he wishes any doubts about his performance to be resolved (see NHS Executive, 2001).

There are many professional regulatory bodies that oversee the behaviour of healthcare practitioners. The General Medical Council (GMC) regulates doctors, the Nursing and Midwifery Council (NMC) regulates nurses and midwives, the General Dental Council (GDC) regulates dentists, and the Health Professions Council (HPC) regulates the professions allied to medicine, such as physiotherapists, radiographers and dieticians. Pharmacists, opticians, chiropractors and osteopaths are also subject to professional regulation. Following the *NHS Plan* (2000b), in which the Government stated an intention to incorporate all of the professional regulatory bodies as part of a single body, the NHS Reform and Healthcare Professions Act 2002 provides for the Council for the Regulation of Healthcare Professionals (s 25). The general functions of the Council will be to promote 'the interests of patients and other members of the public in relation to the performance of their functions by the [regulatory] bodies'; to 'promote best practice'; to 'formulate principles relating to good professional self-regulation'; and to 'promote co-operation between regulatory bodies'.

As an example of professional regulation this chapter will concentrate mostly on the regulation of doctors, but reference to the other bodies will be made where appropriate. Like the other regulatory bodies, the GMC was established and its regulatory powers are defined by statute: s 1 of the Medical Act 1983 (as amended). Under the Medical Act 1983 (Amendment) Order 2002, the GMC has been streamlined and will maintain the following committees: the Education Committee, one or more Interim orders Panels, one or more Registration Decisions Panels, one or more Registration Appeals Panels, the Investigation Committee and one or more Fitness to Practice Panels (s 3 of the Medical Act 1983 (as amended)). When reading the cases, note that the Investigation Committee and the Fitness to Practice Panel will, in future, deal with any cases previously dealt with by the Health Committee, the Preliminary Proceedings Committee (PPC) or the Professional Conduct Committee (PCC). For a brief overview of reforms to the fitness to practice procedures, see www.gmc-uk.org/cg/fact_sheets/ftp_reforms.pdf.

Under s 2 of the Medical Act, the GMC is required to maintain a register of qualified medical practitioners who are suitable to practice. Although the practice of medicine is not limited to registered practitioners, it is a criminal offence to pretend to be a registered practitioner (s 49) and certain areas of practice are restricted, including: the prescribing of certain drugs; abortion (Abortion Act 1967); assisting childbirth (along with registered midwives); the removal of organs or tissue for transplantation (Human Tissue Act 1961); and medical certification (death, sick leave, etc – s 48 of the Medical Act 1983). Under s 47 of the Medical Act 1983, only certain appointments – eg, as prison doctors, or doctors in public hospitals, or doctors in the armed forces – can be held by registered practitioners.

As indicated by the different Committees, the GMC has a number of functions, which includes: overseeing and determining educational standards (s 5); advising on medical ethics and standards of practice (s 35); investigating an allegation that a doctor's fitness to practice is impaired (s 35C); determining a practitioner's fitness to practice due to ill health (s 37); dealing with a practitioner whose performance is seriously deficient (s 36A of the Medical Act 1983 (as amended by s 1 of the Medical (Professional Performance) Act 1995)); and dealing with a practitioner accused of misconduct (s 36). Sanctions include admonishment, conditional registration, suspension from the register or being struck off. These sanctions are usually applied after a hearing before the relevant committee; however, where a doctor faces sufficiently serious allegations, the Interim Orders Panel may make an order suspending the doctor's registration for up to a maximum period of 18 months. The order must be reviewed within the first six months and then at least every three months (s 41A inserted into the Medical Act 1983 by Article 10 of the Medical Act 1983 (Amendment) Order 2000). See also the GMC, *Interim Orders Committee: Referral Criteria* (2000) (at www.gmc-uk.org/probdocs/criteria.htm), and the General Medical Council, *(Interim Orders Committee) (Procedure) Rules Order of Council* (2000). If a doctor's name is erased from the register he must now wait five years before applying for restoration (Article 9 of the Medical Act 1983 (Amendment) Order 2000), but any sanction may be challenged by appeal to the Privy Council (s 40 of the Medical Act 1983). A decision by the GMC may also be challenged by judicial review.

15.1   The regulation of professional conduct

Guidance is published by the GMC in a number of booklets. General guidance is provided in the booklet entitled *Good Medical Practice* (2001). It states: 'Patients must be able to trust doctors with their lives and well-being. To justify that trust, we as a profession have a duty to maintain a good standard of practice and care and to show respect for human life … Serious or persistent failure to meet the standards in this booklet may put your registration at risk.' The other regulatory bodies publish similar guidance: for example, the GDC publish *Maintaining Standards* (1997–2001) and the NMC publish a *Code of Professional Conduct* (2002), which is produced to inform both practitioners and other members of the public of the standards expected of those professionals registered to practice.

Jeetle v GMC (1995): Serious professional misconduct includes moral impropriety

Facts

The appellant had behaved indecently and entered into a sexual relationship with one of his patients. The patient complained to the police and the appellant was discovered naked in the patient's bedroom by two police officers. One of the charges before the GMC was that the doctor had prescribed opiates for his patient in order to facilitate his sexual advances. The appellant was found guilty of serious professional misconduct and his name was erased from the register. He appealed on the grounds that the allegation regarding the reason for his prescribing the drugs was not stated in the charge and there was no direct finding.

Decision

The Privy Council dismissed the appeal. Whether or not the drugs had been prescribed to facilitate sexual advances, the PCC had sufficient grounds to justify their finding of serious professional misconduct.

Comment

One of the duties required of doctors by the GMC is that they 'avoid abusing ... [their] position as a doctor'. In *De Gregory v GMC* (1961), a doctor was struck off for serious professional misconduct when he began a relationship with a married woman. The woman and her family had been the doctor's patients but, prior to the relationship becoming physical, the woman removed herself (although not her children) from the doctor's list. Despite the woman not being the doctor's patient the Privy Council upheld the GMC's finding of serious professional misconduct because 'he gained his access to the home in the first place by virtue of his professional position'.

Doughty v General Dental Council (1988): Serious professional misconduct is not restricted to 'dishonesty or moral turpitude'

Facts

The PCC of the GDC found the plaintiff dentist guilty of serious professional misconduct. The charges against him were that: he had failed to retain patients' x-rays for a reasonable period and failed to submit them to the Dental Estimates Board when required; he failed to exercise a proper degree of skill when treating patients; and, on a number of occasions, he failed to complete treatment to the patient's satisfaction. The GDC held that his name should be erased from the register. The appellant appealed to the Privy Council.

Decision

The Privy Council dismissed the appeal. Their Lordships stated:

... what is now required is that the General Dental Council should establish conduct connected with his profession in which the dentist concerned has fallen short, by omission or commission, of the standards of conduct expected among dentists and that such falling short as is established should be serious.

Comment

This case established an objective standard as one: 'judged by proper professional standards in the light of the objective facts about the individual patients ... the dental treatments criticised as unnecessary [were] treatments that no dentist of reasonable skill exercising reasonable care would carry out.'

McCandless v GMC (1996): Serious professional misconduct includes seriously negligent treatment

Facts

The appellant was found guilty of serious professional misconduct for making diagnostic errors for three patients and for failing to refer them to hospital. The PCC directed that his name should be erased from the register. He appealed to the Privy Council.

Decision

The Privy Council dismissed the appeal, stating: 'Serious professional misconduct was not restricted to conduct which was morally blameworthy but could include seriously negligent treatment measured by objective standards.' Their Lordships approved *Doughty* and held that it also applied to doctors.

Comment

A single act that satisfies this standard of 'serious negligence' may be sufficient to incur liability for serious professional misconduct. Thus, in one case, an anaesthetist who failed to obtain the patient's consent for the use of a rectal suppository inserted while the patient was anaesthetised was guilty of serious professional misconduct (see Mitchell, 1995. See also *R v Statutory Committee of the Pharmaceutical Society of Great Britain ex p Sokoh* (1986)).

Silver v GMC (2003): The Committee must specifically consider whether a negligent act is sufficient to amount to serious professional misconduct

Facts

The appellant was a GP who had negligently failed to ensure that a patient received prompt medical care after she had fallen at home. The Committee held that there had been a 'managerial, organisational and communications failure' within the GP's practice and the appellant was found guilty of serious professional misconduct. The appellant appealed, arguing that it was an isolated incidence and the sanction was too severe.

Decision

The Privy Council allowed the appeal. While the appellant's conduct was obviously negligent and might amount to professional misconduct, this was not certain and the Committee had failed to specifically consider whether the appellant's negligence did constitute serious professional misconduct.

Spofforth v General Dental Council (1999): It is the duty of the PCC to ensure that any penalty imposed is appropriate to the nature and gravity of the offence

Facts
The appellant had been convicted of seven counts of forgery and false accounting amounting to £5,826. The convictions related to falsified invoices required to support a claim for certain grant monies. There was no allegation that he had not incurred the expenditure or would not have been entitled to the grant; he had simply failed to keep the required proof which he subsequently forged. The only sanction available to the GDC under s 27 of the Dentists Act 1984 was to erase his name from the register. The GDC refused leave for adjournment despite the fact that the appellant was suffering from profound depression and unable to give proper instructions for the conduct of his case. The dentist appealed.

Decision
The Privy Council allowed the appeal. The PCC had a duty to satisfy itself that any criminal convictions were so grave as to demonstrate that the dentist was unfit to practise before resorting to the sole and draconian power of erasure from the register. Since none of his patients had suffered, and there had been no improper claims on the NHS, the appellant had a case to make before the GDC and there was no good reason for refusing his request for adjournment.

Comment
See also *Dad v General Dental Council* (2000), in which the Privy Council held that suspending a dentist's registration for two motoring offences unconnected with his professional practice was unjustified. In *Crabbie v GMC* (2002), the doctor was dependent on alcohol and had been convicted of causing death by dangerous driving and driving while over the limit. The Privy Council held that if the offences were serious enough to justify erasure, then there was no obligation to refer to the Health Committee, which did not have the power to erase the doctor from the register. In *R (on the Application of Toth) v GMC* (2003), the High Court further held that the PCC did not have the power to refer a case to the Health Committee unless it had first excluded erasure from the register as a possible sanction.

Under the General Medical Council Preliminary Proceedings Committee and Professional Conduct Committee (Procedure) Rules 1988, a 'minor motoring offence' will not constitute grounds for a disciplinary hearing. However, in *Patel v GMC* (2003), the Privy Council held that dishonesty was at the top end of the spectrum of misconduct.

In *Bijl v GMC* (2001), the Privy Council held that it was excessively harsh to erase a practitioner's name from the register where the allegations concerned errors of judgment and he did not pose a risk to the public: conditional registration would have been a more appropriate sanction.

Under s 22 of the Nursing and Midwifery Order 2001, complaints may be brought before the NMC where the allegation relates simply to misconduct or where the practitioner is convicted of or cautioned for a criminal offence. See *Balamoody v*

UKCC For Nursing Midwifery and Health Visiting (1998), which held that the terms of the Nurses, Midwives and Health Visitors (Professional Conduct) Rules 1993 covered all criminal offences irrespective of how serious they were or whether they had been committed by the applicant in a professional capacity. While not all offences would require further sanction by the regulatory body, some would and that was for the body to determine. The reasoning behind the decision in this case probably survives the passage of the Nursing and Midwifery Order and the establishment of the NMC to replace the now defunct UK Central Council.

R (on the Application of X) v GMC (2001): The Interim Orders Committee may suspend a doctor pending a criminal trial where it is necessary to protect the members of the public

Facts

The applicant was awaiting trial for charges of indecent assault against two of his nieces. The Interim Orders Committee suspended him from the register under the power granted by s 41A of the Medical Act 1983. The applicant applied for judicial review of the decision, arguing that there was no evidence he posed a risk and that the GMC were wrong to act prior to a conviction.

Decision

The High Court refused the application. The GMC's decision could not be said to be 'manifestly wrong', involving – as they do – charges of offences against the person and alleged breaches of trust, and the 1983 Act did not preclude the power to suspend prior to a conviction.

Comment

Note that, by virtue of the Medical Act 1983 (Amendment) Order 2002, the Interim Orders Committee has been replaced by an Interim Orders Panel. Section 41A provides:

(1) Where an Interim Order Panel or a fitness to Practise Panel are satisfied that it is necessary for the protection of members of the public or is otherwise in the public interest, or is in the interests of a fully registered person, for the registration of that person to be suspended or to be made subject to conditions, the Panel may make an order: (a) that his registration in the register shall be suspended (that is to say, shall not have effect) during such period not exceeding eighteen months as may be specified in the order ('an interim suspension order'); or (b) that his registration shall be conditional upon his compliance, during such period not exceeding eighteen months as may be specified in the order, with such requirements so specified as the Panel think fit to impose (an 'order for interim conditional registration').

Roylance v GMC (1999): The misconduct complained of must be related to the profession of medicine

Facts

The appellant was the Chief Executive Officer of the United Bristol Healthcare NHS Trust. He was also a registered doctor. The appellant was charged with failing to take remedial action on being made aware of an excessively high mortality rate of children undergoing corrective heart surgery. He was found guilty of serious professional misconduct and his name was erased from the medical register. One of the grounds of his appeal was that the allegations against him did not concern his professional judgment as a doctor and were therefore not capable of being professional misconduct under s 36 of the Medical Act 1983.

Decision

The Privy Council dismissed the appeal. There was a sufficiently close link between the duties of a Chief Executive and the profession of medicine since both required a duty to care for the safety and well-being of the patients in his charge. Clyde LJ stated:

'Misconduct' is a word of general effect, involving some act or omission which falls short of what would be proper in the circumstances. The standard of propriety may often be found by reference to the rules and standards ordinarily required to be followed by a medical practitioner in the particular circumstances. The misconduct is qualified in two respects. First, it is qualified by the word 'professional' which links the misconduct to the profession of medicine. Secondly, the misconduct is qualified by the word 'serious'. It is not any professional misconduct which will qualify. The professional misconduct must be serious.

Brown v General Dental Council (1990): The standard of proof required is the criminal standard of beyond reasonable doubt

Facts

A nine-year-old boy died following a prolonged anaesthetic. The dentist was charged with administering an overdose. He was found guilty of serious professional misconduct and his name was erased from the register. He appealed.

Decision

The Privy Council allowed the appeal. The prosecution had failed to show, on the criminal standard of proof, that an overdose had been administered or that the appellant had failed to adequately monitor the patient or exercise proper skill.

Comment

See also De Gregory v GMC (1961), in which their Lordships held: 'A high standard of proof is required, and judgment should not be given on a mere balance of probabilities.' In the NHS Plan (2000b), the Government suggested that the GMC should consider introducing a civil burden of proof and the Privy Council has now held that the standard of proof is not the same for all of the GMC's committees. In Sadler v GMC (2003), the Privy Council considered, amongst other things, the standard of proof required in a case before the Committee on Professional Performance. Because this Committee's role was rehabilitative rather than punitive, the Privy Council held that proof should be judged on the civil 'balance of probabilities' standard.

R v GMC ex p Arpad Toth & Jarman (Interested Party) (2000): Where there is a conflict of evidence, it is for the PCC and not for the preliminary screener or the PPC to determine that the case cannot succeed

Facts

Mr Toth accused Dr Jarman of serious professional misconduct after his child died. The screener decided that because there was a conflict of evidence between the doctor and Mr Toth, there was no chance of the charge satisfying the criminal standard of proof. The screener therefore decided that there was no question of serious professional misconduct. The GMC accepted that the screener's decision had not followed proper procedure and was legally flawed. They were prepared to consent to an order quashing the decision. Dr Jarman objected that this would be unfair to him.

Decision

The High Court held that Mr Toth had a legitimate interest in obtaining an investigation that was not outweighed by any adverse effects or unfairness to Dr Jarman. It was not for the screener or the Preliminary Proceedings Committee (PPC) to determine the likelihood of success based on conflicting evidence. The screener and the PPC should be slow to halt proceedings and any doubt should be resolved in favour of proceeding. The screener's decision would be quashed and the complaint remitted to a different screener.

Comment

The role of the screener is to act as a filter to prevent inappropriate cases from proceeding. The screener should determine if the charges are *capable* of amounting to serious professional misconduct or unfitness to practise, and not consider the likelihood of success based on the evidence. Once past the screener, the role of the PPC is to determine whether any case 'ought to be referred for inquiry' to the PCC or the Health Committee (s 42 of the Medical Act 1983). The PCC is not a fact-finding body, but should consider whether there was an arguable case of serious professional misconduct, while avoiding making a value judgment concerning the merits of the case: see *R (on the Application of Holmes) v GMC* (2002) CA and (2001) HC.

Under r 6(3) of the GMC Preliminary Proceedings Committee and Professional Conduct Committee (Procedure) Rules 1988 (as amended), the screener must refer a case 'if he is satisfied from the material available in relation to the case that it is properly arguable that the practitioner's conduct constitutes serious professional misconduct'. In *Woods v GMC* (2002), the High Court held that this meant that the test for the screeners to apply before they can refuse to refer a case is simply whether there is 'effectively, no arguable case'. As far as the PPC is concerned, the High Court approved an aide memoire, formulated by two senior barristers, for the GMC's use. This stated that:

1   In conduct cases the PPC's task is to decide whether, in its opinion, there is a real prospect of serious professional misconduct being established before the PCC. Serious professional misconduct may be considered in the context of conduct so grave as potentially to call into question a practitioner's registration whether indefinitely, temporarily or conditionally.

2   The 'real prospect' test applies to both factual allegations and the question whether, if established, the facts would amount to serious professional misconduct. It reflects not a probability but rather a genuine (not remote or fanciful) possibility ...

3   ... the PPC ... (2) is entitled to assess the weight of the evidence; (3) should not, however, normally seek to resolve substantial conflicts of evidence ... (7) ... should lean in favour of allowing the complaint to proceed to the PCC.

GMC v Spackman (1943): The GMC must follow the rules of natural justice

Facts

In divorce proceedings involving one of his patients it was found that Dr Spackman had entered into an adulterous relationship with one of his patients. The GMC removed his name from the medical register on the basis of the divorce court's finding. The GMC refused to allow Dr Spackman the opportunity to introduce evidence to controvert that finding. Dr Spackman applied for certiorari.

Decision

The Privy Council allowed the appeal. The GMC had failed to satisfy the requirements of natural justice.

Comment

Such a refusal would today also fall foul of Article 6 (the right to a fair trial) of the Human Rights Act (HRA) 1998. In *Madan v GMC* (2001), the court held that Article 6 was engaged and that this required the Committee to give reasons and explain why the sanction was a proportionate response (on the need to give reasons, see also *Stefan v GMC* (1999) and *Gupta v GMC* (2001)). The duty to give reasons, however, is limited to the findings of facts and the explanation as to why they amounted to serious professional misconduct. There was no duty to give reasons as to why evidence was rejected or accepted: see *Luthra v GMC* (2004). In *Misra v GMC* (2003), the Privy Council upheld an appeal where the GMC had introduced prejudicial material that was unrelated to the professional misconduct charge. However, in *Tehrani v UKCC* (2001), the Outer House held that, under Article 6 (right to a fair trial), Schedule 1 to the HRA 1998, the conduct committee of the UKCC was not required to meet all the conditions of an independent and impartial tribunal because there was an automatic right of appeal to the Court of Session.

Taylor v GMC (1990): A case may only be reserved for reconsideration before the expiry of a sanction if it is necessary for the practitioner's progress to be monitored

Facts

The appellant had been found guilty of serious professional misconduct for irresponsible prescribing of methadone. Prior to the hearing he had been convicted of four criminal offences of unlawfully prescribing controlled drugs. The PCC suspended his registration for 12 months but intimated that this would be reconsidered before the expiry of that term. The committee subsequently twice extended the suspension for 12 months. The doctor appealed to the Privy Council.

Decision

The Privy Council allowed the appeal. A case should only be reserved for reconsideration where it is necessary to monitor the doctor's progress, in which case the reasons should be given. Since the suspension did not relate to his fitness to practice, nor was there anything that would require the committee to assess his fitness to resume practice, the extension was quashed. Where a disciplinary hearing is consequent to a criminal conviction or results in a finding of serious professional misconduct, the sanction has a punitive element. Lord Bridge held that:

... a practitioner who is suspended ... is entitled to conclude that his criminal behaviour or professional misconduct was not regarded by the committee as sufficiently grave to warrant erasure and that the period of suspension directed was thought sufficient to provide any necessary punitive element ... It can never be a proper ground for the exercise of the power to extend the period of suspension that the period originally directed was insufficient to reflect the gravity of the original offence or offences.

Comment

In *Srirangalingham v GMC* (2001), the Privy Council held that subsequent sanctions should be consistent with the intention of the Committee in reserving a case for reconsideration. Thus, where conditional registration is imposed to ensure an improvement in clinical practice, the GMC should not subsequently suspend the doctor for a failure to comply. However, in *Ghosh v GMC* (2001), a GP (whose problem had been one of unreliability as well as poor performance) had 'failed miserably' to meet the conditions imposed on her registration, and had compounded the problem by failing to visit a patient promptly. The Privy Council held that she had completely undermined the possibility of trusting her further and it upheld the GMC's decision to erase her name from the register.

Although in *Taylor* Lord Bridge mentions a punitive element to a finding of serious professional misconduct, in *R (on the Application of Abrahaem) v GMC* (2004) Newman J held that the GMC sanctions are aimed at protecting the public, not punishing the doctor. This may reflect s 1A of the Medical Act 1983 as amended by the 2002 Order, which reads: 'The main objective of the General Council in exercising their functions is to protect, promote and maintain the health and safety of the public.'

Whitefield v GMC (2002): Appropriate sanctions imposed by the GMC will not constitute a breach of the doctor's rights under the HRA 1998

Facts

The appellant suffered from alcohol dependency. The Health Committee imposed a complete alcohol ban and required random breath, blood and urine tests as conditions of registration. The appellant argued that these conditions were a breach of his rights under Article 8, Schedule 1 to the HRA 1998 (the right to private and family life).

Decision

The Privy Council dismissed the appeal. The appellant had brought his private life into conflict with his public life and his private 'rights' could be restricted because of the public interest in protecting his patients. Even if there was an interference with Article 8(1), this was permitted under 8(2) as lawful, proportionate and necessary to protect the health of others.

***Gosai v GMC* (2003):** The GMC's power, under s 41(6) of the Medical Act 1983, to suspend the doctor's right to apply for restoration (following two unsuccessful applications) to the register is absolute

Facts
The appellant had been erased from the register for serious professional misconduct after he failed to provide an adequate standard of care to a young woman, and then lied in his written evidence to the coroner investigating her subsequent death. He applied for restoration on two occasions and was refused both times because he showed insufficient insight into his behaviour. The GMC then suspended indefinitely his right to make further applications. The appellant appealed, arguing that the power should only be exercised in clear cases where it was in the public interest.

Decision
The Privy Council dismissed the appeal. The wording of s 41(6) was unrestricted and, on the facts of the case, the order was – in any case – appropriate.

15.2   Appeals against GMC disciplinary decisions

***Graf v GMC* (1998):** Appeal from decisions of the Health Committee must usually be on a question of law

Facts
The Health Committee suspended the appellant's registration for a period of 12 months. He appealed on the ground that he was not suffering from a mental illness sufficient to seriously impair his fitness to practice within the meaning of s 37 of the Medical Act 1983.

Decision
The Privy Council dismissed the appeal. There was no issue of law or procedure. The question of mental unfitness was for the Health Committee to decide and their Lordships would not interfere with that decision.

Comment
Under s 40 of the Medical Act 1983 (as amended), this point applies to decisions of both the Health Committee and the Committee on Professional Performance. By virtue of the Medical Act 1983 (Amendment) Order 2002, it will also apply to decisions made by the Fitness to Practice Panels: see also *Stefan v GMC (No 2)* (2001). The court may be prepared to overrule a decision on a finding of fact but it will be extremely slow to do so: see *Moneeb v GMC* (2004). A decision will only be overruled if the finding of fact was so unreliable that no reasonable tribunal would have accepted it: see *Razak v GMC* (2004).

Where a sanction is unduly lenient it may be challenged before a court by the Council for the Regulation of Healthcare Professions under s 29 of the NHS Reform and Healthcare Professions Act 2002: see *Council for the Regulation of Healthcare Professions v The NMC, Truscott* (2004). Whether a sanction is too lenient would be determined by considering whether it was a reasonably appropriate decision when all the relevant factors were taken into account: see *Council for the Regulation of Healthcare Professions v The GMC* (2004a). This power also applies to cases acquitted by the GMC: see *Council for the Regulation of Healthcare Professions v The GMC* (2004b).

Libman v GMC (1972): Appeals to the Privy Council are not simply opportunities to rehear the case

Facts

The appellant had sexual intercourse with one of his patients – whose medical condition was partly psychological – and subsequently offered his patient and her husband sums of money to persuade them not to pursue the issue with the GMC. The Disciplinary Committee found him guilty of serious professional misconduct and suspended his name from the register for six months. He appealed under s 36(3) of the Medical Act 1956 (as amended by s 14 of the Medical Act 1969).

Decision

The Privy Council dismissed the appeal. The appeal was basically against the findings of the committee on a question of fact. There was ample evidence to justify their decision. Their Lordships determined that:

... although the jurisdiction conferred by statute is unlimited, the circumstances in which it is exercised in accordance with the rules approved by Parliament are such as to make it difficult for an appellant to displace a finding or order of the amity unless it can be shown that something was clearly wrong either (i) in the conduct of the trial or (ii) in the legal principle applied or (iii) unless it can be shown that the findings of the committee were sufficiently out of tune with the evidence to indicate with reasonable certainty that the evidence had been misread.

Comment

See also *Hossack v General Dental Council* (1998), in which the Privy Council held that they could reverse a finding of fact of the GDC PCC, if that finding of fact was out of tune with the evidence to the extent that the evidence must have been misunderstood. Also, in *Balfour v The Occupational Therapists Board* (2000), the Privy Council held that to find someone guilty of infamous conduct in a professional respect was a question of fact and degree. This was for the Disciplinary Committee to decide and the court would not replace the Committee's decision with its own opinion.

In *Ghosh v GMC* (2001), the Privy Council clarified its role and held that it was:

... appellate, not supervisory. The appeal is by way of a rehearing in which the Board is fully entitled to substitute its own decision for that of the Committee. The fact that the appeal is on paper and that the witnesses are not recalled makes it incumbent upon the appellant to demonstrate that some error has occurred in the proceedings before the Committee or in its decision, but this is true of most appellate processes.

Because the Privy Council lacks the expertise in judging appropriate professional medical standards it 'will accord an appropriate measure of respect to the judgment of the Committee ... But the Board will not defer to the Committee's judgment more than is warranted by the circumstances'.

Harding-Price v GMC (No 1) (2001): It may be reasonable for the GMC to suspend a doctor from the register despite a pending appeal to the Privy Council

Facts

The appellant had been found guilty of professional misconduct and his name had been ordered to be erased from the register. This took place 28 days after the direction and the GMC suspended him from the register in the meantime. The appellant lodged an appeal to the Privy Council and applied to the High Court to have his suspension lifted so that he could return to practice while waiting for his appeal to be heard.

Decision

The High Court dismissed the appeal, as the GMC's decision was not unreasonable. Garland J stated:

We have to ask ourselves whether the decision reached by the Professional Conduct Committee was wholly wrong or a decision which a Professional Conduct Committee really could not have reached if it was applying its mind to the issues in a fair, balanced and reasonable way. We do that looking both at the finding of serious professional misconduct and at the finding of danger underlying the suspension imposed and with which we are immediately concerned.

USEFUL INTERNET LINKS

Note: all sites listed start http://www except *** which are just http://

Internet sites related to law

dca.gov.uk	Department for Constitutional Affairs: information about new and pending legislation
courtservice.gov.uk	Transcripts of court judgments
lawreports.co.uk	Weekly Law Reports website: includes summaries of recent judgments
bailii.org	British and Irish Legal Information Institute
austlii.edu.au	Australasian Legal Information Institute
hcourt.gov.au	Judgments from the High Court of Australia
lexum.umontreal.ca/csc-scc	Judgments from the Supreme Court of Canada
echr.coe.int	Information and judgments from the European Court of Human Rights
***europa.eu.int/eur-lex/en/index.html	EU legal information
***curia.eu.int/en/index.htm	European Court of Justice
markwalton.net/index.asp	Mental health law website with links to many other sites
parliament.uk	UK Parliament
direct.gov.uk	Government information and some publications
legislation.hmso.gov.uk	UK legislation
ukcle.ac.uk	UK Centre for Legal Education
***webjcli.ncl.ac.uk	Web Journal of Current Legal Issues: all areas of law, peer reviewed, full text on-line
solent.ac.uk/law/mjls/default.htm	Mountbatten Journal of Legal Studies: all areas of law, peer reviewed, full text on-line
murdoch.edu.au/elaw	Murdoch University (Australia) Electronic Journal of Law: all areas of law, peer reviewed, full text on-line
***www3.oup.co.uk/medlaw	On-line index and abstracts for the Medical Law Review

Internet sites related to healthcare

bmj.com	Full access to the British Medical Journal on-line
bma.org.uk	British Medical Association
ncbi.nlm.nih.gov/entrez/query.fcgi	Free access to PubMed for the US National Library of Medicine: a comprehensive database of references (and many abstracts) of all medical and related publications
who.org	World Health Organization: articles and fact sheets
wma.net/e	The World Medical Association: includes the Declaration of Helsinki (research ethics) and the Declaration of Lisbon (patient's rights)
gmc-uk.org	General Medical Council: free guidance available to download, also information about pending hearings
gdc-uk.org	General Dental Council
nmc-uk.org	Nursing & Midwifery Council
hpc-uk.org	Health Professions Council
dh.gov.uk	Department of Health
hfea.gov.uk	Human Fertilisation and Embryology Authority

Internet sites on bioethics

corec.org.uk/index.htm	NHS Central Office for Research Ethics Committees
ethics-network.org.uk	UK Clinical Ethics Network: a site to support clinical ethics committees
nih.gov/sigs/bioethics	Links to many resources
nuffieldbioethics.org	Nuffield Council on Bioethics
***bioethicsweb.ac.uk	Bioethics gateway, run by the Wellcome Trust

BIBLIOGRAPHY

Aristotle, Thomson, JAK (trans), *Nicomachean Ethics*, 1953 (revised 1976), London: Penguin.

Arlidge, A, 'The trial of Dr David Moor' [2000] Crim LR 31.

Bartlett, P and Sandland, R, *Mental Health Law: Policy and Practice*, 2nd edn, 2003, Oxford: OUP.

Beauchamp, TL and Childress, JF, *Principles of Biomedical Ethics*, 5th edn, 2001, New York: OUP.

Bok, S, *Lying: Moral Choice in Public and Private Life*, 1978, Hassocks: Harvester.

BMA (British Medical Association), *Advance Statements About Medical Treatment – Code of Practice*, 1995, available from www.bma.org.uk/ap.nsf/Content/codeofpractice.

BMA (British Medical Association), *Medical Ethics Today*, 2nd edn, 2003, London: BMJ Books.

Brazier, M and Miola, J, 'Bye-Bye *Bolam*: a medical revolution?' (2000) 8 Med L Rev 85.

Brazier, M, *Medicine, Patients and the Law*, 3rd edn, 2003, London: Penguin.

The Bristol Royal Infirmary Inquiry, 'Learning from Bristol: the report of the public inquiry into children's heart surgery at the Royal Bristol Infirmary 1984–1995', Cm 5207, 2001, available at www.bristol-inquiry.org.uk.

Brody, H, *The Healer's Power*, 1992, New Haven, CT: Yale University Press.

Buchanan, A, 'Medical paternalism' (1978) 7 Philosophy and Public Affairs 370.

Callahan, D (ed), 'The goals of medicine: setting new priorities' (1996) 26 Hastings Center Report Special Supplement S1.

Caplan, AL, 'Informed consent and provider-patient relationships in rehabilitation medicine' (1988) 69 Archives of Physical Medicine and Rehabilitation 312.

Charlesworth, M, *Bioethics in a Liberal Society*, 1993, Cambridge: CUP.

Chief Medical Officer (CMO), *The Removal, Retention and Use of Human Organs and Tissue from Post-mortem Examination*, 2001, London: DoH, available at www.dh.gov.uk/assetRoot/04/06/50/47/04065047.pdf.

Chief Medical Officer (CMO), *Making Amends: A Consultation Paper*, 2003, London: DoH, available at www.doh.gov.uk/assetRoot/04/06/09/45/04060945.pdf.

Confidentiality & Security Advisory Group for Scotland, *Protecting Patient Confidentiality – Final Report*, 2002, available at www.show.scot.nhs.uk/sehd/publications/ppcr/ppcr.pdf.

DoH, *NHS Indemnity – Arrangements for Clinical Negligence Claims in the NHS*, 1996, Catalogue No 96 HR 0024, London: DoH, available at www.dh.gov.uk/assetRoot/04/01/44/58/04014458.pdf.

DoH, *Code of Practice for the Diagnosis of Brain Stem Death – Including Guidelines for the Identification and Management of Potential Organ and Tissue Donors*, 1998, HSC 1998/035, London: DoH.

DoH, *Mental Health Act 1983 Code of Practice*, 1999, London: HMSO, available at www.dh.gov.uk/assetRoot/04/07/49/61/04074961.pdf.

DoH, *Effective Care Co-ordination in Mental Health Services: Modernising the Care Programme Approach*, 2000a, London: DoH.

DoH, *The NHS Plan*, 2000b, Cm 4818-I.

DoH, *An Investigation into Conditional Organ Donation: The Report of the Panel*, 2000c, available at www.dh.gov.uk/assetRoot/04/03/54/65/04035465.pdf.

DoH, *Families and Post Mortems*, 2003a, HSC 2001/23, available at www.dh.gov.uk/ PolicyAndGuidance/HealthAndSocialCareTopics/Tissue/TissueGeneral Information/TissueGeneralArticle/fs/en?CONTENT_ID=4002253&chk=pjRv4o.

DoH, *Confidentiality: NHS Code of Practice*, 2003b, available at www.dh.gov.uk/ assetRoot/04/06/92/54/04069254.pdf.

Donchin, A and Purdy, LM (eds), *Embodying Bioethics: Recent Feminist Advances*, 1999, New Jersey: Rowman & Littlefield.

DTI, *Implementation of EC Directive on Product Liability: An Explanatory and Consultative Note*, 1985, London: DTI.

Dworkin, G, 'Paternalism' (1972) 56 The Monist 65.

Dworkin, G, *The Theory and Practice of Autonomy*, 1988, New York: CUP.

Ellin, J, 'Lying and deception: the solution to a dilemma in medical ethics', in Mappes, TA and Zembaty, JS (eds), *Biomedical Ethics*, 3rd edn, 1991, New York: McGraw-Hill.

Fenn, P, Diacon, S, Gray, A, Hodges, R and Rickman, N, 'Current cost of medical negligence in NHS hospitals: analysis of claims database' (2000) 320 British Medical Journal 1567.

Gavaghan, C, 'Use of preimplantation genetic diagnosis to produce tissue donors: an irreconcilable dichotomy' (2003) 6 Human Fertility 23.

GDC, *Maintaining Standards*, 1997–2001, available at www.gdc-uk.org/pdfs/ ms_full_nov2001.pdf.

Gillon, R, *Philosophical Medical Ethics*, 1985, Chichester: John Wiley.

Gillon, R, 'Patients in the persistent vegetative state: a response to Dr Andrews' (1993) 306 British Medical Journal 1602.

Glover, J, *Causing Death and Saving Lives*, 1977, London: Penguin.

GMC, *Seeking Patients' Consent: The Ethical Considerations*, 1999, London: GMC.

GMC, *Confidentiality: Protecting and Providing Information*, 2000, London: GMC.

GMC, *Good Medical Practice*, 3rd edn, 2001, available at www.gmc-uk.org/standards/ default.htm.

Graber, GC, 'Basic theories in medical ethics', in Monagle, JF and Thomasma, DC (eds), *Health Care Ethics: Critical Issues for the 21st Century*, 1998, Maryland: Aspen Publishers.

Hare, RM, *Moral Thinking: Its Level Method and Point*, 1981, Oxford: Clarendon.

HFEA, *Code of Practice*, 6th edn, 2003, available at www.hfea.gov.uk/HFEA Publications/CodeofPractice.

HFEA, *Sex Selection: Options for Regulation*, 2003, available at www.hfea.gov.uk/ AboutHFEA/Consultations.

Lord Irvine, 'The development of human rights in Britain under an incorporated convention on human rights' [1998] PL 221.

Jackson, E, 'Conception and the relevance of the welfare principle' (2002) 65(2) MLR 176–203.

Joint Committee on the Draft Mental Incapacity Bill Report, 2003, HC 1083-I Session 2002–03, HL Paper 189-I, available at www.publications.parliament.uk/pa/jt/jtdmi.htm.

Jones, R, *Mental Health Act Manual*, 8th edn, 2003, London: Sweet & Maxwell.

Jonsen, AR, *The New Medicine and the Old Ethics*, 1990, Cambridge, MA: Harvard UP.

Keown, J, 'Restoring moral and intellectual shape to the law after *Bland*' (1997) 113 LQR 481.

Khan, M and Robson, M, 'What is a responsible group of medical opinion?' (1995) 11 Professional Negligence 4.

Kluge, E-HW, 'Health information, the fair information principles and ethics' (1994) 33 Methods of Information in Medicine 336.

Laing, JM, 'Rights versus risk? Reform of the Mental Health Act 1983' (2000) 8 Med L Rev 210.

Law Commission, *Mentally Incapacitated Adults and Decision-Making: Medical Treatment and Research*, Consultation Paper No 129, 1993, London: HMSO.

Law Commission, *Mental Incapacity*, Report No 231, 1995, London: HMSO.

Lee, RG and Morgan, D, *Human Fertilisation and Embryology*, 2001, London: Blackstone.

Lipkin, M, 'On lying to patients', in Mappes, TA and Zembaty, JS (eds), *Biomedical Ethics*, 3rd edn, 1991, New York: McGraw-Hill.

Lord Chancellor, *Making Decisions*, Cmnd 4465, 1999, London: HMSO.

Maclean, AR, 'Organ donation, racism and the Race Relations Act' (1999) 149 NLJ 1250.

Maclean, AR, 'Resurrection of the body snatchers' (2000) 150 NLJ 174.

Maclean, AR, 'Crossing the Rubicon on the human rights ferry' (2001) 64(5) MLR 775.

Maclean, AR, 'Consent, sectionalisation and the concept of a medical procedure' (2002a) 28(4) JME 249.

Maclean, AR, 'Beyond *Bolam* and *Bolitho*' (2002b) 5(3) Medical Law International 205.

Maclean, AR, 'An Alexandrian approach to the knotty problem of wrongful pregnancy: *Rees v Darlington Memorial Hospital NHS Trust* in the House of Lords' [2004] 3 Web JCLI, available at http://webjcli.ncl.ac.uk/2004/issue3/maclean3.html.

Mappes, TA and Zembaty, JS, 'Biomedical ethics and ethical theory', in Mappes, TA and Zembaty, JS (eds), *Biomedical Ethics*, 3rd edn, 1991, New York: McGraw-Hill.

Mason, JK, McCall Smith, RA and Laurie, GT, *Law and Medical Ethics*, 6th edn, 2002, London: Butterworths.

Mason, JK, 'Wrongful pregnancy, wrongful birth and wrongful terminology' (2002) 6 Edinburgh Law Review 46.

McGrath, P, 'Autonomy, discourse and power: a postmodern reflection on principlism and bioethics' (1998) 23 Journal of Medicine and Philosophy 516.

Mill, JS, 'On liberty', in Gray, J (ed), *On Liberty and Other Essays*, 1991, Oxford: OUP.

Mitchell, J, 'ABC of breast diseases: a fundamental problem of consent' (1995) 310 British Medical Journal 43.

Montgomery, J, *Health Care Law*, 2nd edn, 2003, Oxford: OUP.

National Audit Office, *Handling Clinical Negligence Claims in England*, 2001, HC 403 Session 2000–01, London: The Stationery Office, available from www.nao.gov. uk/pn/00-01/0001403.htm.

NHS Executive, *Introduction of Supervision Registers for Mentally Ill People*, 1994, HSG(94)5.

NHS Executive, *Assuring the Quality of Medical Practice: Implementing Supporting Doctors Protecting Patients*, 2001, Leeds: NHS.

NMC (Nursing & Midwifery Council), *Code of Professional Conduct*, 2002, available at www.nmc-uk.org/nmc/main/publications/codeofprofessionalconduct.pdf.

O'Sullivan, D, 'The allocation of scarce resources and the right to life under the European Convention on Human Rights' [1998] PL 389.

Parks, JA, 'A contextualized approach to patient autonomy within the therapeutic relationship' (1998) 19 Journal of Medical Humanities 299.

Ramsey, P, *The Patient as Person*, 1970, New Haven, CT: Yale University Press.

Randall, F and Downie, RS, *Palliative Care Ethics*, 1996, Oxford: OUP.

Rawls, J, *A Theory of Justice*, 1972, Oxford: OUP.

Raz, J, 'Autonomy, toleration, and the harm principle', in Gavison, R (ed), *Issues in Contemporary Legal Philosophy*, 1989, Oxford: Clarendon.

Ross, WD, *The Right and the Good*, 1930, Oxford: Clarendon.

The Royal Liverpool Children's Inquiry Report (2001) HC 12, available at www.rlcinquiry.org.uk.

Savulescu, J and Momeyer, W, 'Should informed consent be based on rational beliefs?' (1997) 23 JME 282.

Secker, B, 'The appearance of Kant's deontology in contemporary Kantianism: concepts of patient autonomy in bioethics' (1999) 24 Journal of Medicine and Philosophy 43.

Secretary of State for the Home Department, *Reforming the Coroner and Death Certification Service: A Position Paper*, Cm 6159, 2004, available at www.official-documents.co.uk/document/cm61/6159/6159.pdf.

Stewart, A, 'Damages for the birth of a child' (1995) 40 Journal of the Law Society of Scotland 298.

Thomson, M, 'After *Re S*' (1994) 2 Med L Rev 127.

Tong, R, *Feminist Approaches to Bioethics*, 1997, Boulder, CO: Westview.

Veatch, RM, 'Models for ethical medicine in a revolutionary age' (1972) 2 Hastings Center Report 5.

Waitzkin, H, 'Doctor-patient communication: clinical implications of social scientific research' (1984) 252 Journal of the American Medical Association 2441.

Lord Woolf, 'Are the courts excessively deferential to the medical profession?', inaugural lecture in the Provosts Lecture Series, University College London, (2001) 9 Med L Rev 1.

World Medical Association, 'Proposed revision of the Declaration of Helsinki' (1999) 147 Bulletin of Medical Ethics 18.

INDEX